TEACHING WITH
THE INSTRUCTIONAL
Cha-Chas

4 Steps to Make Learning Stick

Foreword by Rick Wormeli

LEANN NICKELSEN & MELISSA DICKSON

Solution Tree | Press

555 North Morton Street
Bloomington, IN 47404
800.733.6786 (toll free) / 812.336.7700
FAX: 812.336.7790

email: info@SolutionTree.com
SolutionTree.com

Visit **go.SolutionTree.com/instruction** to download the free reproducibles in this book.

Printed in the United States of America

Library of Congress Cataloging-in-Publication Data

Names: Dickson, Melissa, author. | Nickelsen, LeAnn, author.
Title: Teaching with the instructional cha-chas : four steps to make learning
    stick / Melissa Dickson and LeAnn Nickelsen.
Description: Bloomington, Indiana : Solution Tree Press, [2018] | Includes
    bibliographical references and index.
Identifiers: LCCN 2018023639 | ISBN 9781945349959 (perfect bound)
Subjects: LCSH: Teaching. | Lesson planning. | Learning, Psychology of. |
    Educational tests and measurements. | Academic achievement.
Classification: LCC LB1025.3 .D525 2019 | DDC 371.26/2--dc23 LC record available at https://lccn.loc.gov/2018023639

Solution Tree

Jeffrey C. Jones, CEO
Edmund M. Ackerman, President

Solution Tree Press

President and Publisher: Douglas M. Rife
Editorial Director: Sarah Payne-Mills
Art Director: Rian Anderson
Managing Production Editor: Kendra Slayton
Senior Production Editor: Tonya Maddox Cupp
Senior Editor: Amy Rubenstein
Copy Editor: Ashante K. Thomas
Proofreader: Evie Madsen
Text and Cover Designer: Abigail Bowen
Editorial Assistant: Sarah Ludwig

Acknowledgments

This book would not have been written without the wonderful opportunity, encouragement, and examples from the Anne Arundel County School teachers and administrators in Maryland—Bobbi Pedrick, Martha Lehman, Pam Courson, Maureen Gerrity, Erin Belcher, Dina Miller, Marty McConnell, Sue Wilson, Beth Harpel, and Jessica Haynie, and all the amazing SERTs. We have been working with the K–12 teachers to incorporate the instructional cha-chas since 2009. The results are astounding. Thank you to all the other schools that have taken the instructional cha-chas challenge to close their gaps. Thank you for dancing with us, trying the strategies, and sharing your success stories and frustrations on this amazing journey that leads to powerful learning. We aren't finished yet; the song is still playing.

Thank you to Douglas Rife and Claudia Wheatley for inspiring us to write this book. Thank you to our amazing editors, Amy Rubenstein and Tonya Cupp. You are absolutely gifted with the big picture, organization, word choice, idea meshing, details, and how to handle two traveling authors and presenters! Thank you also to Ashante K. Thomas and Evie Madsen, as well as the rest of the Solution Tree staff who made this book outstanding. Behind a great book are many authors and contributors!

Thank you to the following coaches, educators, and friends who have formed what we know and how we teach, coach, and live life: Eric Jensen, Rick Wormeli, Diane Heacox, Richard Cash, Katie McKnight, Ron Coniglio, Betty Hollas, Jim Grant (we miss you), Lynne Ecenberger, Kim Geddie, Linda Allen, Cheryl Dick, Bryan Harris, Shauna King, Jenny Severson, Tracie Steel, Eric Larison, Jim Ewing, Laura Smith, Sharon McClelland, Melinda Donnellan (and the Conroe Independent School District literacy coaches), Kathy Clark, Melodye Pinson, Mary Donohoe, and Pam Guthrie. Many thanks to the team of people at Staff Development for Educators (SDE), who got us started on our presenting journey. A special thank-you goes to Dr. Bryan Harris for assisting with the research. A special thank-you goes to Dr. Eric Jensen, who gave me the opportunity to write and learn with him for the past twenty years. Invaluable!

Other districts we want to thank for being on the instructional cha-chas journey long term include Lansing, Michigan, schools, Lorris Elementary (Myrtle Beach), Maryvale Public Schools (New York), Olathe Public Schools (Kansas), Pittsfield Public Schools (Massachusetts), Riverton and Green River schools (Wyoming), Westlawn Elementary School and Theron Jones Elementary School (Texarkana), Vero Beach Elementary (Florida), Rose and Alex Pilibos Armenian School (Los Angeles), Reo and Cavanaugh Elementary (Lansing, Michigan), Phoenix Academy (Annapolis, MD) and many more.

—LeAnn and Melissa

Thank you Joel, my BFF and twenty-six-year love of my life, for always supporting my passion to teach and train. I could not keep up with everything without your help, love, and patience! Keaton and Aubrey, my college kiddos, thank you for sharing with me what you love about your teachers and daily learning experiences. You have taught me more than you know. I'm blessed! Thank you Mom for encouraging me to become a teacher and showing me that my belief in my students will show in their achievement. Last and most, I thank my Lord, who gives me daily strength and power.

—LeAnn

Special thanks to my sons, Josh, Shane, and Drew (who I miss every day). You three formed my philosophy as to *why* we must differentiate. When facing life's challenges, I hope you dance. Mom and Dad, my first and best teachers. Leading by example, you taught me everything worth knowing. Brett, the best brother in the world. You keep me dancing and laughing. Rock on!

—Melissa

Solution Tree Press would like to thank the following reviewers:

Ashley Bingenheimer
Technology Integration Specialist
School District of River Falls
River Falls, Wisconsin

Angie Evans
Learning Coach
Red Mountain Elementary School
Ivins, Utah

Tara Looney
K–6 Reading Interventionist
Concordia Elementary School
Concordia, Missouri

Jeanette Brosam
Instructional Coach
Franklin STEAM Academy
Champaign, Illinois

Luane Genest
Fifth-Grade Teacher
Sunset Heights Elementary School
Nashua, New Hampshire

Visit **go.SolutionTree.com/instruction** to download
the free reproducibles in this book.

Table of Contents

Reproducible pages are in italics.

CHAPTER 6
Take Step Three: Check (Evaluate) 117

CHAPTER 7

Take Step Four: Change (Differentiate) 159

CHAPTER 8
Finesse the Chunk, Chew, Check, and Change Cycle: A Beautiful Classroom Dance

EPILOGUE
Swing Into Action With the Four Steps: Time for Your Solo

About the Authors

LeAnn Nickelsen, EdM, is an educator, coach, author, and trainer. She presents nationally and internationally on topics such as closing the gaps in high-poverty schools through differentiation strategies and evidence-based researched strategies; balanced literacy strategies and processes; and enhancing engagement, memory, and transfer in learning environments. She is known for delivering a wealth of information in an active, fun format with very specific, practical classroom examples. Participants leave with many ideas for maximizing learning for all students.

LeAnn believes that training is not enough for teachers to implement high effect size tools and strategies. Coaching is needed to bring full transfer from trainings, and she works with teachers one-to-one and in small groups to help them achieve their educational goals. She is a parent of college-age twins and applies the research to the hardest jobs out there—parenting and teaching.

LeAnn earned a master's degree in educational administration from the University of North Texas.

To learn more about LeAnn's work, visit Maximize Learning (www.maximizelearninginc.com) or follow @lnickelsen1 on Twitter.

Melissa Dickson, EdM, is an outstanding presenter and educator. She is passionate about providing teachers with research-based ideas and strategies that they implement immediately. In her decades as an educator, Melissa has been a literacy coach, staff developer, site-based team leader, mentor teacher, inclusion teacher, classroom teacher, and early childhood teacher. She supports a balanced literacy classroom model. Melissa presents internationally at conferences and seminars and provides custom training for schools and districts. Her ability to provide relevant information with humor and enthusiasm makes her a very popular presenter. Participants leave her sessions with a wealth of ideas to immediately implement in their classrooms.

She has a bachelor's degree in education and a master's degree in reading from Sam Houston State University.

To learn more about Melissa's work, follow @mdickson221 on Twitter.

To book LeAnn Nickelsen and Melissa Dickson for professional development, contact pd@SolutionTree .com.

Foreword

by Rick Wormeli

In the 2000 film *Billy Elliott*, starring Jamie Bell and Julie Walters, eleven-year-old Billy has had a rough time auditioning for the Royal Ballet Theater, and an even more difficult time getting his family to support his dream to be a dancer. After receiving skeptical views of his rebellious dance audition and a scolding for punching another boy auditioning for the same slot in the ballet company, Billy is sure he's failed and makes his way to the door. The judges stop him, however, and ask, "What does it feel like when you're dancing?" The camera closes in and Billy responds with raw honesty:

> Don't know. Sorta feels good. Sorta stiff and that, but once I get going . . . then I like, forget everything. And . . . sorta disappear. Sorta disappear. Like I feel a change in my whole body. And I've got this fire in my body. I'm just there. Flyin' like a bird. Like electricity. Yeah, like electricity.

Billy's epiphany conveys the same emancipation as psychologist Mihaly Csikszentmihalyi's (2008) flow and so beautifully expressed in "High Flight," the classic poem by John Gillespie Magee Jr. (, an American pilot serving in the Royal Canadian Air Force during World War II. Remember those lines from the poem: "Oh! I have slipped the surly bonds of earth, and danced the skies on laughter-silvered wings," and later, "High in the sunlit silence. Hov'ring there . . . " To shed one's affectations and displace worldly angst while lost in the music and dancing is a cathartic moment of self-discovery; we come alive. In that electric moment, we experience robust belonging, daring hope, and real liberation. And to do this with a dance partner or team moving with you in synchronicity? We slip the surly bonds and become more than we were; we flourish.

Notice, though, that Billy's *soaring* dance and Magee's *hov'ring* are both grounded in the physics of their realities. Neither is supernatural, but what they achieve is in direct response to their grounded realities turned powerful trebuchets. Billy dances with swinging arms and high-stepping cadence along the narrow rims of brick walls. He slams his body against encroaching walls to the beat of a primal rhythm only he can hear, practically leaping out of his skin, purging pent-up anger and catalyzing joy. He is released, just as Magee feels, emancipated from gravity, but deeply influenced by reality and fundamentals.

And so, we dance; music please . . . hear it? Now, we go: walk forward, back, forward, back, sidestep together, sidestep together—other direction now—sidestep together, sidestep together, rock step, rock step . . . and, one, two, cha-cha-cha! We're off!

In their book, *Teaching With the Instructional Cha-Chas: Four Steps to Make Learning Stick,* highly accomplished educators (our dance instructors) LeAnn Nickelsen and Melissa Dickson show us how to push one foot into new territory then bring the other foot to join the journey, all in a coordinated effort to maximize student learning. Notice how grounded they are in classroom reality and instructional truths at every turn, however. Who knew those elements could help us soar like this? One, two, cha-cha-cha—and cha! Twice the fiery, two-step *pasodoble*, this is a four-step dance done in a teacher's favorite style—*practical*. It's the *baile práctico de cuatro pasos*: chunk, chew, check, and *change*!

In our first foray to the dance floor as we read, several factors become apparent. First, LeAnn and Melissa know their neuroscience and the practical applications thereof. In fact, they are among the most studied educators I know, and even better, they are gifted communicators who make the latest in what we know about learning and the brain actionable—not in some fake, school-catalog-perfect classroom, but in classrooms that reflect our diverse realities and challenges. True to their professionalism, they reference recent and time-tested research, revisiting many of our education research heroes, and providing multiple references for follow-up study. It's hard to be both scholarly and practical, vetting the research and activating teacher creativity, but wow—they do it well.

Second, LeAnn and Melissa are not just in favor of students owning their learning and acting on it, but also for teacher self-efficacy. A clear theme in these pages is that gradual release of responsibility for students, which Douglas Fisher and Nancy Frey (2015) promote, and also for teachers to run with as well. *There's no sense in being beholden to the mere descriptions in this book simply because they are printed here.* They intone, *So use these tools and make them your own!* Thankfully, we're granted behind-the-scenes intimacy with lesson planning—serious, warts and all, truly reflecting a teacher's daily experiences—something other professional books mistakenly avoid. The authors are immediately inspiring, yes, but they provide teachers with specific tools to augment, revise, and differentiate each strategy to reflect their own style and students' challenges, cultivating instructional dexterity. With these tools we are responsive to current needs and versatile with those down the road. And particularly appropriate here: there's not one foo-foo-fluff activity in the group. All strategies included herein are substantive, resulting in real learning. Any National Board Certified teacher reflecting highly accomplished practice would be proud to use these ideas.

And good golly, let's hear it for each time they include a Bumping It Up, Breaking It Down, and, Specializing For section! Fortunately, they end every description of their strategies with this tag triad, demonstrating how to raise complexity and challenge, break the learning experience down, or extend the learning experience for those who might not find it accessible otherwise, so we can truly skip the differentiation platitudes and make it real for our classrooms. Their next book should be on just providing these three responses to fifty or more commonly used teaching techniques today. It would sell a lot of copies. ·

As someone who works with adult learners more and more, I'm excited about how many of these strategies can be adapted easily for professional development experiences. I'm grabbing ideas right and left as I read, upping my game as a teacher of teachers. Talk about engagement and making learning stick! I'm going to do the big picture, dynamic duo, and several chew strategies, for sure.

We're grateful, too, that LeAnn and Melissa put their considerable expertise in technology and assessment to wise use in these pages. They incorporate many technology integrations, and make an ample number of website and app recommendations, some of which I've used, and many of which I'm excited to try. They are ceaselessly attentive to the power of formative assessment and feedback in each of the cha-chas as well. Their approach reflects modern assessment thinking. While there is an emphasis on language arts and reading and writing examples, they applied the strategies to other subjects as well, and for that, I'm grateful too.

They don't mention it specifically, but there's a subtle theme of, *Let's activate joy and music in student learning and teacher lesson planning* that runs through many of their descriptions. My colleagues and I are so stoked by the creativity in these pages. In fact, we want to put down the book and go try the ideas right away, much like walking into a large hardware store and breathing it all in; we feel like we're going to pop unless we start building something right away! Just in reading their strategy sequence—*I do, we do, two do, you do*—I'm riffing on Frank Sinatra and wondering what else in teaching might have a rhythm I've missed all these years. In our stressful lives as educators, including local and national politics, racism, poverty, equity, demoralizing accountability measures, and increasingly limited resources, this stuff is not only refreshing, but it sustains us.

American country music singer Lee Ann Womack and songwriters Mark D. Sanders and Tia Sillers (2000) knew it all along. In their song, "I Hope You Dance," they invite us to never lose our sense of wonder, not to fear the mountains in the distance, or to settle for the path of least resistance. With LeAnn and Melissa's inspiration here, we can do these great things for and with our students. And, really, when given the chance to sit it out or dance, we hope you'll dance.

It's always stunning and a little humbling to discover the power of our students and their daily realities to breathe life into our classroom lessons. Let's stay vigilant in looking for it. Combine that newly tapped power of student realities with the instructional fundamentals from cognitive science, and students thrive. Well coached and cared for, we all dance; well grounded, we fly.

Then comes the music. Come, take my hand, turn the page, and let's dance. Instructional cha-chas indeed.

Brenman, G., & Finn, J. (Producers), & Daldry, S. (Director). (2000). *Billy Elliot* [Motion picture]. England: BBC Films.

Csikszentmihalyi, M. (2008*). Flow: The psychology of optimal experience*. New York: Harper Perennial.

Magee, J. (1989). The *complete works of John Magee, the pilot poet*. Gloucestershire, United Kingdom: This England Books.

Sanders, M. D., & Sillers, T. (2000). I hope you dance [Recorded by L. A. Womack]. On *I hope you dance* [CD]. Nashville, TN: MCA (September 1999).

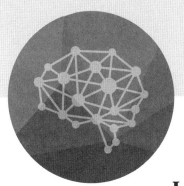

INTRODUCTION

Maneuver Your Footwork With Four Steps

Delivering content and effectively using the formative assessment process can be quite overwhelming to some teachers. We wondered how we could make this powerful, highly differentiated process more doable. Because we love to dance, rhyme, chant, and make content easier, we came up with the cha-chas chant.

> Chunk it, we teach a bit
> Chew it, they think about it
> Check it, do they know?
> Change it, to watch them grow (Jensen &
> Nickelsen, 2014, p. 186)

This Book's Focus

Neuroscience and evidence-based research have changed how we eat, sleep, move, think, learn, teach—how we live our lives. Neuroscientists explore our brains to show how they respond to different environments. For example, physical exercise not only benefits the physical body, but it also benefits mental capabilities (Erickson et al., 2011). Aerobic exercise can increase hippocampus volume leading to cognitive improvements and the "alleviation of depression and anxiety" (Sleiman et al., 2016). The hippocampus is a part of the brain associated with long-term memory and learning transfer. When it improves and grows, so does cognitive

function and memory. These factors have positive implications for memory performance and suggest that fitness protects against brain volume loss (Erickson et al., 2011).

Another example is University of California Berkeley professor Marian C. Diamond's (2001) seminal research revealing that the brain responds to enriching environments. She was the first to prove that the brain can change and improve with experience. She examined some of Albert Einstein's brain, where she found an abundant amount of support cell—more than average. And her research with rats that showed novel toys (rotating the type of toys), companions, healthy food, space in a cage, and other factors changed the anatomy of the brain. Her research concludes that impoverished environments can lower capacity to learn, while enriched environments increase plasticity, learning, and memory. The bottom line is that much research, the past and present, supports how important environment is. (There is even an ongoing conflict regarding whether we can grow new brain cells, known as neurogenesis in the hippocampus. The implications are important.)

This book will explore cognitive and behavioral sciences as well as other evidence-based research that help us determine how to reach students more efficiently and effectively. This scientific basis is our book's foundation along with the formative assessment process and differentiation efficacy—which back the multitude of strategies we offer.

The *formative assessment process* says the following (Schimmer, 2018).

- Learning never ends. It is an iterative process.

- Assessment is for evaluating information and moving students forward faster with their learning. It allows the teacher and student to partner in the process of closing the gap between the student's current work or thinking and the desired learning.

- Teachers and administrators don't discipline students for not learning something by a certain date but rather, they partner with them to update the growth toward the standards.

- The latest assessment is the most accurate—no matter what quarter.

Learning is all about students reaching the learning target, goal, outcome, or objective in an engaged, enjoyable manner. Learning is a rough draft and can be quite sloppy at times. This is to be expected, and formative assessment is part of it.

Differentiation and the formative assessment process go hand in hand. You can't separate them. They have the same goals for student learning, and they mirror our goals for students as well.

- We want students to joyfully learn the curriculum and more.

- We want students to be active learners with opportunities to make the content more meaningful and connected to their lives and their world.

- We want students to be independent thinkers, so they can use powerful strategies that allow them to learn faster and more efficiently.

- We want to partner with our students to guide, facilitate, help, support, and cheer them on to do their very best thinking daily.

- We want students to take on the responsibility of monitoring their own learning, reflecting on it, and determining next best steps with our guidance, teaching, and facilitation.

- We want students to be prepared for life outside the classroom and to be productive citizens who help lead us successfully into the future.

To that end, we've included dozens of strategies so K–8 teachers around the world could see effective instruction and differentiation as *doable* and as a *must do*. You will see templates filled in as examples throughout the book. Elsewhere in the book, and online at **go.SolutionTree.com/instruction**, you can access blank versions of these templates. Here, teachers see the brain-based evidence that proves that using daily formative assessment and differentiation is not a choice, but rather a necessity. As teachers, we put this process into play in our own classrooms with great success, and as educators and consultants, we saw teachers' mindsets and toolkits, as well as students' engagement and achievement, change throughout the years we coached. This book is a mindset changer. *Teaching With the Instructional Cha-Chas: Four Steps to Make Learning Stick* will introduce four steps into your instruction: (1) chunking, (2) chewing, (3) checking, and (4) changing. Content mastery and greater student achievement will result.

This Book's Strategies

Each strategy in chapter 2 through chapter 6 includes the grouping method (whole group, small groups, partners, or individual), directions, an example or template (or both), simple suggestions for differentiation (ways you can *change* the lesson by bumping it up for advanced students, breaking it down to scaffold for learners who are struggling, and specializing it for some of the other challenges you face in your classroom), and how to incorporate technology (including links to useful websites and apps). Because websites frequently change, you can visit **go.SolutionTree.com/instruction** for a list of current websites.

Every strategy we included addresses a variety of learning preferences, and literacy components (reading, writing, listening, and speaking). While you won't see those features specifically called out, you can use the strategies in confidence knowing they are there. Also, be aware that chapter 7 addresses more purposeful differentiation strategies.

You shouldn't give the strategies independently as worksheets, but rather use them as thinking and discussion templates, and as part of the gradual release of responsibility model (Fisher & Frey, 2015; Pearson & Gallagher, 1983), which requires the teacher to model each strategy (*I do*), provide opportunities for guided practice (*we do*), and small-group or partner practice (*two do*) before expecting students to demonstrate the strategy independently (*you do*).

Chapters 4 and 5 talk more about this model, but table I.1 shows how our four-step instructional cha-chas cycle correlates with Douglas Fisher and Nancy Frey's (2008) gradual release of responsibility. While most lessons follow the gradual release in the order here, a teacher may choose to change this. For example, a lesson might start with a *you do* that has a question to activate prior knowledge. Either way, the goal in each lesson is to have all four types of release, done gradually and based on the checkpoints and data received from those checkpoints.

Table I.1: *Gradual Release of Responsibility in the Instructional Cha-Chas Cycle*

Step in Four-Step Cycle	Gradual Release of Responsibility	What Does the Teacher Do?	What Does the Student Do?
Chunk	*I do* Direct instruction	• Shares learning target—the lesson's purpose • Makes content relevant and interesting; gets student buy-in • Models the skill or explains or shows content (via a think-aloud) • Directs instruction • Provides engaging tools • Chunks for ten to fifteen minutes (depending on student grade)	• Actively listens and watches • Sits near the teacher • Possibly takes notes • Might form general questions, *How does this connect with me* questions, and *I wonder* statements
Chew, check, and change	*We do* Guided practice	• Provides interactive instruction • Guides students • Asks questions to ascertain learning • Prompts and cues to support students • Listens to conversations to assess • Starts to release some responsibility so students try the learning • Differentiates when needed (change instruction) • Pulls small groups based on what is seen or heard • Gives feedback to move work closer to learning target	• Responds to questions • Practices what he or she just learned • Asks questions for clarification • Seeks peer help, for example, turn and talk • Makes thinking visible (via annotations, graphic organizers, two-column notes, mind maps, whiteboards, and so on) so teacher can assess • Receives feedback and changes work accordingly
Chew, check, and change	*Two do* Collaboration	• Creates opportunities for student conversations via purposeful groups • Creates question and statement stems to help with discussions • Has word walls available so students can use academic and domain-specific vocabulary terms • Listens to and observes students • Documents the daily data for where students are with the learning target • Organizes data and makes changes based on the data • Gives feedback to move work closer to learning target	• Discusses what he or she learns in structured manners with domain-specific vocabulary • Practices, in an interactive, fun group format, what he or she learns • Receives feedback from peers and changes work accordingly • Makes connections • Reflects and assesses productiveness of his or her group work time • Might play games to reinforce learning target

continued on next page ⇒

Step in Four-Step Cycle	Gradual Release of Responsibility	What Does the Teacher Do?	What Does the Student Do?
Chew, check, and change	*You do* Independent practice	• Confers with students; possibly pulling a small group of students to reteach, give extra support, and scaffold (differentiate) • Observes and documents student understanding • Gives feedback to move work closer to learning target • Clarifies confusions	• Works in school • Strategically applies what he or she learns in the lesson to complete the assessment (evidence of learning target mastery) • Assesses personal progress toward learning target

Source: Adapted from Fisher & Frey, 2008.

During each phase of the gradual release of responsibility, as the students chew on the content, you will check their understanding and change instruction as you need to. We'll go into this in more detail in chapters 6 and 7 (page 117 and 159, respectively).

We firmly believe this book will enhance your teaching in many ways. You will enjoy the strategies that are in line with high-quality standards. They are rigorous, highly engaging, and easy to implement with any topic in grades K–8. They are not suppositions. They have and are producing results in classrooms across the world.

This Book's Organization

Because we know that dancers never step on stage without choreographing their routine and effective teachers never step into a classroom without first choreographing their instruction, we've split the book into two parts, the first of which guides your planning. The second guides your step-by-step instruction implementation.

Part I includes chapters 1–3. Chapter 1 examines the formative assessment process and introduces our four-step instruction cycle to help you maximize learning. Chapters 2 and 3 focus on the planning required to effectively frame your instruction before embarking on the four-step cycle. Specifically, chapter 2 deals with how to design effective daily learning targets and formative assessments to ensure that each student meets the standard. We present a lesson-planning template to get you started. You'll see this template in later chapters as well. Chapter 3 explores the importance of knowing

your students academically, socially, and emotionally, and planning the most effective methods for instruction. That includes strategies for preassessing, activating prior knowledge, pre-exposing, and priming their brains for the content.

Part II includes chapters 4–8. In each chapter, we'll share strategies that help you accomplish each step in the instructional cha-chas and provide ways to differentiate for students as well. Chapter 4 introduces the first step of our instructional cha-chas cycle: chunking, or breaking, the content into manageable pieces for students. We'll examine some of the best strategies to ensure that every student receives relevant, rigorous, and robust content. Chapter 5 covers the second step of the cycle: providing an opportunity for students to chew, or engage with, the content. We'll share some of our favorite strategies for reaching the variety of learners in your classroom to ensure that all students master the content. Chapter 6 examines the third step: checking, or evaluating, where students are in mastering the standard. This is the formative assessment step. We'll explain why it is crucial to examine evidence every day for every student and provide strategies that make that possible. Chapter 7 covers the final step of the instruction cycle: changing, or differentiating, the instruction. We'll share strategies that allow teachers to more purposefully differentiate their instruction, grouping, pacing, practice, and more based on their formative assessment results. Chapter 8 provides a sample lesson plan that shows you how to bring all the dance steps together for a quality lesson designed for maximum learning. We also include a lesson-plan template, checklists, and self-assessment to help you teach this way.

Let's dance!

Part 1

SETTING UP YOUR CLASSROOM DANCE FLOOR

Building a dance floor starts with design. Then, you deliver quality materials. After that, you nail down the boards and sand the wood to provide a seamless finish fit for dancing.

The same premise is necessary when creating the "dance floor" in our classrooms. The design is the teacher's mindset and how they establish, manage, and encourage a passion and enthusiasm for learning. The materials are the research-based best practice strategies a teacher uses to ensure student success, and the framework is of course, the standards. Part I of this book sets the stage. First, get familiar with the formative assessment process: chunk, chew, check, and change in chapter 1. Start planning your daily learning target and formative assessment in chapter 2. Continue planning by learning how to get to know your students in chapter 3. By the end of part I you will understand the frame you need to provide a seamless finish fit for learning.

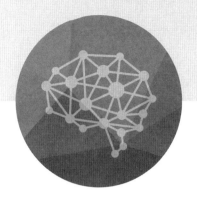

Choreograph Your Instruction With the Cha-Chas Steps

You can sum up brain research, the formative assessment process, and differentiated instruction in four steps: (1) chunk, (2) chew, (3) check, and (4) change. When you dance all four steps daily during all content area instruction and practice, planning instruction gets easier, and the results will amaze you. Before we can swing into our four steps, we must answer the following questions.

- What does neuroscience say about learning?
- What is the formative assessment process?
- What is differentiated instruction?
- Is there research to support differentiated instruction?
- How did we merge neuroscience, the formative assessment process, and differentiated instruction into four steps?

What Does Neuroscience Say About Learning?

Giving students frequent opportunities to quiz themselves or take brief teacher- or computer-designed quizzes to recall information, along with giving them effective feedback, has an effect size of more than 0.80 (more than one and a half years of growth) on student achievement (Adesope, Trevisan, & Sundararajan, 2017; Cranney, Ahn, McKinnon, Morris, & Watts, 2009). *Effect size* is a number that represents the difference between two groups to show effectiveness. In this case, it shows how effective one agent is on student achievement. Retrieving information from the brain—the memory—about what was learned that day and previous days is more effective than rereading the text, taking notes, or listening to lectures again (Agarwal, Roediger, McDaniel, & McDermott, 2013).

This study also finds that recalling and writing an answer to a flash card question (before flipping over flash card) or equation improves learning more than thinking the student knows the answer and flipping over the card prematurely. Bottom line? Researchers say to educators to pull information *out* of student brains rather than place more information into their brains and provide feedback to students about their learning (Agarwal et al., 2013). Retrieval represents the *chew* and feedback represents a *check* and *change* in our instructional cha-chas. Both are critical components for memory and learning.

What Is the Formative Assessment Process?

Formative assessment isn't a one-time thing. It is a process that both teachers and students use throughout their work together; each gives feedback to the other so the teacher can change instruction and improve students' achievement (Popham, 2013). Since educators *always* want to improve students' achievement, they should view *all* assessments through a formative lens—even the main formative assessment. Figure 1.1 shows the progression from preassessment to summative assessment. If you use the preassessment data collected prior to instruction to determine what to teach, who to teach, and how to teach, then it becomes a type of formative assessment because it *informs* your upcoming instruction. (Chapter 3 on page 22 talks about preassessment in detail.) Ongoing formative assessments occur throughout a lesson and allow you to correct misconceptions or misunderstandings; provide feedback; and change grouping, pacing, content, and assignments.

These daily, ongoing formative assessments inform your instruction on the spot, the next day, or at a future date. Teachers don't give summative assessments until after many formative assessments and much feedback. It makes sense that if we catch student errors early, they should do better on future assessments as long as we are assessing the same thing at different times in the unit or quarter. If we catch mistakes early and respond to them (with feedback, reteaching, different pacing, and other differentiation), they will learn it before the summative assessment. Teachers should only grade summative assessments. Many teachers and students mistakenly think the assessment process is complete at that point. If you view summative assessments through a formative lens, you can determine areas for student growth from graded work. Technically, *any* assessment is formative if it informs the teacher and student of how learning is going and how to change instruction versus just recording it.

We'll answer these questions in the following sections.

- What are the characteristics of the formative assessment process?
- Is there research to support the formative assessment process?

What Are the Characteristics of the Formative Assessment Process?

The characteristics of the formative assessment process are multifaceted, with specific criteria.

- All instruction centers around the learning target, which is a mini step toward achieving the standard. The learning target is small enough to ensure mastery within approximately one to two days. To achieve a standard, you make a progression of mini learning targets

Assessments Drive Instruction

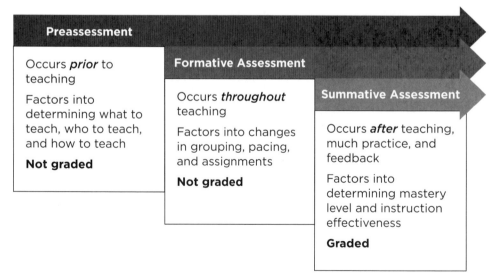

Preassessment

Occurs *prior* to teaching

Factors into determining what to teach, who to teach, and how to teach

Not graded

Formative Assessment

Occurs *throughout* teaching

Factors into changes in grouping, pacing, and assignments

Not graded

Summative Assessment

Occurs *after* teaching, much practice, and feedback

Factors into determining mastery level and instruction effectiveness

Graded

Instructional choices and day-to-day decisions such as unit formation, learning targets toward standards, student grouping, strategies, pacing, and so on

Figure 1.1: *Assessments drive instruction.*

to lead learners to a broad, deeper standard. For example, if the standard is to "determine the main idea of a text and explain how it is supported by key details; summarize the text," a possible learning target might be *identify the main idea and any supporting details* (National Governors Association Center for Best Practices & Council of Chief State School Officers, 2010a). The learning target is one step toward mastery of a larger standard. The plan for instruction, the activities for practice, the questions you ask, the assessment method you use, the criteria required for success, and the information you provide for feedback are all based on helping students accomplish the learning target.

- The focus is on the depth of learning, rather than the grade, which allows you to use a variety of tools and strategies throughout the process. For example, students could practice the learning together, thus using their strengths and supporting their growth opportunities as they approach mastery.

- The assessment *informs* the student and teacher about where the student is with the learning target (also known as *outcome*, *objective*, and *standard subskill*).

- Formative assessments, whether they are short and sweet or long and deep, are ongoing and woven into every lesson, all day long, with all students. These formative assessments give the teacher feedback on his or her teaching. He or she can see how effective it is based on the student work.

- Examined assessments lead to differentiated instruction. Based on the evidence, teachers adjust instructional activities to accomplish the goal at hand, and students apply metacognition to gauge their level of understanding and tell the teacher what they need next. The teacher can give feedback or lead students into self-assessment on that work so any gaps can be closed.

- Response to these data—the differentiated instruction—should occur seconds, minutes, or days from the initial examination (not weeks or months).

In summary, the formative assessment process is an ongoing, planned (and sometimes spontaneous), daily process. You can more easily implement this process with the students when you thoroughly plan, so you can respond wisely when the unexpected comes. These unexpected challenges happen daily. For example, while teaching mathematics, you notice a common error that four students are making. Because your plan involved several strategies to use during that lesson, you realize you need to teach a specific strategy sooner versus later.

Is There Research to Support the Formative Assessment Process?

Educational researchers Paul Black and Dylan Wiliam (1998) are instrumental in establishing that the formative assessment process is transformational, asserting that, done properly, it helps students learn markedly better. Their research concludes that student gains from this process are "amongst the largest ever reported for educational interventions" (Black & Wiliam, 1998, p. 61). In fact, the effect sizes were between 0.40 and 0.70. Any effect size greater than 0.40 is significant and will produce achievement gains. Black and Wiliam (1998) find that using assessment can make learning faster. The formative assessment process can literally help students learn twice as fast.

John Hattie (2009), in his book *Visible Learning*, finds that providing formative evaluation of student learning via interventions produces a 0.90 effect size on achievement. That's almost a two-year leap. It's about the:

> Power of feedback to teachers on what is happening in their classroom so that they can ascertain, "How am I going?" in achieving the learning intentions they have set for their students, such that they can then decide "Where to next?" for the students. (Hattie, 2009, p. 181)

Hattie (2009) explains that it's the teacher's attention to what students are doing, making, saying, or writing—in other words, focusing on mastery evidence—that enables him or her to determine how to respond. He says a teacher's openness to seeing where students are struggling and to innovating that are what matter most (Hattie, 2009). Achievement raises drastically when teachers take the time to examine daily evidence and respond *soon*.

Black and Wiliam's (1998) effect size differs some from Hattie's (2009). That difference stems from the total participants pooled, as well as the variety and types of research. Hattie pooled hundreds of related research to conclude his effect size. He (2009) explains that "some types of feedback are more powerful than others" (p. 174). Cues or reinforcement are crucial. The form matters also. Video, audio, or instruction feedback by computer work well, as does relating feedback to learning goals. Finally, students have to interpret and act on the feedback (Hattie, 2009).

Since about 1978, many others have conducted research reviews on feedback and other aspects of formative assessment (Fuchs & Fuchs, 1986; Shavelson, 2006). The big takeaway, according to Dylan Wiliam and Siobhán Leahy (2015), is that the less time that passes between collecting and responding to evidence, the bigger the impact. In fact, the research concludes that responding six seconds to ten minutes after examining the evidence has the biggest impact. In other words, checkpoints during the lesson should drive immediate feedback. Leahy and Wiliam's (2012) research in schools shows that:

> When formative assessment practices are integrated into the minute-to-minute and day-by-day classroom activities of teachers, substantial increases in student achievement—of the order of a 70 to 80% increase in the speed of learning—are possible, even when outcomes are measured with externally-mandated standardized tests. (p. 67)

Bottom line: respond to the visible, daily data as soon as possible and ensure your students do, too. Using the formative assessment process daily will highly benefit students, teachers, and the rest of a school. Teachers will have less reteaching and fewer students who struggle.

What Is Differentiated Instruction?

In a nutshell, *differentiated instruction* is meeting students' unique, diverse needs so they successfully meet the learning target. Students may not arrive at those goals on the same day and in the same way. This approach is based on a mindset that all students can improve their skills and understanding to achieve the daily learning target and eventually the standard—it just might take more time, different tools, and more teacher support. Rick Wormeli (2018), author of the updated

Fair Isn't Always Equal, says "differentiated instruction is doing what's fair for students" with best practices, "including giving them the tools to handle anything that is undifferentiated" (p. 3). Wormeli (2018) asserts that differentiation "isn't individualized instruction, though that may happen from time to time as warranted. It's whatever works to advance the students. It's highly effective teaching" (p. 3).

Every teacher we've ever worked with has wanted his or her students to succeed. The challenge has always been finding the right tools and strategies to make it happen, and using these tools and strategies strategically and habitually.

Is There Research to Support Differentiation?

Though research doesn't use the term *differentiation* specifically, it does strongly support all the pieces that go into differentiation as we define and explain them in this book. For example, we know formative assessment has strong effect sizes, and that responding to student needs is the last step in the process. This is differentiation. To move students forward, you look at their learning (evidence) and make changes. Then, we give feedback, which has a very strong effect size of 0.73 (Hattie, 2009). When you take time to differentiate, you can move all students to "Got it" with their own tools, support, and time.

There are so many ways to differentiate, and we must choose the most powerful evidence-based strategies for efficiency. For example, one differentiation technique is to provide texts at the students' instructional level, so they can better comprehend it. Another technique is to preteach vocabulary words to English learners (ELs) before beginning a science lab. If your students are struggling to comprehend text and disengaging during reading, you might want to try the strategy reciprocal teaching (chapter 5, page 81), which has an effect size of 0.74 (Hattie, 2009). When teachers base their teaching on students' prior learning, there is an effect size of 0.85 (Hattie, 2009). Reteaching is part of this response; data from the previous lesson tells you to base a new lesson on what students need.

Responding to student needs further looks like relating to students and conveying competence. When students perceive that their teacher is credible, the effect size on student learning is 0.91 (about two years of growth). Hattie (2009) defines *teacher credibility* as a teacher's passion about his or her work, trust, and a teacher's competence. Finally, we must mention one more effect size: when teachers work collectively to improve student achievement and believe their major role is to evaluate their impact on student learning, there is an effect size of 1.57 (Hattie, 2009). That is about three years of growth. That's worth it. We would call this *team differentiation*—using the data from their classrooms to reflect, discuss, and create a response plan for the goal of improving student achievement. All of these effect sizes support the practice of differentiated instruction.

How Did We Merge Neuroscience, the Formative Assessment Process, and Differentiated Instruction Into Four Steps?

We have taken the formative assessment process and added what we've learned about neuroscience and differentiation to develop a four-step cycle for successful instruction. Figure 1.2 shows that cycle.

Three critical questions are part of Hattie's (2009) and Black and Wiliam's (1998) feedback effects, which form a process for teaching. Each leads to the next.

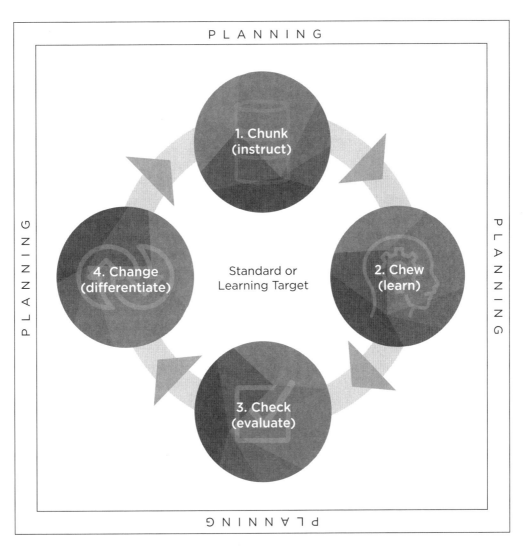

Figure 1.2: *The framed four-step instructional cha-chas cycle.*

1. Where am I going? (Planning includes the teacher sharing learning targets and criteria for success toward this learning target; students understand these learning intentions and can use them to give self-feedback.)

2. Where am I right now? (The teacher has taught, or chunked, and students are showing what they know, or chewing. To know where students are right now, the teacher must check for understanding.)

3. How do I close the gap to get to the learning intentions? In other words, how do I get from here to there? (The teacher, via change, helps students see the gap and guides students as they determine the next steps.)

Notice that the steps are a continuous feedback loop, a cycle. In other words, after you *change* instruction, you might move forward with the next chunk, or you might need to respond differently. It's all based on what you learn during the check. The cycle can occur several times in one lesson. You could also look at this cycle as a daily one: the last checkpoint in the lesson should tell us how to change the next day's learning target, and thus, the cycle starts over with the next day's lesson.

Notice also that all four steps of the instructional cha-chas cycle revolve around the standard or daily learning target. Achieving the daily learning target and reaching the standard are the goals of every lesson. And finally, notice the cha-chas cycle is framed by planning. Of course, we know that no teacher ever steps in front of class without first planning. In fact, we believe that planning is the foundation for quality lessons. Therefore, we framed our four steps to remind you that the cycle is only powerful if you *plan* for all four pieces. This planning frame is so important that the cycle can be thrown off if planning isn't thorough. Once you plan, it's time to instruct using the steps, which the following sections explain in more detail.

Chunk (Instruct)

This is where we look at evidence-based instructional strategies and brain research to determine how to teach the lesson, so students can receive it powerfully for stronger retention. Researched tools from Robert J. Marzano, Debra J. Pickering, and Jane E. Pollock's (2009) *Classroom Strategies That Work* book, show us what works, but not all tools will work perfectly for all students. Because students differ in the way they learn, differentiating how we teach the content is very important.

We take the copious content we need to teach in order for students to understand the learning target and start *chunking* the content into meaningful, smaller, similar, interrelated sections. That helps the brain perceive each section as a coherent group of ideas. The teacher craftily ensures that students are making these chunks meaningful, and therefore, more memorable. You can present the chunks as a short video clip, reading sections, online research, software programs, learning centers, teacher directed, student led, and more.

The first chunk should always introduce the learning target. Students should know what they are supposed to learn, why they are learning it, and how they will know where they are within the learning process each day. Chapter 4 (page 49) talks about chunking in detail and offers approximate time limits and strategies.

Chew (Learn)

During this step, students *chew*, or process, the chunk to enhance their learning. Sometimes we give them choices in their chews and other times we give one chew directive for the whole class. Let them decide how to think about the content. It's what the students *do* with what they just learned—create a website, graph, sort, act out, analyze, synthesize, research—that encourages retention. Chapter 5 (page 81) talks about chewing in detail and offers strategies. Advance to the third step while the students are doing, making, thinking, or writing about their learning.

Check (Evaluate)

Checking for understanding happens while the students are chewing the content. This formative assessment checkpoint allows you to offer regular descriptive, actionable feedback about where the students are in relation to the learning target. Students can also check their own learning. Teach them to self-assess and self-monitor. Chapter 6 (page 117) talks about checking in detail and offers a variety of strategies for checking.

Change (Differentiate)

Let students practice what they learn and revise their work based on feedback from you, other students, or self-reflection. This might be a time to reteach or enrich. This *change* is differentiated instruction. Teachers differentiate during each cha-chas step in a simpler fashion, and yet, this final step is the major differentiation response. It is during this step that you gather data to determine whether you should make bigger changes, such as your pacing, grouping, or assignments. Realize that this final step in the instructional cha-chas cycle might not be the final one in helping all students go from *get it* to *got it*. It's an ongoing process. Chapter 7 (page 159) talks about changing and offers more purposeful differentiation strategies to help you do so.

In closing, you're setting up students for success in learning.

Summary

Setting up your classroom dance floor requires you to understand why you make the choices you make. We hope that this chapter has helped you understand the research behind differentiated instruction and the formative assessment process. More importantly, we hope we have made these concepts easy to remember with our instructional cha-chas. Now that you understand why it's worthwhile to choreograph your instruction with the steps, it's time to examine how we begin planning for them, starting with the standards.

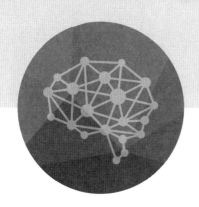

CHAPTER 2

Move Smoothly From Broad Ideas to Smaller Ideas

Every excellent lesson plan, like a choreographed dance routine, has non-negotiables. To successfully plan, you must know your district curriculum and standards. (Knowing your dance partners—your students—is equally important, and chapter 3 on page 21 details that effort.) Once you know your standards, you create daily learning targets to support your students in taking little steps toward the broader standard. Determine what students will do, say, make, or write to show their achievement toward the learning target. You can even create a variety of methods to provide choice for the students, which will likely increase their motivation. Create the criteria for success so students know exactly what they must do to show what they know. This evidence, along with other pieces of evidence you have observed—informal, on-the-fly data gleaned during class—drive your instruction.

State standards tend to be very broad and are written from an educator's perspective; students rarely understand them. For example, one of the National Governors Association Center for Best Practices and Council of Chief State School Officers' (NGA & CCSSO, 2010b) Common Core State Standards for mathematics asks that second-grade students "fluently add and subtract within 100 using strategies based on place value, properties of operations, and/or the relationship between

addition and subtraction" (2.NBT.B.5). Most second graders do not know what the word *fluently* means, and it's the first word in the standard.

A student-friendly learning target helps students determine the goal and expectations for each lesson. The target helps them determine where they are in relation to the broader standard. Authors Susan M. Brookhart and Connie M. Moss (2012) explain that *learning targets*:

> Describe, in language that students understand, the lesson-sized chunk of information, skills, and reasoning processes that students will come to know deeply. We write learning targets from the students' point of view and share them throughout today's lesson so that students can use them to guide their own learning. (p. 3)

Teachers usually plan several *checks* within a lesson to measure student progress toward the learning target, as well as one bigger formative assessment, often referred to as the *class assignment*. The latter is often something tangible, like a written response or a presentation and is the hard evidence showing whether the student mastered the day's learning target. As you plan this, consider the details, the rigor, and the thinking that you want your students to exhibit. It's the start of a beautifully choreographed lesson.

To plan for instruction, we must answer the following questions.

- How do you identify the standard?
- How do you identify the learning target?
- How do you choose the main formative assessment?
- How do you choose criteria for success?

How Do You Identify the Standard?

Which standard will you be partially or wholly assessing in the lesson? We know that teachers touch on several standards within a lesson, but focus on one to make it easier for student to self-assess and for you to determine what you are assessing. When you have learning targets in place, you are partially assessing a standard. Sometimes the learning target for that lesson is the actual standard because you have taught all the learning targets in that progression toward the standard. Table 2.1 shows several standards broken into learning targets.

How Do You Identify the Learning Target?

It takes several learning targets to get to the big, broad standard. How many learning targets will students need to reach the standard? Ideally, you will accomplish this identification with your teacher team. Together, you separate each standard into skills, content or concepts, and context. Breaking apart the standard will help you determine what prerequisites to teach so students can reach mastery. Each prerequisite is a potential learning target depending on whether you teach them to the whole class, a small group, or to individuals who need it (which is an example of differentiation). The flowchart in figure 2.1 demonstrates this breaking apart. For more details about how to do this process with your team, see chapter 2 in *Design in Five* by Nicole Dimich Vagle (2015).

It helps to create a learning target progression to get your students to the standard. The Delaware Department of Education (n.d.) has examples of these progressions for Common Core English language arts standards on its "Curriculum Development for English

and Language Arts (ELA)." For example, the following is a nine-step adapted progression that the Delaware Department of Education (n.d.) gives for the NGA and CCSSO (2010a) Reading standard "Determine two or more main ideas of a text and explain how they are supported by key details; summarize a text" (RI.5.2).

1. I can determine the main idea of a text.
2. I can explain the difference between main ideas and key details in a text by showing examples from the text.
3. I can graphically represent the relationship between main idea and details.
4. I can explain how the different text features add up to the main idea.
5. I can organize the ideas in a text.
6. I can analyze how a text is organized.
7. I can give examples of how the author supports the main idea with the details in the text.
8. I can write a summary including the main ideas and key details of a text.
9. I can determine two or more main ideas of a text and explain how key details support them; I can summarize the text.

Note that the last learning target is the standard. All the previous learning targets lead a student to the big, broad, challenging standard. Each learning target becomes a one- or two-day lesson using the instructional cha-chas cycle.

Notice the following characteristics of a strong learning target. (Visit **go.SolutionTree.com/instruction** to download the reproducible version of this list, "Characteristics of a Strong Learning Target.")

- **Each learning target has a verb and specific content:** The verb is the *do* and the content is the *know* that the students will *show* within that lesson's main formative assessment.

- **Learning targets have verbs that you can visualize and measure:** Examples of verbs include *synthesize, analyze, determine, compare and contrast,* and *explain.* Vague verbs such as *understand, learn, know, comprehend, appreciate,* and *realize* are hard to visualize and measure. The verbs focus on the type of thinking students will engage in versus the activities they will do.

- **Learning targets have the positive, student-friendly, goal-oriented statement *I can:*** All brains are different, and students will reach the learning target in different ways on different days, but most should be able to accomplish the learning target within a one- or two-day lesson plan. If the majority of students cannot master the learning target within a few days, then you may need to break down your learning target further or provide interventions.

- **The phrase *at the end of this lesson* appears in the learning target:** For example, *At the end of this lesson, I can distinguish between main idea and details.* This helps students understand the precise expectation for that lesson.

Table 2.1: *Breaking a Standard Into a Learning Target*

Standard	Learning Target
With prompting and support, identify major events in the story (RL.K.3).	I can identify major events in this story.
Ask and answer questions about key details in a text (RL.1.1).	I can ask and answer questions about key details in the text orally and in writing.
Describe in depth a character, setting, or event in a story or drama, drawing on specific details in the text (e.g. character's thoughts, words, or actions; RL.4.3).	I can describe a character based on specific details in the text.

Source for standard: NGA & CCSSO, 2010a.

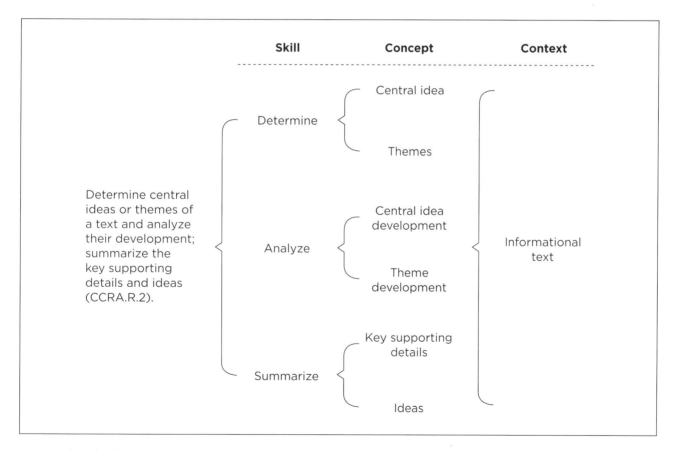

Source: Adapted with permission from Anne Arundel County Schools, 2018.

Source for standard: NGA & CCSSO, 2010a.

Figure 2.1: *Unwrapping a standard with a flowchart.*

Visit go.SolutionTree.com/instruction for a free reproducible version of this figure.

- **Students can self-assess where they are with that learning target:** Hattie (2009) finds that the act of self-assessment has a 1.44 effect size on student achievement. We will share in chapter 3 (page 21) many ways to help students own this learning target.

Choosing the main formative assessment is the next step in lesson planning.

How Do You Choose the Main Formative Assessment?

You will informally check for student learning throughout the lesson, but deciding what formative assessment will be the biggest—but not summative—evidence of proficiency. It should be substantial and produce higher-level thinking. One- or two-page writings, short essays, graphic organizers, and role-playing are some of our favorite substantial formative assessments for those reasons.

Just giving students a chew does not mean they will engage in higher-level thinking. For example, if you ask them simply to write about what they learned without giving them the criteria for success for that writing, you are unlikely to get quality, higher-level thinking within that writing product. Brainstorm what qualities you expect in this writing. Determine this assessment's characteristics. We take you through the steps to creating the criteria for success in the next section.

We encourage you to explore Norman L. Webb's (1997, 1999) Depth of Knowledge (DOK) to design more level two, three, or four products or chews to truly challenge your students. Author Eileen Depka (2017) offers question help for English language arts (figure 2.2) and science (figure 2.3).

You may also consider other taxonomies, including Bloom's (1956; Anderson & Krathwohl, 2001) revised taxonomy and universal design for learning (Meyer, Rose, & Gordon, 2014).

DOK Level	English Language Arts Example
Level one: Recall and reproduction	Who is the main character in the story?
Level two: Skills and concepts	Identify the theme in the story. Provide evidence from the story to support the theme you have chosen.
Level three: Strategic thinking	Compare the Wicked Witch from *The Wonderful Wizard of Oz* to the Queen of Hearts in *Alice's Adventures in Wonderland*. How are they similar and how are they different? Provide evidence.
Level four: Extended thinking	Read two different stories by the same author. Describe similarities and differences in the writing style of the author.

Figure 2.2: Using DOK in an English language arts lesson.

DOK Level	Science Example
Level one: Recall and reproduction	Describe the process of photosynthesis.
Level two: Skills and concepts	You notice that a plant in your classroom is not doing well. How would you determine the cause?
Level three: Strategic thinking	You have little direct light in your bedroom, but would like to have a plant. What plant would you choose, and why?
Level four: Extended thinking	Research and plan a garden that will adequately supply vegetables for a family of four. Include a minimum of four vegetables. Include planting times, size of garden, number of plants, cost, and potential yield.

Figure 2.3: Using DOK in a science lesson.

How Do You Choose Criteria for Success?

The criteria for success is proof, or evidence, of mastering the learning target. It's a student-friendly tool that makes them aware of exactly what the formative assessment asks of them, so they can assess their current performance in light of the learning target. The criteria are linked to the task or performance—the main formative assessment. It's a list of attributes that you want to see in their assessment. Choose criteria that align with the learning target. You can request a checklist, rubric, self-assessment, exemplar, or nonexemplar.

We highly recommend having students watch you complete an exemplar and nonexemplar while they work toward the main formative assessment. We like to ask our students to explain what we expect to confirm their understanding. Every now and then, we develop them with our students, getting their buy-in and ideas. For example, some students might request to use a different website to gather information rather than the one you provide on the checklist. This criteria for success helps you differentiate and give better feedback.

Figure 2.4 is an example of how the learning target, formative assessment, and criteria for success come together to form an engaging, higher-level-thinking lesson (as shown in the student example on the bottom left). It's just the beginning of the process. Alignment of all three is critical. It works as one more support for the

Fourth-Grade ELA classroom	Learning Target + Formative Assessment + Criteria for Success

Learning Target:
I can make a reasonable inference about a character's feelings based on his or her actions and dialogue.

Standard RL.4.1

Group A: Book Club Chapter Response

<u>Very Important Part</u> Criteria for Success

❑ I will make an accurate <u>inference</u> about my character based upon what I read today.

❑ I will back up my inference using <u>details</u> about what the character <u>said</u> and/or <u>did</u>. [Clue: Think about <u>how</u> the character said something.]

Conventions:

❑ I will <u>capitalize</u> all sentences and proper nouns.

❑ I will end each sentence with <u>punctuation</u>.

❑ I will reread my response to make sure that it sounds right and that I answered <u>all</u> parts of the questions.

Scaffolded Criteria for Success

Student Example:

By: Amal

The most important thing that Matt did was go to war with George Washington. This was important because he could have got really hurt. The most important feeling that Matt had was worried. Matt was worried because he was stuck in the time of the Revolutionary War.

Group B: Book Club Chapter Response

<u>Very Important Part</u> Criteria for Success

Sentence starters: The most important thing that _____ did was _____ because _____.

The most important feeling that _____ had was _____ because _____.

❑ I will make an accurate <u>inference</u> about my character based upon what I read today.

❑ I will back up my inference using <u>details</u> about what the character <u>said</u> and/or <u>did</u>. [Clue: Think about <u>how</u> the character said something.]

Conventions:

❑ I will <u>capitalize</u> all sentences and proper nouns.

❑ I will end each sentence with <u>punctuation</u>.

❑ I will reread my response to make sure that it sounds right and that I answered <u>all</u> parts of the questions.

Source: D. Hafner, E. Kirby, & J. McKinlay, Maryvale Primary School, New York, 2018.
Source for standard: NGA & CCSSO, 2010a.

Figure 2.4: *Alignment example—the learning target, formative assessment, student example, and criteria for success.*

students who are working to master the learning target. Notice that the fourth-grade teachers provided two different criteria for success checklists so they could meet the needs of a few students who needed sentence starters.

Figure 2.5 shows the first part of the lesson-plan template. The highlighted, added portions of the lesson-plan template in subsequent chapters show the elements each chapter discusses. You will see the progression of this template's completion throughout the chapters, with the completed lesson plan in figure 8.2 (page 188). Find "The Main Idea and Detail Tabletop Graphic Organizer"

reproducible on page 104, and visit **go.SolutionTree .com/instruction** to download a free reproducible form for recording what your students have mastered, their preferred learning modality, notes for teaching the lesson or unit, and so on.

Effective teachers know their standards and their students and plan accordingly. With the decisions in place from this chapter, you have completed step one in the planning phase. Now you're set up to powerfully implement the remaining steps. It's time to incorporate student data into the plan.

Daily Lesson Plan

Subject or unit: Reading: Main Idea—Details   **Grade:** 5

Standard: Determine two or more main ideas of a text and explain how they are supported by key details; summarize the text (RI.5.2).

Learning target (do and know): I can describe or graphically represent the relationship between main idea and details.

Main formative assessment (show): Students complete "The Main Idea and Detail Tabletop Graphic Organizer" (page 104) to show how the details (table legs) support the main idea (tabletop) based on a given paragraph.

Criteria for success (check type):	Criteria for success (explain details): Students self-assess their work and complete a checklist with the following criteria for success.
☐ Rubric ☑ Self-assessment ☑ Checklist ☐ Peer assessment ☐ Exemplars ☐ Nonexemplars ☐ Verbal ☐ Other: _____	☐ I can write accurate details on the legs. ☐ I can write the accurate main idea on the tabletop. ☐ I can write an explanation, in complete sentences, of how the details and main idea are connected.

Source for standard: NGA & CCSSO, 2010a.

Figure 2.5: *Reviewing the sample lesson plan for alignment.*

Summary

You always create a song list before beginning to dance, just as you create a learning list for your students before beginning instruction. We hope that this chapter guided you through the process of providing a seamless learning sequence by showing you how to break a broad standard into smaller learning targets that students can master within a few days, and how to design formative assessments that accurately evidence learning target mastery.

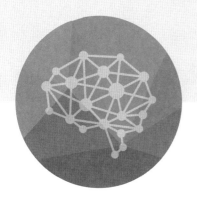

C H A P T E R   3

Get to Know Your Dance Partners

Dance instructors determine how proficient their dancers are prior to placing them in a dance class. They want to find out if their students know the dance vocabulary, the steps, whether they've danced a particular style, and if they've partnered before. While teachers can't control who is in their classroom, we can and should find out as much as we can about our students so we can choreograph an effective lesson.

This chapter will focus on knowing your students—learning about students academically, socially, and emotionally by way of preassessment. This information helps you plan the most effective instruction. The remainder of the chapter presents preassessment strategies that you can use to expose students to the content as well as prime their brains to activate and build on prior knowledge.

It might seem as if you should design content-driven lessons rather than student-driven lessons. After all, you are required to teach standards and students are supposed to master content. The most effective teachers we know are "students of their students" (Tomlinson, 2014, p. 4) who design lessons that are both content driven and student driven. They differentiate for a variety of readiness levels as well as for learning *preferences* (which is simply how students learn best).

To know students, teachers must answer the following questions.

- How can you learn about students?
- Why are preassessing, activating prior knowledge, pre-exposing, and priming worthwhile?
- What strategies can you use?

How Can You Learn About Students?

Teachers can get to know their students through observation, direct questions, or the kinds of assessments and inventories offered online. Search online for the inventories or surveys that fit your grade level. The multiple-intelligence survey provided at Surf Aquarium (www .surfaquarium.com/MI/inventory.htm) is one we like.

Students learn many ways, so table 3.1 (page 22) has considerations for different modalities. Ask these questions during student-teacher conferences or provide them in written format to students or parents.

The more you know about your students, the easier it is to plan your instruction. For example, if you realize a student struggles with bright lights, you may choose to use lamps rather than the overhead fluorescent lights.

Table 3.1: *Factors in a Student Learning Preference*

Learning Preference	Description *(Teachers will ask the following questions for each factor.)*	Information Aspect
Learning modality	Do they learn best visually, aurally, kinesthetically, or a combination of these? Do they like noise or quiet? Do they work best alone or in a group? Do they prefer lots of light or a darker area? Are they affected by room temperature?	Academic, emotional
Cognitive style	Do they think in more concrete or abstract manners? Do they start their thinking process more part-to-whole or whole-to-part? Do they prefer a collaborative or competitive situation? Are they more inductive or deductive in their reasoning?	Academic, social
Intelligence preferences	How is their brain wired for learning? Are they verbal linguistic, logical-mathematical, visual spatial, bodily-kinesthetic, musical rhythmic, interpersonal, intrapersonal, or naturalists according to Howard Gardner's (1993) multiple intelligences?	Academic
Culture and gender	Does their culture or gender affect the way they learn, what they value, or how they interact with one another?	Social, emotional
Interests	What do they like to do outside the classroom? Can you use their interests to help them see the relevance in the lesson?	Social

Source: Gardner, 1993.

Visit **go.SolutionTree.com/instruction** *for a free reproducible version of this table.*

If there are lots of student athletes in your classroom, you might have students read sports articles and biographies, use trading cards to locate hometowns on maps, or debate about whether location determines success in certain sports.

Why Are Preassessing, Activating Prior Knowledge, Pre-Exposing, and Priming Worthwhile?

Preassessing, activating prior knowledge, pre-exposing, and priming enhance memory, increasing how well students learn content. They are important teaching tactics that occur at different times with different intentions.

Preassessing

Not only do you want to find out about how students best learn, but where they are with the content standards *before* planning the lesson. Preassessments can be formal, with a teacher-made test or quiz, or even by administering the post-test, or informal, by adding a warm-up or exit ticket question. Preassessing students' content knowledge allows you, the teacher, to determine *what*

to teach, *who* to teach, and *how* to teach in a way that best promotes learning. We typically ask the following questions while reviewing preassessment results. (Visit **go.SolutionTree.com/instruction** to access a reproducible version of them.)

- What do my students already know about these standards? Can I eliminate or combine learning targets?

- What major concepts are missing from their background knowledge? How might I build them within this unit? Do I need to create additional lessons? Should I prime their brain with these missing concepts before I even start teaching the unit? If so, how will I do this?

- What learning targets might I need to spend more or less time teaching?

- Will I teach these learning targets and standards to the whole group or a small group? If it is small-group instruction, what will the rest of the students do while I'm instructing?

- What misconceptions do they have about this unit or learning target? How can I address these misconceptions early?

These questions lead teachers to the following kinds of decisions.

- If the students already know the content, then there is no need to instruct the skill. We might integrate that skill or knowledge into other lessons.

- If some of the students know the content and others don't, we may create different assignments adjusted to their background knowledge. (We call this differentiation *tiered assignments*.) This allows us to provide instruction and practice for students who need it and deeper, more rigorous work for students who would benefit from a deeper understanding of the content. Tiered assignments are explained in chapter 7 (page 171).

- If none of the students know the content, then we provide whole-group instruction.

Activating Prior Knowledge

We often get the question, How are preassessments different from activating prior knowledge activities? They both activate students' background knowledge on the topic at hand. They both get students focused on the current lesson. They both give you, the teachers, valuable information about where your students are with the learning targets. One difference is *when* you give the activity. It is a preassessment if you give it one to seven days before teaching the lesson. It gives you plenty of time to plan with the preassessment results in mind. If you use an activity to see what they know a couple of *minutes* before you teach it, that is considered activating prior knowledge. You don't have much time to change your instruction, but it helps students make meaning and connections. Also, this powerful process promotes connections in the brain and improved memory.

Preassessments give *the teacher* a big advantage since there is time to change how he or she will teach the unit or lesson. Activating prior knowledge gives *the students* a big advantage since the neural networks are ready to make connections with the new learning. They are both excellent ways to prepare students for upcoming information, which can enhance the learning process, for both the teacher's planning and the students' learning (Shing & Brod, 2016).

Pre-Exposing

Pre-exposing students to content, or *pre-exposure*, is teaching bits of content and skills in advance—days, weeks, months, or even years before accountability. This tool, worth taking advantage of, is also known as *building background knowledge*, *spiral curricula*, or *purposeful scaffolding*. Some classroom examples follow.

- Attending on-site or mini field trips before the unit

- Visiting virtual museums before the lesson

- Preteaching vocabulary words and elaborating on them

- Providing realia or artifacts connected with the content

- Showing pictures or viewing video clips related to the topic

Providing students with rich instruction focused on the content they are reading, or are about to read, increases the likelihood that students' comprehension will improve (Graves, 2006). Preteaching vocabulary supports comprehension, particularly for students who struggle academically (Fisher, Frey, & Pumpian, 2012).

Priming

Priming happens minutes—even seconds—before exposure to a learning event. Research shows that cognitive priming is worth the time (Wexler et al., 2016). The Wexler et al. (2016) study shows that a five-minute game just before mathematics or reading boosts comprehension on those curricular games, and that "doing three 20-minute brain training sessions per week for four months increased gains on school-administered math and reading achievement tests compared to control classes tested at the same times without intervening brain training." Classroom priming examples follow.

- Sharing and discussing the daily learning target

- Using vocabulary words while speaking or discussing the learning

- Standing by a poster that reads *brain alert* when telling them something important

- Creating a standard web, or thinking map, showing all the learning targets, concepts, and products that they will encounter in the unit and referring to it every time you teach one of the targets.

Getting to know students this way to more effectively plan and instruct is not more work or a waste of time. All the techniques are easy to use.

What Strategies Can You Use?

Some common types of preassessments fall into two categories: (1) already designed and (2) teacher designed. Already-designed preassessments follow.

- Unit pretests or unit summative tests
- Benchmark tests
- Chapter questions
- Reading inventories
- Interest inventories
- Surveys for learning preferences and multiple intelligences

Teacher-designed preassessments follow.

- Student-led conferences
- K-W-L charts
- Entrance or exit tickets
- Essay, short answer, and journal responses
- Running records and anecdotal notes
- Anticipation guides
- Knowledge framing

We're sure that you are familiar with many of the preassessments here. Most teachers have given students an interest inventory or multiple-intelligence survey; conducted conferences with students to determine their learning strengths and growth areas; and given students Donna M. Ogle's (1986) K-W-L chart to complete (what I *know*; what I *want* to know; and what I *learned*). You've surely given students essay questions, short-answer questions, and journal responses to learn what they know about an upcoming standard; used running records taken during guided reading to plan the following day's instruction; and added a question about an upcoming learning target to your daily exit ticket.

The strategies in this chapter offer even more choices. Like the others listed here, you're not limited to using them during preassessment only. These strategies work for most formative assessments. Unit tests and chapter questions are often given *after* teaching—but think how much better you could plan and differentiate your lesson if you gave them *before* teaching. In fact, you could give many of the assessments in this chapter at different points in the lesson, but we'll be examining them as preassessments that help you learn more about your students.

On the following pages, we will describe in more detail the teacher-designed preassessment strategies that you may not be as familiar with.

Create-a-Cloze

Create-a-cloze is a preassessment strategy for individual students. During create-a-cloze, students fill in the blanks with key terms. This will help you see what vocabulary and key concepts your students already know, and then you can omit them from your lesson.

Directions

Create or download a passage about the topic your students will be studying. Delete key words within this passage and create a separate list of these words so students have terms to choose from while trying to figure out which word goes in the blank.

Example

See figure 3.1 for an example of a create-a-cloze.

Suggestions for Differentiation

The following suggestions can help you differentiate this strategy.

- **Bumping it up:** Do not provide a word bank. Students must come up with the appropriate words on their own. Delete more challenging words from the passage.

- **Breaking it down:** Divide the text into paragraphs with a word bank for each paragraph. Present fewer blanks. Give students the first letter of the appropriate word.

- **Specializing for students with fine motor challenges:** Number the blanks and allow students to write the number beside the word in the word bank. Allow students to draw a line connecting the blank to the word.

Suggestions to Incorporate Technology

Build Custom Cloze Activities (http://edhelper.com /cloze.htm) and The Teacher's Corner (worksheets .theteacherscorner.net/make-your-own/fill-in-the-blank) will help you develop create-a-cloze activities. (Visit **go.SolutionTree.com/instruction** to access live links to the websites mentioned in this book.)

Name: _____   Date: _____

American Revolution Summary Quiz

After the _____ War, King George III taxed the colonists heavily. He said that England needed more money because of the cost of the war. The colonists were forced to pay _____ to England although they had no representation in _____, the English governing body that makes the laws. They refused to pay a tea tax, and further expressed their anger over this tax by participating in the _____. The colonists especially hated the tax law called the Stamp Act, which caused them to _____ stamped goods.

As anger grew, both the colonists and the _____ prepared for war. On March 5, 1770, a crowd gathered around several British soldiers and shouted insults and threw rocks and snowballs at them. The soldiers opened fire, and three colonists were killed. This event became known as the _____. Some people became _____, or people who supported England. Some people became _____, or people who wanted freedom from England. The people who didn't support England were accused of committing _____. Some people who didn't support the war at all and remained _____.

The first major battle was at Concord and _____. British soldiers marched on the colonists during the night, but _____ received a warning that the British were coming. He galloped across the countryside, warning the colonists. They were ready on a minute's notice, and therefore, got the nickname _____. This was the first battle of the _____.

On July 4, 1776, the _____ was approved by members of the Continental Congress. The war went on for years, and soldiers in the _____ Army faced many hardships because they had few supplies, food, or clothing during the winters. They continued to receive support from the colonists.

The American victory at _____ in 1781 forced the British to surrender. In 1783, the _____ was signed, and it named the United States as a new nation with a _____ government. It finally became _____, free from England.

Word Bank

independent	neutral	Patriots	Boston Massacre
democratic	Treaty of Paris	Continental	Revolutionary War
taxes	Boston Tea Party	Loyalists	Declaration of
Paul Revere	treason	Parliament	Independence
boycott	Minutemen	Redcoats	
Yorktown	Lexington	French and Indian	

Source: Nickelsen, 2003.

Figure 3.1: *Example of create-a-cloze.*

Self-Evaluation Graffiti Corners

Self-evaluation graffiti corners is a preassessment strategy for small groups of students. During this activity, teachers label the room's corners and students move to corners of the room that represent their knowledge about the topic. The benefit is seeing how students feel about their level of knowledge and the students consolidating their knowledge with their group.

Directions

Create the signs (*know very little, know some, know more,* and *know a lot*) for each corner. Share the topic with the students. Have them reflect individually and write their knowledge level on a sticky note prior to moving to the appropriate corner. In their corners, students can use chart paper or construction paper to design a graffiti chart of things they know about the topic. Students may share their chart orally with the class or visually, by leaving them posted in the corner and moving around the room examining each other's chart. Students can add to the chart as they continue gaining knowledge throughout the unit of study.

Example

See figure 3.2 for examples of two self-evaluation graffiti corners on plants. As you can see, one group's knowledge is very basic, containing key concepts and a simple visual, while the other group shows much deeper knowledge and a more complex visual.

Suggestions for Differentiation

The following suggestions can help you differentiate this strategy.

- **Bumping it up:** Have students include an analogy, simile, or metaphor to their chart; ask them to draw lines connecting various concepts on their graffiti chart. Or, allow them to develop some inquiry questions about the topic and then provide time to research the answers.

- **Breaking it down:** Give students key terms to include on their chart; have some images ready for them to choose from. Or, allow students who are struggling to examine books and websites on the topic for several days to help them build some background knowledge.

- **Specializing for students who do not participate or need accountability:** Give each student a different colored marker and have them take turns writing something they know. If they can't think of anything, they wait

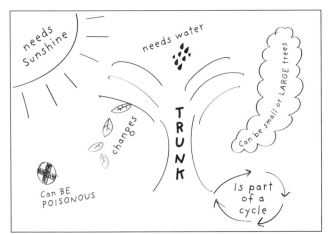
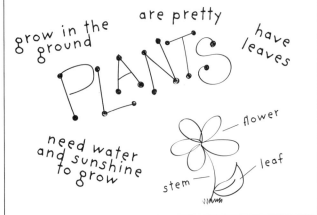

Figure 3.2: *Examples of two self-evaluation graffiti corners on plants.*

for five seconds before passing it to the next student, allowing them more time to consider their next response. Have each member sign his or her name or use a different color marker so you can determine what each student knows.

Suggestions to Incorporate Technology

The following website and app will help you develop self-evaluation graffiti corners.

- Graffiti Creator (www.graffiticreator.net) has wild graffiti styles.

- MindNode (https://mindnode.com) has more organized mind maps.

Anticipation Guide

Anticipation guides are a preassessment strategy for individual students. The benefit is seeing key concepts your students already know, therefore moving onto content that they still haven't mastered.

Directions

Use the "Anticipation Guide" reproducible (page 40) with some key statements about the unit. Statements should be true or false. Students place a check mark in the Before Learning column to explain whether they agree or disagree with the statement. After the learning or reading, ask students to place a check mark in the After Learning column based on what they learn. Invite them to go back to the text or notes to determine if they were correct and write the page numbers where they verify the information. Students correct any false statements by making them true within the Statement column.

Example

See figure 3.3 (page 28) for an example of an anticipation guide.

Suggestions for Differentiation

The following suggestions can help you differentiate this strategy.

- **Bumping it up:** Include more abstract, complex, or inferential statements. Make some of the statements half true and half false. Change the Agree and Disagree boxes on both sides to include a continuum (a two-sided arrow) with Strongly Agree and Strongly Disagree.

- **Breaking it down:** Choose statements that the text specifically answers.

- **Specializing for kinesthetic learners:** Consider making the anticipation guide more kinesthetic with one of the following versions.

  - *Vote with your feet*—Let students know which side of the room represents agreement and which side of the room represents disagreement. Have them read the statement and then physically walk to the side of the room that represents their thinking.

  - *Vote with your toes*—Students stand in rows of about five, making sure you can see their feet. Tell students to read the statements silently as you read them aloud. Provide about ten seconds of think time after reading each statement before asking students to vote. Students vote by turning their bodies so that their toes face right for statements they believe to be true, and left for statements they believe to be false. Observe to determine areas that need clarification.

Suggestions to Incorporate Technology

The following website and app will help you develop anticipation guides.

- Kahoot! (https://kahoot.it) works well if you are a one-to-one school and every student has a device.

- Plickers (www.plickers.com) allows one device to gather students' responses without the need for student devices.

Spooky Animals: Some Scary-Looking Species Are All Fang and No Bite

Directions before learning: Read each of the following statements. Indicate whether you agree or disagree with the statement by placing a check in the appropriate box.

Directions after learning: Revisit each statement and mark your thinking. For any changed responses, record the page numbers that support your thinking.

Before Learning		Statement	After Learning		Page or Pages
Agree	Disagree		Agree	Disagree	
✓		Tarantulas are dangerous to people.		✓	1
	✓	Some tarantulas are so big that you cannot hold them in your hand.	✓		1
✓		There are vampire bats, vampire squirrels, vampire squids, and vampire deer.	✓		2
✓		Vampire bats bite humans and drink their blood.		✓	2
✓		A slow loris is a primate with a venomous tongue.		✓	2

My new learning:

- Tarantulas are <u>not</u> dangerous to people.
- Tarantulas can grow so big you might have trouble holding one in one hand.
- Vampire bats definitely drink blood, but seldom go after humans.
- A slow loris' arms hide glands full of toxins.

Figure 3.3: *Example of anticipation guide.*

Draw It, Web It, Write It

Draw it, web it, write it is a preassessment strategy for individuals or small groups. During this activity, students choose how to display their knowledge about the upcoming topic. The benefit is seeing what key concepts your students already know.

Directions

Distribute the "Draw It, Web it, Write It" reproducible (page 41). The *draw it* area of the room will have supplies for students to quickly draw what they know about the topic. The *web it* area will have supplies for students to create a web of words related to the topic. The *write it* area will have writing supplies, so students can construct a paragraph about what they know on the topic. For students who wish to do all three (draw, web, and write), provide the draw it, web it, write it template. Present students with the topic of study. They reflect on the topic at hand, determine whether they would rather draw, web, or write their responses, and then move to that area of the room and begin sharing their knowledge about the content. Students can explain their product when they finish.

Example

See figure 3.4 for an example of draw it, web it, write it.

Suggestions for Differentiation

The following suggestions can help you differentiate this strategy.

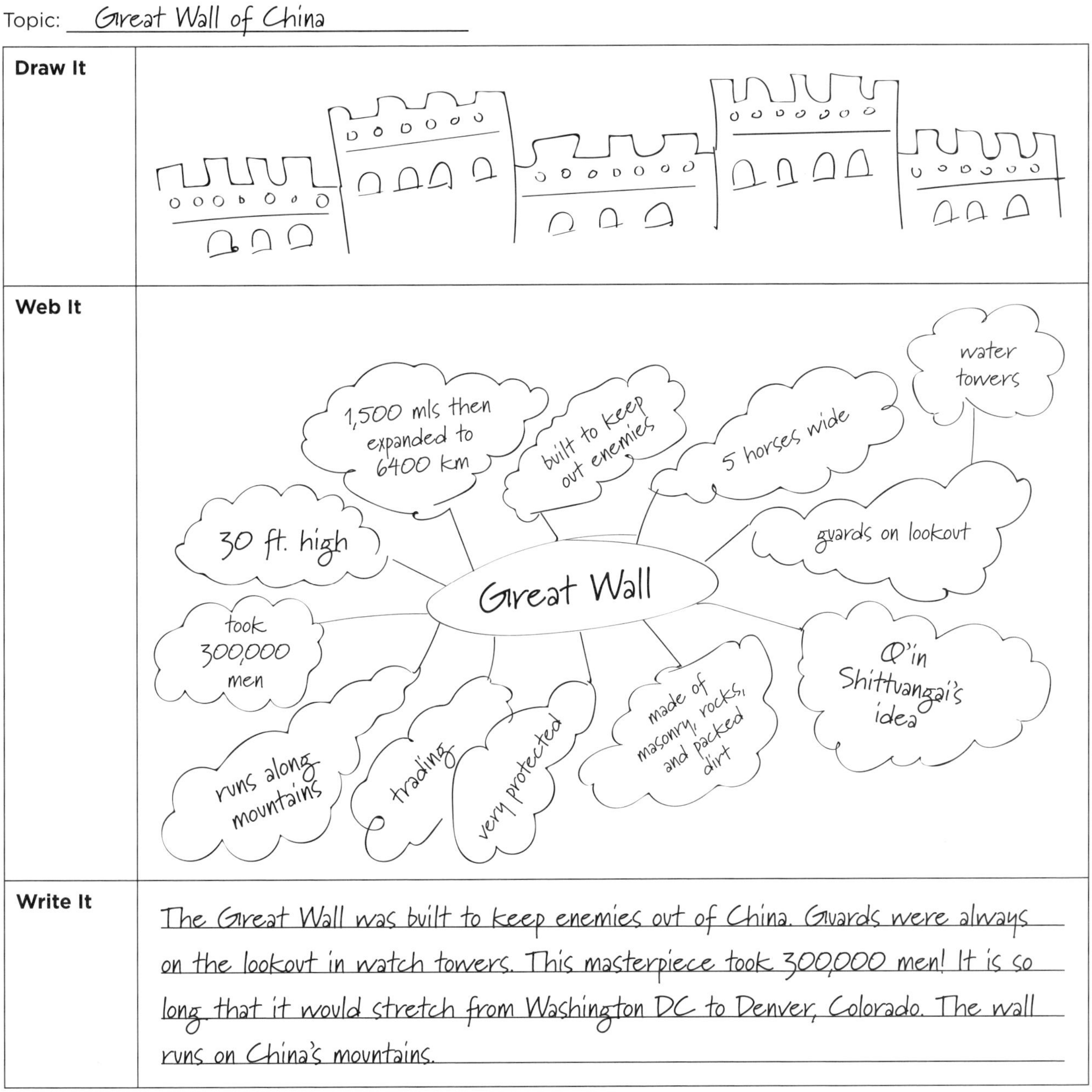
Topic: Great Wall of China
Draw It
Web It
Great Wall
1,500 mls then expanded to 6400 km
built to keep out enemies
5 horses wide
water towers
guards on lookout
30 ft. high
took 300,000 men
Q'in Shittvangai's idea
made of masonry, rocks, and packed dirt
very protected
trading
runs along mountains
Write It
The Great Wall was built to keep enemies out of China. Guards were always on the lookout in watch towers. This masterpiece took 300,000 men! It is so long that it would stretch from Washington DC to Denver, Colorado. The wall runs on China's mountains.

Figure 3.4: *Example of draw it, web it, write it.*

- **Bumping it up:** Increase the complexity of what you require them to draw, web, or write by adding more criteria. You can do this by adding more vocabulary words for them to include in the picture, web, or writing.
- **Breaking it down:** Decrease the complexity of what they draw, web, or write by limiting the criteria necessary. Provide sentence starters in the writing section. Provide picture books on the topic for the drawing center (to help them draw the object). Be prepared to help students start their webs.
- **Specializing for students who do not participate or need accountability:** Put students into small groups. Give each student a different color marker and have him or her take turns adding to the group's drawing, web, or paragraph until each student depletes all that he or she knows. Have each member sign his or her name in his or her color marker so you can determine what each individual student contributes.

Suggestions to Incorporate Technology

The following websites will help you develop the draw it, web it, write it strategy.

- Paper (www.fiftythree.com/paper) is a good resource for students who want to draw.

- MindMeister (www.mindmeister.com), MindNode (https://mindnode.com), and Popplet (http://popplet.com) are good resources for students who want to create a web.

- Reading Rockets' "Paragraph Hamburger" (https://bit.ly/1YmdgeJ) offers an outline, templates, and books to practice writing paragraphs.

Knowledge Framing

Knowledge framing is a preassessment strategy for individual students that can continue on throughout the learning. During this activity, students fill in the graphic with information that they know and want to know. They complete the remaining sections as they continue their learning. The benefit is seeing what key concepts your students already know, and therefore you don't need to teach, as well as it being a checkpoint to see what they are learning. You can also use it after a chew to see if they can summarize the learning.

Directions

Provide students with the "Knowledge Framing Prior to Reading the Text" reproducible (page 42). Students complete the top and bottom section of the picture frame, stating what they know and what they want to learn about a specific topic. As students continue to learn, they complete the sides of the frame, explaining their new learning. Finally, students complete the middle of the picture frame by drawing a visual representation and by writing a summary of the learning. The summary can be a paragraph, poem, or song. If there isn't enough room, students continue the summary on the back.

Example

See figure 3.5 for an example of knowledge framing.

Suggestions for Differentiation

The following suggestions can help you differentiate this strategy.

- **Bumping it up:** Ask these students to write more statements about what they think they know on the back of the graphic organizer. Ask

them to include vocabulary words that they know relate to this topic, and encourage them to write a topic sentence and details for their summary.

- **Breaking it down:** Give these students a summary frame of *who*, *did what*, *where*, *when*, *why*, and *how*. Encourage students to look through picture books to *jog their memory* about what they know about this topic. Allow these students to use Google Images (https://images.google.com) if drawing is a challenge, and give them question stems to help them generate their *What do I want to know?* questions.

- **Specializing for ELs:** Partner the students with a grade-level, English-speaking student. While both students participate in the discussion, the native English speaker, or a student who is proficient in English, would do the writing, while the English learner would draw the image.

Suggestions to Incorporate Technology

The following apps will help you develop the knowledge-framing strategy.

- The iOS device app Ghostwriter (https://apple.co/2t2I90P) allows students to draw their own organizer and allows you to upload the graphic as a PDF for students to use.

- Explain Everything (www.explaineverything.com) is amazing for combining new and existing media, annotations, and text to create unique visual stories. It also helps get everyone on the same page by sharing projects for continuous development and feedback.

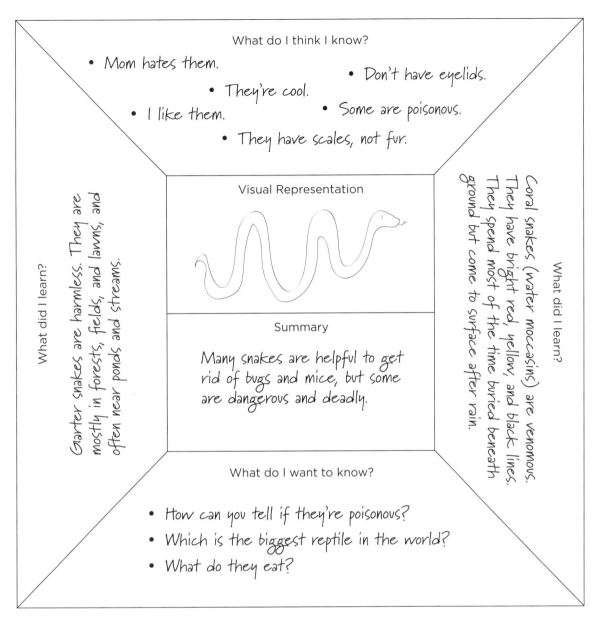

What do I think I know?
- Mom hates them.
- They're cool.
- I like them.
- Don't have eyelids.
- Some are poisonous.
- They have scales, not fur.

Visual Representation

Summary

Many snakes are helpful to get rid of bugs and mice, but some are dangerous and deadly.

What did I learn? (left)
Garter snakes are harmless. They are mostly in forests, fields, lawns, and often near ponds and streams.

What did I learn? (right)
Coral snakes (water moccasins) are venomous. They have bright red, yellow, and black lines. They spend most of the time buried beneath ground but come to surface after rain.

What do I want to know?
- How can you tell if they're poisonous?
- Which is the biggest reptile in the world?
- What do they eat?

Figure 3.5: *Example of knowledge framing prior to reading the text.*

Find an Expert

Find an expert is a preassessment strategy that allows the whole group to activate their prior knowledge by discussing key questions about the content. During this activity, students move around the room in search of an expert to answer one of the questions on the handout. The benefits are seeing which students are knowledgeable about the upcoming content and might be experts during the teaching and allowing all students to think about and discuss the content prior to instruction.

Directions

Create nine questions about an upcoming unit of study and record them in the boxes on the "Find an Expert" reproducible (page 43). Have students walk around the room to *find an expert* who can respond to one of the questions. After responding verbally, the student who responded writes his or her initials in the box. Students circulate until all boxes are initialed or time is called. Students may give incorrect answers. You may want to mingle to clarify during the activity or share an answer key at the end of the activity.

Examples

See figure 3.6 for an example of find an expert. See figure 3.7 for a find-an-expert example for nonreaders.

Suggestions for Differentiation

The following suggestions can help you differentiate.

- **Bumping it up:** Create a separate find-an-expert template with more complex questions. Require students to both answer and defend

their answer prior to initialing. Have them design the questions that go inside the boxes.

- **Breaking it down:** Create a separate find-an-expert template for these students with questions that are more simply worded. If using the same sheet, have them get a tic-tac-toe of responses rather than completing the entire page. Use a student who is struggling to model the activity. Have him or her approach a classmate with a lot of background (or with you). Now this student has one answer correct and can be the expert for that question.

- **Specializing for nonreaders or students with limited English skills:** Put pictures in the boxes and have them discuss what they know about the pictures. Make some of the items something they can act out or do physically. For example, Without saying a word,

Find an Expert

| **Directions** |
| Complete the following two steps. The goal is to activate your prior knowledge in the content area and to gather new ideas. |

1. Walk around the room and find someone who can respond to one of the statements in each box. After responding verbally to your question, the person should initial in the square.

2. A person can only answer and initial one square on your card. Feel free to discuss the answer too.

Label the parts of this equation. Product and factor 1,500 x 15 = 22,500	Create a multiplication and division fact family.	Explain how fact families can help with division. Give an example.
How is repeated subtraction related to division?	How is repeated addition related to multiplication?	How does an array help you with division and multiplication?
Label the parts of this equation. 9 8⟌72 (quotient, divisor, dividend)	Draw an array to represent. 6 x 4	Show with manipulatives: 3 groups of 5.

Figure 3.6: *Example of find an expert.*

can you "show" me one of this week's vocabulary words? Or, Can you solve the following mathematics problem? Provide a clipboard with paper or a whiteboard for them to record their responses.

Suggestions to Incorporate Technology

The following apps will help you develop the find-an-expert strategy.

- Ghostwriter app (https://apple.co/2t2I90P) allows those with Mac, iPad, and iPhone devices to upload the graphic or take a picture of the graphic for students to annotate directly on it.

- Skitch (https://evernote.com/products/skitch) allows the same capabilities on the same devices.

Find an Expert

Topic: The pond

You will see these pictures in the book we are about to read. Find someone who can tell you the proper name for the object in the picture.

Figure 3.7: Example of find an expert modified for nonreaders.

Show What You Know

Show what you know is a preassessment strategy for small groups of three students. This activity can help students activate prior knowledge as they design questions about upcoming content and ask their classmates to answer them. The benefit is seeing what key concepts your students already know and what questions they want answered about the upcoming content.

Directions

Place students in groups of three. Tell students to think of questions about the topic. Assign one student to be the scribe and list all questions that pop into group members' minds on a sheet of paper. The scribe writes all the questions down quickly. If someone makes a statement, the scribe can write the statement and change it to a question afterward. After questions are generated, ask groups to categorize the questions as closed questions (one-word, simple learning answers) or open-ended questions (variety of answers can be given).

Distribute one "Show What You Know" reproducible (page 44) to each student. Have students choose the four best questions and write them on their individual template. These could be the same four questions for each group member or they could be different questions based on student choice. Students travel around the room and try their best to answer other students' questions. Make sure that students are aware that this is not for a grade and that you will be using the information gathered to plan your teaching. Students must respond to each question, even if all they do is write *I don't know*. Student responses can come in any method they can put in the boxes. Allow student groups to meet again to see which questions they answered and how many questions stumped their classmates. You might need to incorporate their stumped questions into the instruction.

Example

See figure 3.8 for an example of show what you know.

Suggestions for Differentiation

The following suggestions can help you differentiate this strategy.

- **Bumping it up:** Design an inquiry station to allow advanced students to research the unanswered open-ended questions and present those answers to their classmates as a wrap-up to the unit.

- **Breaking it down:** Design an inquiry station that gives each student who is struggling one closed question that he or she must research the answer to and present to his or her classmates as a wrap-up to the unit.

- **Specializing for students reading significantly below grade level:** Provide alternate text at these students' independent reading level or allow them to listen to the text being read so that reading level does not determine whether they know the content standard.

Suggestions to Incorporate Technology

The following websites will help you use the show-what-you-know strategy.

- Rewordify (https://rewordify.com) is a text compactor that simplifies and shortens readings, so students can discuss the same text.

- Newsela (https://newsela.com), Smithsonian's TweenTribune (www.tweentribune.com), and News in Levels (www.newsinlevels.com) offer informational text that are adjusted for high, medium, or low Lexile levels.

Name: _____Becky_____   Date: __10/2_____

Directions: The questions in the following boxes relate to an upcoming unit. This is not for a grade, but rather an opportunity for you to show what you know. I will use this information to plan my teaching. Give it your best try. Good luck!

Topic: Spiders

1. How fast can a spider spin a full web? How long does it take with different kinds of spiders?	2. What is a web made up of? What makes up the thread-like string coming out of the spider?
3. If a spider lost a _____, could it still spin a web?	4. What is a life cycle of a spider? How long do they live?

Figure 3.8: Example of show what you know.

Four-Choice Processing

Source: Adapted from Jensen & Nickelsen, 2008.

Four-choice processing is a preassessment strategy for individual students. This activity allows you to see what students know about a topic. The benefit is seeing what key concepts your students already know and which questions generate the most responses.

read the question choices at the bottom, decide which question they want to answer within the first box, circle that question, and then answer it in the appropriate box. Students follow this same procedure for each subsequent box.

Directions

Make copies of the four-choice processing template. Students write the topic at the top of the sheet, they

Example

See figure 3.9 for a completed example of the template.

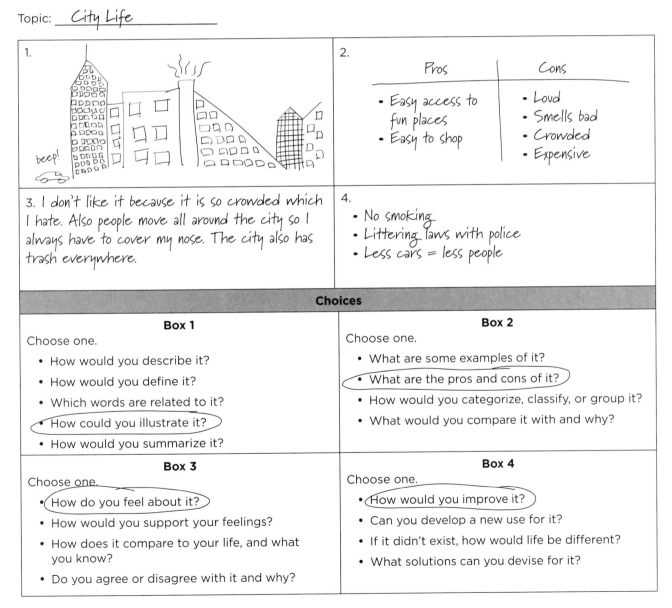

Topic: City Life

1.

2.

Pros	Cons
• Easy access to fun places • Easy to shop	• Loud • Smells bad • Crowded • Expensive

3. I don't like it because it is so crowded which I hate. Also people move all around the city so I always have to cover my nose. The city also has trash everywhere.

4.
- No smoking
- Littering laws with police
- Less cars = less people

Choices

Box 1

Choose one.
- How would you describe it?
- How would you define it?
- Which words are related to it?
- *How could you illustrate it?*
- How would you summarize it?

Box 2

Choose one.
- What are some examples of it?
- *What are the pros and cons of it?*
- How would you categorize, classify, or group it?
- What would you compare it with and why?

Box 3

Choose one.
- *How do you feel about it?*
- How would you support your feelings?
- How does it compare to your life, and what you know?
- Do you agree or disagree with it and why?

Box 4

Choose one.
- *How would you improve it?*
- Can you develop a new use for it?
- If it didn't exist, how would life be different?
- What solutions can you devise for it?

Figure 3.9: *Example of four-choice processing.*

Visit go.SolutionTree.com/instruction for a free reproducible version of this figure.

Suggestions for Differentiation

The following suggestions can help you differentiate this strategy.

- **Bumping it up:** Provide more question choices, use higher-level questions, or both. Have students only complete boxes 3 and 4, which are for more complex thinking. Have students defend and support their answers.

- **Breaking it down:** Limit the question choices, use lower-level questions, or both. Have students complete only boxes 1 and 2, which are for less complex thinking.

- **Specializing for auditory and kinesthetic learners:** Allow students to circulate around the room sharing their thinking prior to *and* after completing the boxes.

Suggestions to Incorporate Technology

The following apps will help you develop the four-choice-processing strategy.

- Bamboo Paper (https://bit.ly/2lfWBhF) is a note-taking and sketching app that you can use to support the four-choice-processing strategy.

- Evernote (https://evernote.com) is a note-taking app that you can use to support the four-choice processing strategy.

Kinesthetic Vocabulary

You can use kinesthetic vocabulary as a preassessment strategy for groups of three or four students if you introduce words prior to a unit. It also can be a priming strategy using words that you have recently taught so you can see whether students retain key vocabulary meanings. This activity's benefit is seeing what key vocabulary you need to cover or seeing what students can quickly retrieve.

Directions

In advance, write up to ten vocabulary words you have recently taught on index cards, small pieces of paper, or on the provided "Kinesthetic Vocabulary Cards" reproducible (page 45). Place students in groups of three to four. This is a game of charades, so do not allow anyone to speak except to announce the word when guessing. Students must correctly pronounce the word when guessing and may use any previous notes for review during the game. Give an identical set of cards to each group of students. Students place the cards face down on a table (no words should be showing) and stand around the cards. Students take turns grabbing a card and acting it out. The other students in the group try to guess the word. Once a group member correctly guesses a word, he or she places the card face up. If group members get stuck, they replace the card face down on the table and choose a new card.

Example

A student who chooses the word *igneous* from the vocabulary cards in figure 3.10 might choose to enact a volcano erupting and then become the lava as it starts to flow and then slowly pools and hardens.

Suggestions for Differentiation

The following suggestions can help you differentiate this strategy.

- **Bumping it up:** Group students who are above proficient and give them more challenging vocabulary. Encourage them to examine any words that gave them trouble and create a method for memory retrieval. Place two words on the same card that they need to act them out so their group can guess both words. (Have them create movements that connect the terms somehow.)

- **Breaking it down:** Group students who are struggling together and provide them with less challenging vocabulary. Encourage them to examine any words that gave them trouble and design a visual to draw on the back of the word card to use as a *memory hook*, to help their brains remember.

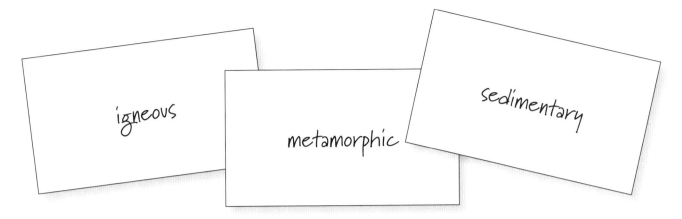

Figure 3.10: *Examples of vocabulary cards.*

- **Specializing for slow processing:** Have the student act out the word twice. Then, set a timer for one minute. Students have one minute of think time to come up with the word before anyone can guess.

Suggestions to Incorporate Technology

The following apps will help you develop kinesthetic vocabulary.

- Endless Alphabet (www.originatorkids .com/?p=564) teaches letter sounds and new vocabulary in the primary grades.

- World's Worst Pet–Vocabulary (https://apple .co/1cz6VnA) is a tool for grades 4–8. It focuses on both Tier 2 vocabulary (general academic words, which include examples like *considerate* and *industry*) and Tier 3 vocabulary (domain specific like *algebra* and *pronoun*; Beck, McKeown, & Kucan, 2002).

- Knowji (http://knowji.com) teaches 1,600 words specifically chosen for popular standardized tests (specifically, the SAT, Graduate Record Examinations, ACT, and Armed Services Vocational Aptitude Battery).

The Big Picture

The big picture is a preassessment strategy for individual students that allows you to preteach students upcoming key vocabulary. The benefit to this strategy is that it takes students deeper than the Frayer model (which provides definition, characteristics, examples, and non-examples) by allowing them to *explain* rather than define the word, form a connection with the word in multiple ways, place the word in the context of a sentence, and design a visual to support memory retention.

Directions

Select three to five vocabulary words that students will encounter in an upcoming reading selection. Choose three to four students to do this activity. Keep track of which students you choose each time and rotate through your list so that everyone gets a chance to participate over the course of a unit or semester. During independent practice time, other classroom transition time, or for homework, give three to four students each a word to preteach to the class the next day. These students complete "The Big Picture" reproducible (page 46) for their word. Provide brief instructions, such as the following.

- **Word description:** Write a definition, in your own words, based on the context.

- **Part of speech and pronunciation:** Use a dictionary or online resources as needed to write the part of speech and pronunciation.

- **Word connections:** Connect the word to yourself, the world, or the text by using similes, metaphors, personal experience, and so on.

- **Word art:** Draw a picture or symbol of the word.

- **Word context:** Write the sentence from the text given to you and then create your own sentence using the word in a new and different context.

Students complete the template and get teacher feedback before teaching the word to the whole class. Students present their words before the class reads the text, using a document camera (a digital overhead that displays real-time images), scanner, or screenshot of their template to enlarge their work for the whole class to view, or allow students to pass their paper around so each student has the opportunity to see it. Encourage students to have fun and be creative with their presentation. They may choose to lead the class in a chant, song, rhyme, or movement. You might also suggest that they use gestures. Remind them that the purpose of their presentation is to help the rest of the class understand and remember the word, so anything they can do to assist with that is good. Place the completed templates on the word wall so all students can see and refer to them during the reading.

Example

See figure 3.11 for an example of the big picture.

Suggestions for Differentiation

The following suggestions can help you differentiate this strategy.

- **Bumping it up:** Choose more challenging vocabulary, possibly words with multiple meanings depending on the context. Challenge students to find additional text that uses the word in a variety of contexts.

- **Breaking it down:** Choose less challenging vocabulary, or preteach the vocabulary to them and provide several options as teaching points. Allow them to choose what they believe is the best way to teach the word to their peers. Ensure that they have time in class, with your support.

The Big Picture

Name: Sarah   Book title: It's All in Your Head by Susan L Barret

Word Descriptions	**Word Connections**
Explain what this word means.	Connect the word (simile, metaphor, or analogy; other synonyms; personal experience).
Ability to sense or know immediately without reasoning or effort, happens automatically	Intuition is like blinking—they both happen fast, they both can benefit us, and they both are subconscious.
Part of speech: noun	

Intuition

Word Context	**Word Art**
Show the word in context.	Show a picture or symbol that assists with memory.
Use the word in a meaningful sentence.	
page 69—It's almost impossible not to be intuitive. The trick lies in being sensitive to what our intuition tells us and knowing when it's steering us in the right direction.	(sixth sense)
Word in a meaningful sentence:	
My intuition told me that the stranger was lying to me about being a relative.	

Figure 3.11: *Example of the big picture.*

- **Specializing for memory challenges:** Provide a variety of product options from which students can choose, including but not limited to sing it, show visual images, and role-play.

Suggestions to Incorporate Technology

The following websites and apps will help you develop the big picture strategy.

- Merriam-Webster's Word Central (www .wordcentral.com) is a gold standard for anything word related.
- Little Explorers (www.enchantedlearning .com/Dictionary.html) looks less polished, but has good content and translations into many languages other than English.

- Wordsmyth (www.wordsmyth.net) has content geared specifically for students K–2.

Summary

Getting to know your dance partners—your students—academically, socially, and emotionally in this cha-cha will help you determine *how* to teach. Preassessing, activating prior knowledge, pre-exposing, and priming will show you how full their dance card might be and help you determine *what* and *who* you teach. The combination of this knowledge allows you to set the stage and frame a beautiful classroom learning dance.

Anticipation Guide

Title:

Directions before learning: Read each of the following statements. Indicate whether you agree or disagree with the statement by placing a check in the appropriate box.

Directions after learning: Revisit each statement and mark your thinking. For any changed responses, record the page numbers that support your thinking.

Before Learning		Statement	After Learning		Page or Pages
Agree	Disagree		Agree	Disagree	

My new learning:

Draw It, Web It, Write It

Topic: _____

Draw It	
Web It	Topic:
Write It	_____

Knowledge Framing Prior to Reading the Text

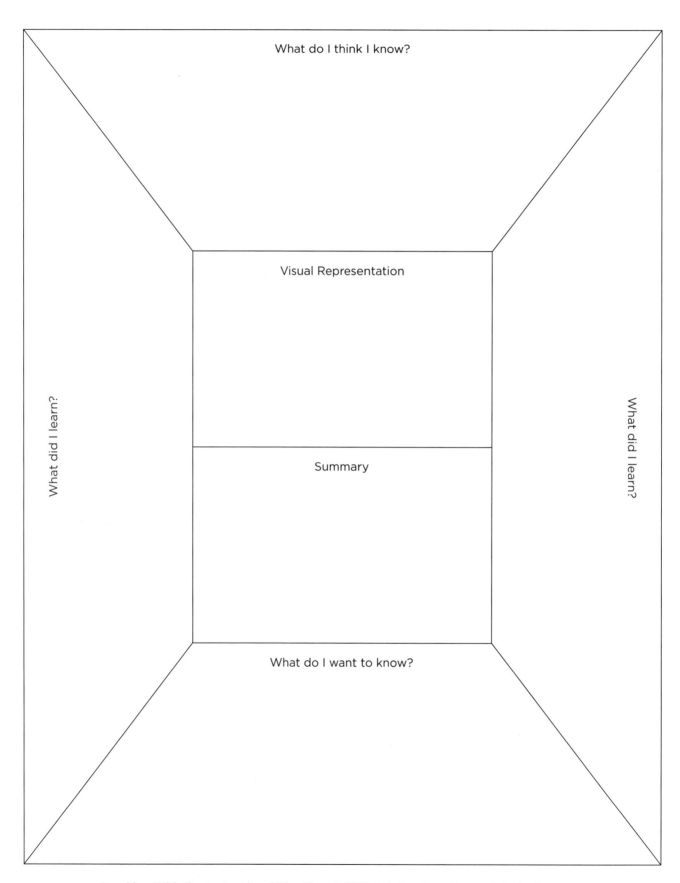

What do I think I know?

Visual Representation

What did I learn?

Summary

What did I learn?

What do I want to know?

Find an Expert

Directions: Complete the following two steps. The goal is to activate your prior knowledge in the content area and to gather new ideas.

1. Walk around the room and find someone who can respond to one of the following statements in each box. After responding verbally to your question, the person should initial in the square.

2. A person can only answer and initial one square on your card. Feel free to discuss the answer too.

Show What You Know

Name: _____ Date: _____

Directions: The questions in the following boxes relate to an upcoming unit. This is not for a grade, but rather an opportunity for you to show what you know. I will use this information to plan my teaching. Give it your best try. Good luck!

Topic:

1.	2.
3.	4.

Kinesthetic Vocabulary Cards

The Big Picture

Name: _____

Book title: _____

Word Descriptions Explain what this word means.	**Word Connections** Connect the word (simile, metaphor, or analogy; other synonyms; personal experience).

Word:

Word Context Show the word in context. Use the word in a meaningful sentence.	**Word Art** Show a picture or symbol that assists with memory.

Part II

PUTTING THE CHA-CHAS STEPS TOGETHER

Part I helped you set up your classroom dance floor and learn about your students. Part II is where you choreograph your dance to meet your students' needs, implementing the four steps that lead you and your students through the instructional cha-chas cycle of instructing, learning, evaluating, and differentiating. Chapter 4 teaches you how, why, and how long to chunk. Chapter 5 guides you through a variety of strategies that allow your students to chew on the content. Chapter 6 leads you through proper, helpful formative assessment so you can check how students are doing. Chapter 7 dives deeply into differentiation so you can change your pacing, instruction, and grouping to deepen student mastery. Chapter 8 offers scenarios and other tools that show how you can bring your classroom dance together.

Take Step One: Chunk (Instruct)

At this point, you have established what dancers call the *frame*. This is your outline, your framework, for success—planning instruction that aligns to standards and learning targets. You know your students' interests, their learning preferences, and their readiness; now it's time to instruct. And when you're instructing, what's happening in a student's brain?

Our brains are built to chunk, and that's what you'll learn how to include in your lessons in this chapter. Dance teachers would never teach an entire dance from beginning to end. Instead, they introduce the dance in eight counts—chunks. Classroom teachers introduce the content in brain-friendly chunks as well. In this chapter, we'll answer the following questions.

- What is a chunk and why does the brain like it?

- How long should a chunk be?

- How do you chunk a daily lesson?

- What teaching elements should chunks include?

- What strategies can you use during chunking?

All this information will help you reach students to maximum effect, so that their learning sticks.

What Is a Chunk and Why Does the Brain Like It?

Chunking is a natural process that occurs during thinking, in which the brain perceives several pieces of information as a single item. Research finds that breaking up a sequence of ideas or information makes it easier to remember and to recall that information in the right order (Ericcson, Chase, & Falloon, 1980; Fonollosa, Neftci, & Rabinovich, 2015). Memory chunking organization has been investigated since the 1950s at least. Experimental psychologist Weston A. Bousfield, in 1953, confirmed that information-carrying items seem to be recalled in associated clusters. Shortly after, psychologist George Armitage Miller (1956) pointed out that limits in our working memory capacity for processing information necessitated organizing them into chunks of what he called the magical number seven. Psychology professor Nelson Cowan (2015) claims the capacity to seven bits is now more like four or fewer, and that changes with age and other factors.

Chunking helps our brains see similarities, connections, and sequences between and among pieces of information. This will require learning how to take the copious amounts of information and determine the smaller sections that have strong associations with each other. While the brain naturally seeks to chunk information into meaningful segments, teachers can facilitate this memory process by planning their lessons in a way that helps students see patterns and chunks in specific content (Fonollosa et al., 2015). That will mean breaking a lesson into smaller pieces rather than leaving it as a large block of information. The brain remembers best that way because that is how it naturally wants to receive information.

These little sections of similar concepts or skills are clumped in a minilesson. Short-term memory holds information for a limited time. Working memory is temporary and where conscious processing occurs. Working memory manipulates what is in short-term memory (Cowan, 2015). The phrases *short-term memory* and *working memory* are often used interchangeably because their functions are still under debate (Sousa, 2017). Information that a teacher presents during a chunk could settle on the part of the brain responsible for long-term storage, but it's new and fragile information. The brain requires review, processing, and retrieval, so the teacher's short, sweet chew moment enhances the memory before going on to the next chunk.

Ideally, the information lives happily ever after in long-term memory, but so many factors determine the strength of that new memory, including but not limited to a student's background knowledge, his or her state of mind at the time, whether misconceptions occurred, and even the time of day he or she received the information (Myers, Stokes, Walther, & Nobre, 2014).

When you analyze your learning target, you will notice many pieces, sections, categories, sequences, or chunks of information. You will have to teach vocabulary words, concepts, visuals, processes, and skills within a daily lesson plan. As you begin instruction, it helps to chunk the information by time limits and using the gradual release of responsibility model (Fisher & Frey, 2015; Pearson & Gallagher, 1983), which can be broken down into the following.

- **I do:** The teacher explicitly teaches this chunk
- **We do:** The teacher and students collaborate to learn more and practice together
- **Two do:** Small groups of students practice and explore the chunk
- **You do:** Students do this chunk independently to determine if they've achieved mastery

How Long Should a Chunk Be?

The issue of chunking in terms of time limits is all about working memory capacity. The real reason we teach in smaller chunks of time is because the brain becomes overwhelmed quickly. Because working memory and attention spans vary widely among students, any hard-and-fast rule or time limit is likely to be problematic. However, most teachers will find success when they limit the amount of input into the following chunk times.

- Grades K–5 students—Four to eight minutes
- Grades 6–8 students—Six to ten minutes

In addition to grade level, consider the following student factors when determining how much time to spend with a chunk of content: how much background knowledge students have, how familiar they are with this content, how relevant the information is to them, how fast they processes information, memory skills (short- and long-term memory plus working memory), their energy level, the content's complexity, and how much content you're providing per minute.

How Do You Chunk a Daily Lesson?

To help you see how this works in the classroom, we have brought together many evidence-based pieces of information, and to simplify planning, we divided the daily lesson plan into the following chunks: beginning chunks of information, middle chunks of information, and the ending chunk. In fact, old but powerful research calls the *primacy-recency effect*, or *serial-position effect*, suggests that most learners can recall best what they learn at the beginning of the list, second best the information that comes at the end of the list, and coming in last, the middle chunks (Ebbinghaus, 1913). More recent brain findings explain why this research is still strong (Botto, Basso, Ferrari, & Palladino, 2014).

The first chunks you teach are within working memory limits; in other words, the small amount of first-mentioned information is not overhauling the working memory, but the later information could exceed the capacity and easily be forgotten. Toward the end of a lesson that has had many processing opportunities, chews have allowed information time to process, so it has been sorted and attached to existing neural networks (Botto et al., 2014).

The closing part of the lesson is not new information, but rather a summary of all the chunks: a consolidation point. This summary alerts the brain for a dopamine dump within the frontal lobe. Dopamine, also called the *motivational chemical*, is a neurotransmitter that can flood the frontal lobe to tell it to focus on this information. Dopamine is the only known neurotransmitter that improves our working memory skills (Bäckman & Nyberg, 2013). In fact, it "is known to play an important role in working memory by increasing the activity of brain circuits relevant to a task and suppressing circuits that distract from that task" (Roffman et al., 2016).

The teacher's guide to chunking in table 4.1 elaborates on the beginning, middle, and closure of a lesson and how you might differentiate within each one.

Overall, the brain notices the novelty or excitement, both of which can send dopamine to the frontal lobe to enhance attention, focus, and memory. So, the more novel, or new, and exciting we can make chunks, the greater the chance your students have of focusing on and retaining the learning. Novelty grabs their attention, like an experiment to get students' attention at the

Table 4.1: *Teacher's Guide to Chunking*

Beginning Chunk: I Do		
Key Points	**What Might Happen During This Chunk**	**Differentiation Possibilities**
• This is the best-remembered chunk in the lesson. • In grades K–5, it will be only the first chunk (because these grades cover less content). In grades 6–8 this might be the first and second chunks. • The most important information should be shared at the beginning of the lesson.	• This portion is usually teacher led, but some lessons start with inquiry or independent work (possibly a review or a prediction). • The teacher shares and explains the learning target in student-friendly language. • The teacher grabs students' attention with novelty, so their brains want to engage and learn. Some examples: show an object or picture; make a mistake; have students perform a quick play, song, or simulation; ask a startling, interesting question; have students make predictions; and play a quick game. These attention grabbers must relate to the learning target and intrigue students. • The teacher activates prior knowledge by asking a few questions for better connections. • The teacher uses strategies to get buy-in from students. He or she shows relevance to students' lives; explain why it's important to their lives currently and future. • The teacher explicitly defines words, shows visuals of words and concepts, shares models, and shows examples. • The teacher uses a variety of ways to help students acquire background knowledge: teacher-led lessons, video clips, images, student reading an article, and student-led jigsaws, for example.	• The teacher uses a variety of content: teacher-led lessons, readings, video clips, inquiry method, and so on. • The teacher finds different Lexile level articles to meet readers' needs. • The teacher includes visual, auditory, and kinesthetic (VAK) strategies. Featuring VAK strategies in every single lesson is a great way to enhance memory. • After preassessing, the teacher chooses vocabulary words to preteach students who show the need.

continued on next page ⇒

Middle Chunks: We Do, Two Do		
Key Points	**What Might Happen During This Chunk**	**Differentiation Possibilities**
• Students retain information during this section least. It requires the most student-processing opportunities. • High engagement needs to happen during these chunks so as not to overload students' working memories.	• The teacher guides students to deeper thinking about the content by sequencing events and providing elaborations, scenarios, more examples, connected content, and what-if situations. • The teacher sequences questions from simple to more complex. • The teacher provides guided, small-group, or partner practice to allow students to think about (chew) the content in a variety of ways.	• After checkpoints during the lesson, the teacher places students in purposeful, flexible groups to reteach or provide extension activities. • The teacher provides a variety of graphic organizers based on student needs. • The teacher plans a variety of leveled questions for groups. • The teacher determines which prompts and cues might move students forward in their thinking. • The teacher determines if students need different activity centers.
Ending Chunk: You Do		
Key Points	**What Might Happen During This Chunk**	**Differentiation Possibilities**
• This is the close of a lesson. • It's the second-best remembered section of a lesson. • The teacher plans the *you do* to show mastery of the learning target and ensure that the independent assignment aligns to the rigor of the upcoming assessments.	• This portion brings all the chunks together. This might take the form of a summary. • The teacher shows or explores the big picture with students. For example, you might create an activity to help students' brains bring together the pieces from the lesson. • An exit ticket helps students demonstrate the degree of mastery of the day's learning target. (This is a formal formative assessment so there is evidence from each student.) • The teacher partners students so they can give a verbal summary and then, the teacher leads a whole-class discussion. (This is an informal formative assessment so you get the gist of where the class is with the learning that day.)	• The teacher designs different exit tickets based on the last checkpoint if students need it. For example, some students may not be ready to show mastery on the exit ticket, so ask them to show you mastery of a particular section of that lesson instead. • The teacher creates different practice pages for students based on preassessment data. • The teacher changes pace with the whole class, small group, or certain individuals based on checkpoint data. • The teacher provides a different amount of support or scaffolding with certain students based on these data.

*Visit **go.SolutionTree.com/instruction** for a free reproducible version of this table.*

beginning of a water cycle lesson (versus just lecturing about what water does during respiration). It's not just the medium that makes something novel, but how the teacher uses it to grab students' attention.

We've observed classrooms where students read an entire text and then answer questions about it, but consider the research indicating that students' reading comprehension improves when you break it into smaller sections and ask them to process *before*, *during*, and *after* reading (National Reading Panel, 2000; Sousa, 2017).

By doing that, you could easily design reading lessons to create a little context for students to respond to before they read to activate prior knowledge. Design a stopping point during reading to discuss the chunk they just read through. Finally, plan a way to wrap up the final section of reading (end of chapter or end of book) with a rich discussion of that content through a processing activity. Teachers who chunk their reading see deeper thinking and comprehension (Nishida, 2013; Pressley & Afflerbach, 1995).

What Teaching Elements Should Chunks Include?

To enhance memory, Eric Jensen says that each chunk should include specific teaching elements, represented in the acronym CARER (personal communication, 2018).

- **Coherent content:** Students must understand what you are explaining and teaching. You must design and sequence every chunk so your students' brains can make logical connections. Can they bring the pieces together to understand the whole? Does one point lead to another point? Do your visuals match the content? Are your definitions clear, concise, and student friendly? Do your activities support the learning target and content? Do your questions help them reach the goal? Do you provide completed examples or models of what they learned so they can study the steps when they need to? Teacher clarity is of utmost importance when it comes to learning content.

- **Active students:** Plan for some type of student movement in your chunks. Some examples include students moving to a different location in the classroom, standing up and finding a partner to process with, sorting objects, combining or manipulating objects, acting out vocabulary words, role-playing a scene, or standing up while learning. Students who are more active and sit less could have longer attention spans, faster cognitive-processing speed, better brain structures and brain functions, and perform better on academic tests than those who are less active. Even little episodes of movement can enhance cognition (Esteban-Cornejo, Tejero-Gonzalez, Sallis, & Veiga, 2015; Ratey & Hagerman, 2008).

- **Relevant content:** If content relates to the students' lives, there is a greater chance attention will occur (Liu & Hou, 2013). Students see or hear a reason to learn the content when you relate it to them; it makes it more meaningful. The brain wants to remember highly relevant content, so the nucleus basalis triggers acetylcholine, a neurotransmitter that forms long-term memories (Luchicchi, Bloem, Viaña, Mansvelder, & Role, 2014). The brain must care about the content in order to store it.

It must say, "This is so important and worthy of learning; therefore, I will store it." Relevance and buy-in strategies need to be part of every chunk.

- **Emotion-evoking strategies or tools:** Humor and laughter are powerful when it comes to remembering content. Role-playing or acting how molecules might act in a solid, liquid, and gas is more memorable than just drawing a circle. Reading a short story such as *Pink and Say* by Patricia Polacco (1994) during your lesson about the American Civil War will evoke a strong emotion and help students bond with the characters, which will enhance their memory of what they learn about the civil war. Emotional content is well remembered.

- **Retrieving the information often:** After students receive a chunk of information, pause and ask the students to retrieve the information in a creative, engaging way. It helps them process and consolidate the information. Working memory overload can happen when we give too much content without retrieval opportunities. Retrieval opportunities allow the brain time to make the content more meaningful, and therefore, more memorable (McDermott, Agarwal, D'Antonio, Roediger, & McDaniel, 2014). Chapter 5 (page 81) shares more in-depth strategies that encourage students to chew content in active ways that strengthen the memory pathways.

You will want to ensure CARER occurs in each chunk so the content sticks in students' minds.

Lesson Plan With Chunks

In figure 4.1 (page 54), we have included only those parts that you've covered to now in the book, and the parts covered in this chapter are shaded gray.

Directions

Choose a learning target and use the teacher's guide to chunking (see table 4.1, page 51) to plan each chunk of the lesson. See how the chunks of knowledge, skills, and concepts are grouped according to their similarities. Think through your content and organize it in a way that your students will understand it. It could be through vocabulary words or concepts. It could also be sequential steps such as the gradual release of responsibility. Group similar concepts and then plan a chewing activity for afterward so that their brains can digest that small chunk. The "Text Chunking" reproducible (page 75) helps you chunk your instruction.

Example

See figure 4.1 for the sample lesson plan for learning chunks. See figure 5.1 (page 84) for the student-processing strategies for this lesson. See figure 5.2 (page 86) for the tabletop graphic organizer, which is the main formative assessment in this lesson plan.

Daily Lesson Plan

Subject or unit: Reading: Main Idea—Details **Grade:** 5

Standard: Determine two or more main ideas of a text and explain how they are supported by key details; summarize the text (RI.5.2).

Learning target (do and know): I can describe or graphically represent the relationship between main idea and details.

Main formative assessment (show): Students complete "The Main Idea and Detail Tabletop Graphic Organizer" (page 104) to show how the details (table legs) support the main idea (tabletop) based on a given paragraph.

Criteria for success (check type):	Criteria for success (explain details): Students self-assess their work and complete a checklist with the following criteria for success.
☐ Rubric ☑ Self-assessment ☑ Checklist ☐ Peer assessment ☐ Exemplars ☐ Nonexemplars ☐ Verbal ☐ Other: _____	☐ I can write accurate details on the legs. ☐ I can write the accurate main idea on the tabletop. ☐ I can write an explanation, in complete sentences, of how the details and main idea are connected.

The Chunk Explained: What Teacher Will Do

Beginning chunks (I do):

Review the definition of *main idea*. Move your arms as large as possible, creating an invisible square in the air, or frame, to represent the big picture.

Define details and make little circles with your hands, going into the invisible square you just motioned. Explain that the little details create the big picture; they help you visualize what the picture looks like.

Middle chunks (we do, two do):

Say, "There are many visuals that we can create to help us understand the relationship between main idea and details. I use the visual of an imaginary frame to represent main idea. The circles inside it represent details. Today, we are going to show another visual: a tabletop with legs supporting it."

Show an anchor chart (a large visual, usually on chart paper) of a tabletop that shows the top of the table labeled Main Idea and the table legs labeled Details. Then, show a paragraph from any of your texts and how the main idea of the paragraph gets written on the tabletop and the details from the paragraph are written on the individual legs supporting the tabletop. Make sure all students can explain that details are the legs of the table that support the tabletop, which represents the main idea.

Share many anchor chart examples: paragraph being separated on the tabletop graphic organizer with main idea on top and details written on the legs.

Ending chunk (you do):

Summarize the day's learning by pointing out what each group does during the lesson and giving positive feedback to each group. (Group work will be explained in chapter 5 on page 83.)

Explain the exit ticket by modeling how to bring the pieces together with a different paragraph (not the one you use to assess students).

Source for standard: NGA & CCSSO, 2010a.

Figure 4.1: *Sample lesson plan for learning chunks.*

Suggestions for Differentiation

The following suggestions can help you differentiate while chunking.

- **Bumping it up:** Create higher-level-thinking questions about your chunks. Combine shorter chunks and ask students to process the sections together by analyzing, comparing and contrasting, or synthesizing.

- **Breaking it down:** Pull students into a small group and break that chunk into smaller sections. Provide more modeling and more chewing opportunities. Provide additional feedback as well.

- **Specializing for working memory challenges:** Break the chunks into even smaller sections and have students retrieve what they learn after each small section. Retrieving the information by recalling it (not looking it up) reinforces memory (McDermott et al., 2014). Give the students a graphic organizer with the content organized by these smaller chunks. Make sure this tool shows the connections among the chunks and content.

Suggestions to Incorporate Technology

The following resources will help you chunk.

- Nearpod (https://nearpod.com) is a classroom tool that helps teachers engage students with interactive lessons.

- Educreations (www.educreations.com) is a community where anyone can teach what they know and learn what they don't. The software turns any iPad or web browser into a recordable, interactive whiteboard, so it easy to create engaging video lessons and share them online.

- Planboard (www.chalk.com/planboard) helps teachers streamline lesson plans, find resources, and collaborate with others.

- Evernote (https://evernote.com) is an app that keeps your notes organized. Memos are synced so they're accessible anywhere, and they are searchable.

- ShowMe (www.showme.com) is an open online learning community where anyone can learn and teach any topic. The iPad app lets you easily create and share video lessons.

What Strategies Can You Use During Chunking?

Remember, when chunking content, the key is to avoid overwhelming the working memory and the hippocampus, one of the storage sites in the brain. Instead, strategically chunk the information and give students many opportunities to chew the content. The strategies in this chapter are designed to support you as you plan each chunk. The first two are templates: one to help you chunk your lesson, and one to help you chunk any reading selection. The remaining strategies help students take in chunks of information so that the processing (chewing) will be easier and more memorable. The chapter ends with student-controlled chunks such as jigsaw learning and rotation stations.

Text Chunking

Individuals, small groups, or whole groups can work with text chunking. The strategy allows you to break the text into manageable pieces. This strategy allows for more focused thinking during reading and deeper comprehension.

Directions

Choose a book and use the "Text Chunking" reproducible (page 75). Figure 4.2 (page 56) is an example. Determine the strategies or tools that you will use from the options listed in the left column and place a check mark in the appropriate boxes. Use the right column to write special details concerning your lesson, such as how you will group students for this reading (partners, small groups, or whole group), and how students will process each section of the book (questions they will answer, thinking jobs during the reading, writing that might occur, and so on).

Figure 4.3 (page 57) has a helpful set of before, during, and after reading questions to help you design the

	Chunk	The Plan (Book or pages to read, words to preteach, student groupings, and processing students will engage in)
Before Reading	❑ Activate prior knowledge with questions such as, What do you already know about this subject? What experiences have you had in this area? ❑ Give the gist of the text and preview it (for example, do a picture walk or focus on text features). ❑ Preteach vocabulary words. ❑ Create a purpose for reading based on the learning target (the thinking job). ❑ Design some before reading prediction questions and have students partner to share their predictions.	Book: *The Happy Hedgehog* by Marcus Pfister (2000) Activate prior knowledge: What's a hedgehog? Show some pictures (or a video clip) of real hedgehogs. Grouping: Whole group Activate prior knowledge: What does happiness look like and sound like? How can you tell someone is happy? Words to preteach: *reptiles, amphibians, absurd, tortoise* Thinking job: While reading, place sticky notes on all the characters the hedgehog is comparing himself to. Be ready to discuss how comparing himself to others made him feel. Predict: What do you think this book is about? What might make him happy? Sad?
During Reading	❑ Students read the section and work on their thinking job during the reading. ❑ Thinking job ideas: graphic organizers filled in; tagging text with sticky notes based on what they need to look for; writing answers to questions; finding the main problem, solution, character, cause, effect, and so on. ❑ Design questions while reading: question for author, question for teacher, question for self (something interesting to research further), question for a friend. ❑ Discuss in small groups or whole group the questions that were created for these sections of reading.	Read pages 1–2 and ask teacher-designed questions about the story. Read pages 3–10 and ask teacher-designed questions. Read from page 11 to the end of the book and ask teacher-designed questions. Use the questions stems in the before, during, and after reading questions in figure 4.3 to design fiction questions at a variety of levels.
After Reading	❑ Share the results of the thinking job in small groups or whole group. ❑ Summarize, bringing all the chunks together. ❑ Reread anything confusing. ❑ Write a response to what was read. Start with a teacher-created prompt. ❑ Discuss teacher-created after reading questions.	Discuss all the characters and what they did in the book. Did their actions create happiness? How do you know? Summarize this story verbally to your reading partner. What made the hedgehog the happiest? How do you feel about this? Why? Writing response: What are the pros and cons of always choosing activities that make you happy?

Figure 4.2: Example of text chunking.

questions you ask students. We have used these question stems for grades 3 and above. We have also used a few of them for K–2 lessons as well by changing some of the language, such as saying *main idea* instead of *gist*. Prior to reading, use the before reading question stems to build background knowledge and set a purpose for reading. After reading each additional chunk, use the during reading question stems to ensure students comprehend each chunk. At the completion, refer to the after reading question stems to extend, enrich, and deepen comprehension of the text.

Example

Refer back to figure 4.2 for an example of text chunking.

Suggestions for Differentiation

The following suggestions can help you differentiate this strategy.

- **Bumping it up:** Design questions and activities that combine sections of the text rather than just one section. Ask students to compare and contrast that text with other texts or other media. Ask

students to analyze and dive deeply into a certain section of text that has multiple meanings.

- **Breaking it down:** Give students a more specific thinking job that enables them to clearly show where they received their answer. Give them sticky notes labeled with potential ways of tagging the text.

- **Specializing for English learners:** Preteach more academic vocabulary terms that students will come across during the reading. Show images of these words. Ask them to define these new words in their own way before asking them to read.

Suggestions to Incorporate Technology

The following websites will help you focus on reading.

- Target the Problem! (www.readingrockets.org/helping/target) helps pinpoint reading comprehension problems.

- Planboard (www.chalk.com/planboard) helps teachers streamline lesson plans, find resources, and collaborate with others. This is a place where you could store these valuable reading lesson plans.

	Nonfiction Question Stems	**Fiction Question Stems**
Before Reading	• What do you think the gist of this text is based on title, headings, pictures, and captions? • What might be the main idea based on the title? • What do you already know about _____? • What do you hope to learn about _____?	• What might this story be about based on cover pages, pictures, title, and so on? • What might be the main problem in this story? What might be the solution? • What do you know about _____? • What other books have we read from this author, and what were they like?
During Reading	• What is an interesting fact that you read? • What details do you think should be part of this text and are not? • What did you learn from paragraph _____? • What supporting details did the author include to help you learn _____? • What does the author mean when he or she says _____? • How does this sentence, passage, or section connect with the rest of the whole text? • What words are confusing or stand out?	• Who did what, where, when, why, and how? • Who is telling this story and why? • Who is the story being written to? • Which words are rich in meaning or create an emotion within you? • How do the characters change based on what they experience (plot events)? • How does the setting impact the plot? How does that impact the characters? • Which words are confusing? • If _____ (word) is changed to _____, how might the meaning change?

Figure 4.3: *Before, during, and after reading questions.*

continued on next page ⇒

Nonfiction Question Stems	Fiction Question Stems
<ul><li>How do the transition words that the author uses help your brain transition between paragraphs or ideas?</li><li>How do the text features help you understand the text better? Would you change any of them?</li><li>How does the author organize this writing? Which text structures did he or she use? Do you agree with the author's choice?</li></ul>	<ul><li>What figurative language or symbols make the visualization process better?</li><li>How does the sequence of the story develop the plot, characters, and climax?</li><li>What major events affect the characters' behaviors?</li><li>What words resonate with you? Which phrases do you love?</li></ul>

	Nonfiction Question Stems	Fiction Question Stems
After Reading	<ul><li>What is the author telling us about this topic (point of view)? Does he or she have any biases?</li><li>What is the author's purpose for writing this?</li><li>Is the author trying to persuade the reader to believe or do something?</li><li>What resources is he or she using to support this topic?</li><li>What does the author want you to believe or understand? What is his or her connotation?</li><li>What facts do you believe are missing from this text?</li><li>What causes _____?</li><li>How can you determine if this author is credible in writing about this topic?</li><li>Research the author's life. What factors in his or her life contribute to this piece of writing?</li><li>What is your opinion about this topic? How would you create an argument for or against it?</li><li>Compare this topic to what we read yesterday about _____.</li></ul>	<ul><li>What does the author want you to believe, understand, or believe and understand?</li><li>What are some themes within this story?</li><li>What tone or mood is the author portraying?</li><li>What assumptions is the author making during _____?</li><li>What two events could have prevented the problem?</li><li>Why did the character do _____ or say _____?</li><li>Does the story describe a culture or belief system?</li><li>Research the author's life. What factors in his or her life contribute to this piece of writing?</li><li>How does this story connect with other stories you read?</li><li>How is this author's style like his or her other book called _____?</li><li>How would you rate this book? Which audience would appreciate this book the most?</li><li>How does the internet site _____ help you understand this book better?</li></ul>

*Visit **go.SolutionTree.com/instruction** for a free reproducible version of this figure.*

Teacher Think-Aloud

A teacher think-aloud involves you verbalizing your thoughts as you teach your chunks. It's a tool that teachers can use during team planning or individually when designing a lesson with a think-aloud. When you use this strategy, you're modeling the reading tools that improve comprehension, and you're reinforcing them throughout the lesson. That way students can imitate that type of thinking during the learning process.

Directions

Select a text. As you read it aloud, model how to use a specific reading-comprehension strategy. Do this by

thinking aloud; figure 4.4 offers some ideas. A think-aloud can happen in fiction, nonfiction, mathematics word problems, or when simply responding to questions that others pose. Follow these steps for an effective think-aloud.

1. Fluently read aloud any type of text in your normal voice.

2. When you get to a place where you need a reading strategy, or when it might aid comprehension, stop reading and instead, share your thinking.

3. Change your voice when you share your thinking out loud with a partner, small group, or the

Reading Strategy		Cue or Phrase That Starts the Thinking Process
Rereading		My mind wandered, so I better go back _____. I wonder what on earth did the author say _____. That didn't make sense. I better _____.
Prediction		I think the following will happen _____. I predict we will learn _____.
Questioning the text or author		What if _____? Why did _____? Who, what, or where _____? Could _____? Should _____?
Clarification		I'm not sure of _____. I was confused when _____. I wonder what the author means by _____.
Summarization		This story is mostly about _____. The main idea is _____. The gist is _____. The most important idea is _____. So far, I've learned _____.
Context clues		I wonder what this word _____ means? Let me look for some clues _____.
Visualization		I am picturing _____. I think it looks like _____.
Connections		This is like _____. This reminds me of _____. This is similar to _____.
Personal response		I agree (or disagree) _____ because _____. My favorite part or fact is _____. I feel _____. I wonder if _____.
Evaluation		My accuracy while reading was _____. My fluency was _____. I comprehended best when _____. I learned _____ about reading strategies today.

Figure 4.4: *Think-aloud strategies and cues.*

*Visit **go.SolutionTree.com/instruction** for a free reproducible version of this figure.*

whole class. You can use a cue or phrase to show what type of thinking you are going to share out loud. (Refer to the think-aloud strategies and cues in figure 4.4 on page 59.) You could even name the reading strategy when speaking to students, like "I'm going to summarize what I just read."

4. Begin reading again and stop when you come across another area where you want to share your thinking.

5. Reflect on the strategies that help you deepen your comprehension.

Example

The teacher is reading a text aloud to the students to model rereading in order to clarify and summarize. She stops, moves to the other side of the room, and says aloud in a low-pitched voice, "Oh my! My brain read that so fast, and I started to daydream. I have no idea what I just read. I better reread that whole section. I might need that information to understand this story." She goes back to the place in the room where she started, rereads the whole paragraph aloud, and then stops. In a different voice—remember to use a variety of inflections so that students know when you are thinking out loud versus reading what the author is saying—in a designated think-aloud location, she says "I'm so glad I reread that section. It was important. In fact, I'm going to summarize what that paragraph says . . ."

Suggestions for Differentiation

The following suggestions can help you differentiate this strategy.

- **Bumping it up:** Group students who are using more strategies than others to practice

their think-alouds with each other. They can challenge one another to use strategies they are not comfortable with.

- **Breaking it down:** Pull students into a smaller group and do a think-aloud with the needed strategy several times. Do not model other reading strategies—just the one the group is trying to learn. Every time you model it, group members place a tally mark on their whiteboard. Stop to discuss why it was or was not an example. Then, ask members to break into pairs to do the same thing with a partner while you observe and give feedback.

- **Specializing for ELs:** Preteach many vocabulary terms before the think-aloud is done with these students in small groups. Focus on modeling word attack skills such as breaking the word into smaller sections, finding the roots and affixes, looking at the pictures around the words, and so on.

Suggestions to Incorporate Technology

The following resources will help you develop think-alouds for teachers.

- Explain Everything (www.explaineverything.com) is a screencasting tool available on Chrome. You use think-alouds in a flipped classroom by creating a screencast that captures your voice as you explain a reading strategy. The tool will capture your voice and anything you write on the screen.

- Flipgrid (https://flipgrid.com) lets students record their thought processes as they solve equations or parse text (Burns, 2018).

Student Think-Aloud

A student think-aloud is a tool used while reading. Students can use it with small groups and partners while practicing, but eventually use it independently (and often) while reading. Think-alouds are beneficial because they help students clarify their thinking by talking through their thinking process. This metacognition can help them pinpoint misunderstandings and can improve their comprehension.

Directions

After you model how to do a powerful think-aloud, it's time to share the steps so students can do their own think-alouds. The steps that follow will help students in grades 3 and above independently work through the think-aloud process. We recommend that for grades K–2, the teacher model these steps and take students through them, one at a time, until students understand the process and can use them independently. Visit **go.SolutionTree.com/instruction** for a free reproducible version of these steps.

1. Fluently read aloud any type of text in your normal voice.

2. When you get to a place where you need a reading strategy, or when it might aid comprehension, stop reading and instead, share your thinking.

3. Change your voice when you share your thinking out loud with a partner, small group, or the whole class. You can use a cue or phrase to show what type of thinking you are going to share out loud. (Refer to the think-aloud strategies and cues in figure 4.4 on page 59.) You could even name the reading strategy when speaking to students, like "I'm going to summarize what I just read."

4. Begin reading again and stop when you come across another area where you want to share your thinking.

5. Reflect on the strategies that help you deepen your comprehension.

These powerful thinking tools produce reflective, metacognitive, independent, strategic readers.

These checklists help student reflect on their reading strategies: "Partner Reading Checklist—Fiction Strategies" reproducible (page 76), "Partner Reading Checklist—Nonfiction Strategies" reproducible (page 77), and the independent reading checklist for content-area reading in figure 4.5. We encourage you not to photocopy these checklists and distribute them. Examples are indispensable, but they are jumping-off points offered as reproducibles only for your easy reference. Be thoughtful about which reading strategies you have already modeled and which you should model more often. Also, be aware of how many might overwhelm students.

Before asking students to use the checklist for content-area reading, provide them with the list of fix-it activities and be sure they are comfortable using them. (Chapter 6, on page 139, has fix-it activities.)

Remember to have students use the think-aloud strategy in other subject areas too: while proofreading someone's writing, reading a newspaper in social studies, reviewing science lab results, and deciphering a challenging mathematics word problem.

Example

See figure 4.5 for an example of a completed independent reading checklist for content-area reading.

Name: _Ann_

Date: _May 1_   **Reading material:** _Lord of the Flies_

Directions: While reading your nonfiction article or book, stop to reflect on your thinking before, during, and after reading. Place tally marks on the lines to show every time you did the action in the different sections. This activity will train your brain to think through reading in powerful ways.

📚 Before Reading
_I_ I preview the section or chapter by looking at and thinking about the boldface or italic headings and vocabulary.
_I_ I skim the chapter to have an idea of how it is organized.
____ I read the sentences around boldface words that are unfamiliar. _No bold_
____ I read the captions, charts, graphs, and diagrams. _None of these_
____ I develop ideas of what I already know about this topic. _I didn't do this_
__ I review the purposes that the teacher (or I) have set before I start to read.

📖 During Reading
_||_ I make a mental picture in my mind of what I am reading.
_||_ I know when I am confused, and I reread to understand.

continued on next page ⇒

***Figure 4.5:** Independent reading checklist for content-area reading.*

Tally	
_|_	I look for information that relates to the purpose I've set or that the teacher or class has set.
_|_	I stop after each section and summarize what I have read.
_|||_	I try to use clues in the sentences, charts, and pictures to figure out new words.
_|_	I record important information in a graphic organizer or special note-taking style.
₶	I jot down questions to ask my teacher, especially when I am confused.
_|_	I use my list of fix-it strategies when I get confused.

💭 After Reading

Tally	
_|_	I discuss ideas or questions that I have with a partner or group.
_|||_	I note new vocabulary in a journal or within a graphic organizer.
_____	I skim to find parts that may answer a question and clarify my purpose for reading. I reread these sections. *I didn't do this*
_|_	I study my notes and reread important parts after each assignment.
_|||_	I celebrate my learning of the content (project, writing, or discussion).

Visit **go.SolutionTree.com/instruction** for a free reproducible version of this figure.

Suggestions for Differentiation

The following suggestions can help you differentiate this strategy.

- **Bumping it up:** Don't give these strategic readers any prompts or tally sheets, but rather, ask them to write a reflection about which reading strategies improve their comprehension. Sometimes, these students can't even tell you which reading comprehension strategies they use—it happens automatically in their brains. This examination encourages metacognition.

- **Breaking it down:** The icons in figure 4.4 (page 59) can help define reading strategies for students who struggle with these words. Decrease the number of reading strategies you ask these students to model during their think-aloud with a partner. Focus on one reading strategy at a time and slowly introduce others when you see they are ready to practice more.

- **Specializing for English learners:** The anchor charts and prompts will help students practice this strategy successfully. Encourage students to create body movements with the reading strategy they are using. For example, interlock your fingers to show a connection and then explain the connection. All students, including highly kinesthetic learners, will remember the reading strategy better.

Suggestions to Incorporate Technology

The following apps will help you develop think-alouds for students.

- **Explain Everything** (www.explaineverything.com) is a screencasting tool available on Chrome. You use think-alouds in a flipped classroom by creating a screencast that captures your voice as you explain a reading strategy.

- **Flipgrid** (https://flipgrid.com) lets students record their thought processes as they solve equations or parse text (Burns, 2018).

Big Picture Note-Taking

Source: Adapted from Pauk & Owens, 2011.

Big picture note-taking is a chunking strategy for individual students and then eventually for whole-group discussions. This strategy benefits students as they organize content into similar, interconnected chunks.

Directions

While you deliver chunks, students can take notes using the "Big Picture Note-Taking Method" reproducible (page 78). This tool will help students organize information from a video, minilesson, PowerPoint presentation, and class readings. The organizer has three columns: (1) The Big Picture, (2) Supporting Details, and (3) Questions and Reflections. Students take notes accordingly based on what they are learning. Model how to take notes in this format before asking them to do it independently. Show them, step by step, how to take notes from all the different types of media.

Most of the information will be written in the middle box—the Supporting Details column. After writing all notes from the various chunks, the learner brings together all the pieces by writing a summary. These notes are useful when studying for a test, since the details will connect to the big picture. Pictures or symbols, questions, and reflections may be written as well to complete the picture in the mind.

The brain loves to attach details to a bigger picture. It's actually how we store information in our brains—similar information gets stored next to other similar concepts or ideas, building on similar neural networks (natural chunking). Teachers can facilitate this process by ensuring the planned chunks are connected to each other. Examples, relevance, buy-in, visuals, and stories can help make the connections, but students ultimately are the meaning makers—at least that is the hope, so retrieval is easier (Sousa, 2017). This linear way of taking notes helps the brain store supporting details next to the appropriate main idea.

Example

See figure 4.6 (page 64) for an example of the big picture note-taking method.

Suggestions for Differentiation

The following suggestions can help you differentiate this strategy.

- **Bumping it up:** Don't give the graphic organizer to students who have strong background knowledge on the topic. Rather, let them design their own tool for taking notes. Explain to them that they will take notes during the learning to show the connections among the details and the main ideas or big concepts of the learning.

- **Breaking it down:** Cut the graphic organizer's chunk sections into separate slips of paper so students focus on one chunk at a time. Deliver the content at a slower pace and then discuss any questions or reflections they have before going on to the next chunk. For grades K–5 or for students struggling with writing, make this a shared writing experience as a whole class or within small groups. Ask the students to do the drawing to represent what they learn.

- **Specializing for kinesthetic learners:** Complete the graphic organizer with your own notes and then photocopy for students. Cut apart each section and ask students to determine which set of details goes with which set of big picture concepts. Create a matching game before teaching this section. After this priming activity, provide a new note-taking page that has words missing that allows students to fill in blanks. (See the create-a-cloze activity on page 24.)

Suggestions to Incorporate Technology

The following apps will help you with the big picture note-taking method.

- Ghostwriter (https://apple.co/2t2I90P) allows students to draw their own organizer, or you can upload the graphic as a PDF for students to use. You can also make the template in Microsoft Word.

- Write! (https://writeapp.co) is a clean, user-friendly word processor that helps minimize distractions.

States of Matter

Name: _____Naomi_____   Date: ____11/20____

The Big Picture	Supporting Details	Questions and Reflections
It can be questions, a concept, or a main idea statement.	List details about the main idea, question, or concept.	While note-taking, jot down questions that pop into your mind or reflections you have about the content.
Chunk one big picture: _Solid_ _____ Molecules very close Picture or symbol: 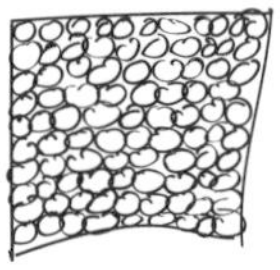	o Has mass o Has volume o Has its own shape o Examples: ice cube, shoes, table, carrots	All <u>matter</u> is in one of the following states: solid, liquid, or gas. They can be transformed too. How?
Chunk two big picture: _Liquid_ _____ Molecules sort of close Picture or symbol: 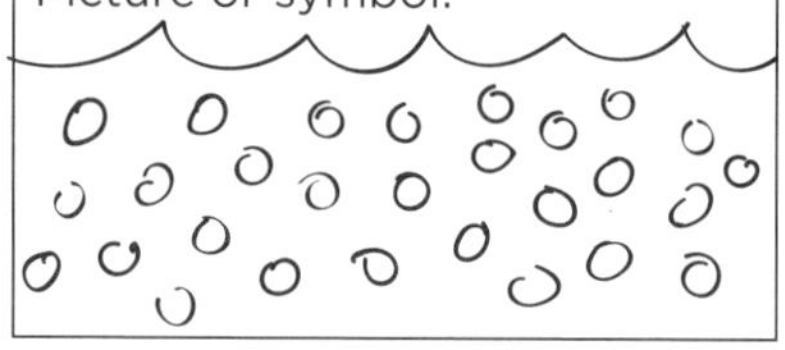	o Takes shape of its container o Has volume o Has mass o Examples: water droplets, coffee, gasoline What?	How can gasoline at a gas station be a liquid? Fact: When you cool a liquid, it could become a solid (ice cube). Can it become something else? Think
Chunk three big picture: _Gas_ _____ Molecules "loose" Picture or symbol: 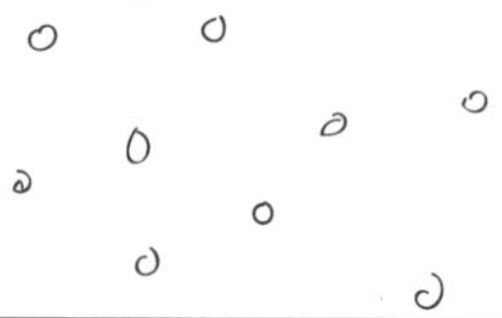	o No shape of its own o No fixed volume o Has mass o Examples: inside a balloon, steam from a teapot, smoke from fire	How can we smell some gasses but not see it or feel it? What causes the scent? Fact: When you cool or compress a gas, it becomes a liquid Think

Summarize all the chunks:

Matter is all around me. Matter is anything that takes space. Matter is either a solid, liquid or gas, and these three states of matter can change if heat or cooling happens at certain levels. There are many ways to change the shape, size, appearance, and texture of these states of matter.

Figure 4.6: *Example of big picture note-taking method.*

Chunk Mind Map

This chunking strategy works for individual students and partners and benefits students by helping them organize into chunks the content they are learning; they must include the details and images supporting the main ideas. This visual web can improve memory of the concepts and their connections.

Directions

Many teachers use word webs with their students. Students organize any information they present or generate (through brainstorming, for instance) so that they pair similar concepts, words, and ideas together in an area on the paper or whiteboard. In other words, the information is chunked. *Mind mapping*, an alternative to webbing, has a few extras such as color, images, symbols, shapes, and highlights. The visuals, location, short phrases, and clustered concepts help the brain store information for easier retrieval. Mind mapping actually extends the chunk into the chew, as students will think about and process the information as they add it to the graphic organizer.

The four steps in creating a mind map follow.

1. Students place the main idea of the whole mind map in the middle of the paper with a circle or rectangle around it.

2. Students represent secondary headings, subheadings, or all the chunks of content to this large main idea in spokes around the main idea and scattered around the paper. We like to use 11" × 17" paper so there is more space for symbols and pictures.

3. While taking notes in class, rewriting notes from several sets of daily student-generated notes, brainstorming what is known, or outlining while reading, students use a pencil or color pencils to group similar facts related to the main topic. Have students use a different color for each secondary section. In figure 4.7 (page 66), for example, they could use brown for all the text and circles in the Saturn section.

4. Students can study their mind maps, share with other students the meaning they made on the topic, or present from it what they learned about the main topic.

Make sure you design a rubric or student check-off sheet for self-assessment and evaluation. See the reproducible "Mind Map Assessment Rubric" (page 79) for possible use. Decide how the students will share these masterpieces: write a summary of the whole mind map, present the chunks to the whole class, write an argument for or against something presented, create an essay about the whole mind map (synthesis), and so on. This is actually the *check* part of the lesson. Unlike some other strategies, mind mapping serves as the chunk, chew, and check all in one.

Example

See figure 4.7 (page 66) for an example of a mind map.

Suggestions for Differentiation

The following suggestions can help you differentiate this strategy.

- **Bumping it up:** Ask students to add more resources to their mind map and to code each one with a different symbol. For example, one resource could have a *#1* next to it and on the back, the citation could be listed under *#1*. Encourage them to make as many connections as possible. Ask them to write a summary to bring all the pieces together.

- **Breaking it down:** Create a template with the main idea and related chunks surrounding it so students can have the foundation for organizing the information.

- **Specializing for kinesthetic learners:** Ask them to write facts about a main idea they are reading about—one idea per sticky note or index card. Students sort these fact cards into like categories and create a category name for each group of facts. They are actually creating a mind map as they start to sort everything and label the categories.

Suggestions to Incorporate Technology

The following apps allow students to show connections among their ideas as well as include symbols and images that represent the ideas.

- MindMeister (www.mindmeister.com), MindNode (https://mindnode.com), and Popplet (http://popplet.com) are good resources for students who want to create a map.

- Coggle (https://coggle.it/?lang=en-US) lets students mind map online, without having to download an app.

- Inspiration Software (www.inspiration.com) offers options for graphic organizers, mind maps, webbing, and more. Kidspiration, for grades K–5, lets you use spoken words as well.

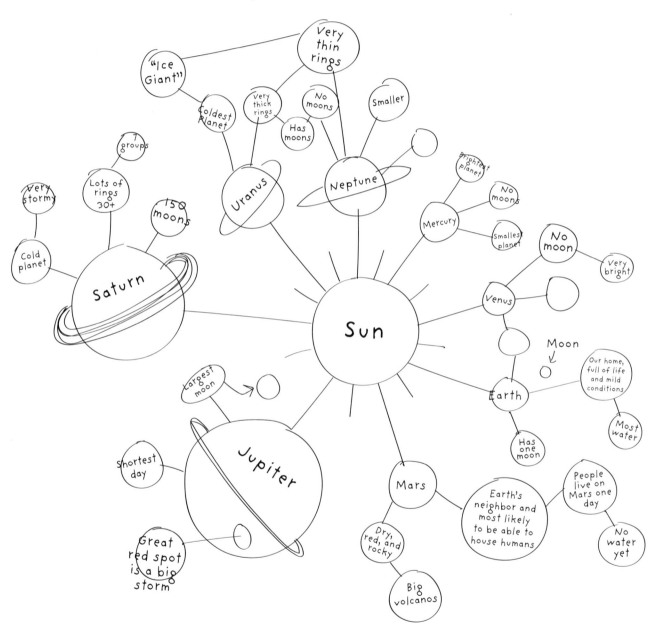

Figure 4.7: *Example of a mind map.*

Color-Coded Nonfiction Chunking

Source: Adapted from Stead, 2006.

This chunking strategy works for individuals, partners, small groups, and whole group. During this lesson, students categorize their learning, which helps them determine if their *What I think I know* is confirmed, not known yet, or a misconception. They also benefit by learning new details, facts, questions, and ideas about the topic.

Directions

Always model this strategy with the whole class until students are comfortable enough to try it with a partner and then independently. Put up five sheets of chart paper, and label them like this: red for What I Think I Know and Misconceptions I Had; green for What I Confirmed, What I Learned, and What I Wonder.

Share the topic with the students. Ask them to "Brainstorm *what you* think you know" about the topic. Each student writes one idea per sticky note and places it on the What I Think I Know chart. Begin reading the text aloud, stopping periodically for students to engage. If something you read is confirmed in the text, move the note to What I Confirmed. Write on a new sticky note and place it on What I Learned. Often when new learning happens, the brain forms questions, which you place on What I Wonder. Occasionally, what students think they know is a misconception. Place those sticky notes on Misconceptions I Had.

After reading, allow students to consolidate the sticky notes from the What I Confirmed and What I Learned charts by sorting the information into like categories. (They can even write a subheading for each category.) At this point, students should be able to retell the information orally or in writing by using the color-coding. Red means *Stop! Don't use this information.* Green means *Go! Use this information.*

Once you model this enough that students are ready to try it on their own, use file folders rather than chart paper. We recommend one trifold for each partner pair. Follow the three steps to assemble your trifold.

1. Obtain one red file folder and one green file folder.

2. Open the folders so they are flat. Tape the left side of the green folder to the right side of the red folder.

3. Fold the folders into one, with the red being the cover.

Place labels on the folders as shown in table 4.2. Visit **go.SolutionTree.com/instruction** to download a reproducible version of the label template.

Example

See figure 4.8 (page 68) for an example trifold for color-coded chunking of nonfiction text (inside).

See figure 4.9 (page 68) for the outside of a trifold for color-coded nonfiction chunking.

Table 4.2: *Color-Coded Nonfiction Chunking—Folder Labels*

Page	Color	Letter	Category
Front cover	Red	Not applicable	Color-coded nonfiction chunking text
First page	Red	K	What I think I know. "I know the following."
Second page	Green	C	What I confirmed. "Yes! I was right."
Third page	Green	L	What I learned. "What new things did I learn?"
Fourth page	Green	W	What I wonder. "What do I still want to know?"
Back cover	Red	M	Misconceptions I had. "I thought it was this but it was not."

Visit go.SolutionTree.com/instruction for a free reproducible version of this table.

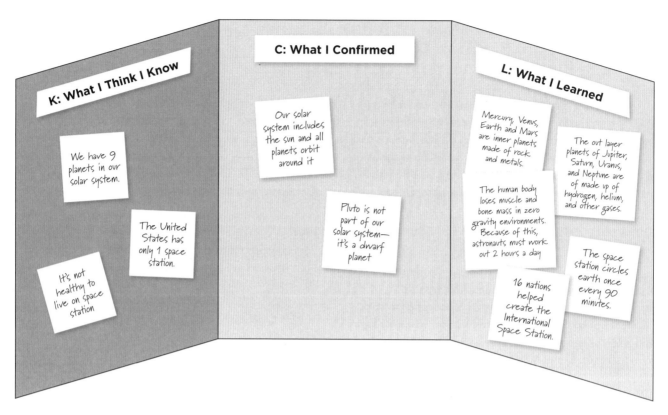

Figure 4.8: Trifold for color-coded nonfiction chunking (inside).

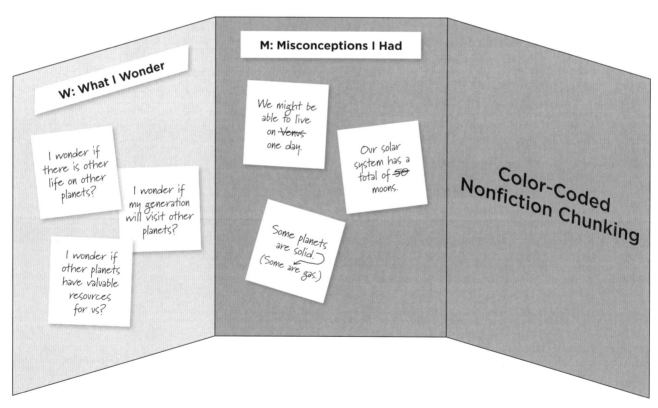

Figure 4.9: Trifold for color-coded nonfiction chunking (outside).

Suggestions for Differentiation

The following suggestions can help you differentiate this strategy.

- **Bumping it up:** Encourage reading from a couple different sources to determine if the facts they brainstorm are accurate or misconceptions. Let them search the internet if the information is not in the texts.

- **Breaking it down:** This group will need more modeling and possibly some priming so the brainstorming phase is more successful. Prime their brains a couple of days ahead of time on the topic they will be reading about. (See page 23 for more about priming.) Support their sticky note organization after the sorting activity so they can organize those green facts into the following manner for better writing: beginning, middle, and end.

- **Specializing for students who struggle to write:** Pair students and assign roles. Have one student read and the other write. If you can find partnerships where one student loves to write and the other one would rather read, that might make a good team.

Suggestions to Incorporate Technology

The following websites will help with color-coded chunking.

- ThinkTank (http://thinktank.4teachers.org) helps students learn how to refine a subject so that it's more manageable for the internet research. We also suggest this website for the What? So what? Now what? strategy.

- Padlet (https://padlet.com) lets students post sticky notes in categories and send them to the teacher for feedback.

What? So What? Now What?

What? So what? Now what? is a chunking strategy for small groups or individuals. It allows their brains to go through a research process based on their interests (What?), why these answers could be helpful to them and others (So what?), and what they might want to explore afterward (Now what?). This strategy provides a thinking process that can lead to applications that are helpful to self and others and at the same time can extend learning.

Directions

First, teach students the difference between an open-ended question (many different answers) versus a closed question (one-word answers). Then, walk them through the three-step inquiry method. Students should brainstorm questions about the topic and write them under step one in the "What? So What? Now What" reproducible (page 80), then choose three questions to research. Encourage them to use as many open-ended questions as possible. Allow them to use technology to research the answers to these questions. Then, have them complete steps two and three.

You might want to do step one together as a whole class and guide their thinking. You can have small groups work together to find the answers. Bring the whole class together to share and discuss what they learned. Then have them explore steps two and three in their small groups and discuss again with the whole class.

Having students explore a topic before receiving explicit instruction can prime their brains for better meaning making and memory. Chapter 3 (page 21) talks more in depth about Wexler and colleagues' (2016) findings that priming information, which happens minutes—even seconds—before exposure to a learning event can improve and enhance memory. Additionally, the information you glean can help you determine what to teach more deeply during that unit or lesson. Suggested topics include world or environmental problems. Those could cover real-world historical, societal, scientific, or mathematical problems.

Example

See figure 4.10 (page 70) for an example of inquiry method What? So what? Now what?

Suggestions for Differentiation

The following suggestions can help you differentiate this strategy.

- **Bumping it up:** Add another concept to some of the questions, such as, How do volcanoes and earthquakes shape the earth's surface? What do they have in common with one another? What are their differences? Challenge them to choose the more complex questions on their step one list.

- **Breaking it down:** Help them find the best websites to answer their questions. You might even provide easy-to-read nonfiction books about the topic so they can look through these books to find answers to their questions. Depending on your students' ages and interests, you might try Saddleback Educational Publishing's (www.sdlback.com/hi-lo-books) Hi-Lo titles. Give these students a list of question stems to them get started with brainstorming.

- **Specializing for English learners:** Preteach some key vocabulary words and share images of these words so they can ask appropriate questions.

Suggestions to Incorporate Technology

These websites will help you with the What? So what? Now what? inquiry method.

- ThinkTank (http://thinktank.4teachers.org) helps students learn how to refine a subject so that it's more manageable for the internet research.

- Google Drive (https://drive.google.com) makes presentation sharing a breeze. You can edit student work and send it right back to them. They can add graphics, pictures, fonts, and more.

- Educreations (www.Educreations.com) lets students create a presentation using an interactive whiteboard format. They can insert photos and even write on the screen.

1. What? State what we want to know about _plants_. ○ Why are there so many different kinds of plants? ○ Why must they be near the sun? ○ Why are they green? ○ Where do they come from? ○ What do they eat? Now, search online for answers.		
Question: Why are they green?	Answer: Their cells have the pigment chlorophyll which absorbs all light except green.	Resource: zmescience.com
Question: Where do they come from?	Answer: Plants come from seeds which come from pollen spreading by bees.	Resource: http://study.com
Question: What do they eat?	Answer: Plants need water, sun, carbon dioxide to make their own food.	Resource: www.scienceforkidsclub.com/ photosynthesis.html
2. So what? ☑ Why is this information important to know? ☑ How can we use this information to improve our life, school, town, state (or province), county, or world? ☑ How does it connect with me? 1. This helps me understand how plants work and how they form around me. 2. We can plant gardens in the community. 3. I eat plants.		
3. Now what? (What should we explore next?) We should explore different plants like trees, flowers, and bushes.		

Figure 4.10: *Example of inquiry method What? So what? Now what?*

Interest Expert Groups Jigsaw

This strategy is best for small groups of four but benefits individuals as they contribute to the learning of others. The benefit is that each student explores a topic of interest and has the opportunity to be the expert on this content when sharing with other group members. All students learn from one another during this process.

Directions

Analyze the upcoming lessons in your unit and find one or two where your students can be in charge of teaching chunks to each other. Collect books or online articles about four different, yet related, topics in the unit and create some questions about each. (For example, if you are studying Native American tribes of the Great Plains, gather materials about the Shoshone, Arapaho, Cheyenne, and Comanche.) Create heterogeneous groups of four students each. Call them *family groups*. Introduce the reading materials you collect and have each student choose one of the topics so that each topic is present within each family group. If more than one person within a group wants the same set of materials, model how to compromise.

After each person in each group makes a selection, group students who are studying the same topics; call these *expert groups*. Together, students in each expert group read the materials and answer the questions. You may want to give them a checklist of what they need to learn so they can teach their content more effectively to their family group. They can also do an online search for any additional questions they may have. They collaborate to ensure they have everything to go back to their family group to share what they have learned. Rotate among the expert groups to provide help as needed and be sure students understand the content. When all the expert groups finish, have students return to their family groups and teach each other what they have learned about their topic. Optionally, you can provide a checklist of what students are to learn and share about their content.

Example

See figure 4.11 (page 72) to learn how to group students for interest expert groups jigsaw.

Suggestions for Differentiation

The following suggestions can help you differentiate this strategy.

- **Bumping it up:** If there is content that is more challenging to understand, mark that text and content so those in the group know that. Students can choose to learn about it if they are ready for the challenge. You could provide more challenging criteria as well for those who choose it and want it.

- **Breaking it down:** Provide graphic organizers at the tables if students need to organize what they plan to teach. Preteach some vocabulary terms before the whole lesson.

- **Specializing for students who struggle with multiple steps or have weaker working memory capacity:** For students who are unsure of this research process, partner them with someone who feels confident about the multistep process. This could be helpful if you have an odd number of students as well. Break the process into smaller steps, too.

Suggestions to Incorporate Technology

The following websites offer great Lexile level articles to use for jigsaws.

- Newsela (www.newsela.com) delivers daily news articles at five reading levels from grades 3–12. Articles are accompanied by Common Core–aligned quizzes to provide quick, powerful feedback.

- ReadWorks (www.readworks.org) lets students present information on your SMART Board and write notes in text online. The site offers articles sorted by topic, and all the articles come in audio versions.

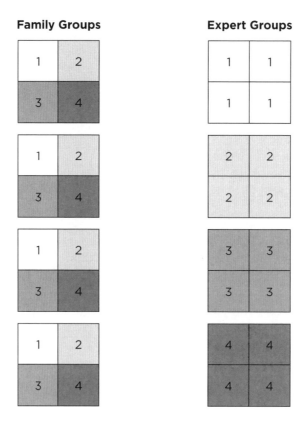

Figure 4.11: How to group students for interest expert groups jigsaw.

Rotation Stations

This small-group strategy lets students explore a particular topic several ways. The whole group has processing activities at each station so there is more engagement and more discussion, and therefore, more learning.

Directions

Divide your content into chunks that you can represent at stations where students can interact with one another and with the content. Each station (placed on desks, open-floor spaces, or tables) reflects a different chunk of information and asks students to engage in the content in different ways. Provide a specific task, written out step by step, at each station. The tasks should include a finished product of some kind that students must complete. Each student is thereby held accountable to document his or her own learning while at that station, but the group must work together to complete the task.

You will need to determine how to group your students.

- Each heterogeneous small group of three to five students includes students with varied background knowledge on the topics at hand, different leadership skills, and different cultural backgrounds.

- Create all heterogeneous groups except one group that is homogeneous. Allow that group to process these stations at higher levels or provide more help and support.

Example

See figure 4.12 for a rotation station planning template.

Suggestions for Differentiation

The following suggestions can help you differentiate this strategy.

- **Bumping it up:** Homogeneously group students and give them a more challenging assignment with analyzing or synthesizing assignments that go along with each station.

- **Breaking it down:** Rotate with the group of students that might need more explanation, definition, modeling, and examples from you.

- **Specializing for students with working memory challenges:** Type and print, on a piece of paper that stands out, a hard copy of the steps so groups can easily see it when they arrive at the station. One student reads the steps aloud. Provide roles and clear routines for rotating and for organizing the assignments at each station.

Suggestions to Incorporate Technology

The following resources will help you work on rotation stations.

- Place computers or tablets at some of the stations so students can research online.

- Place smartphones or tablets at a sorting station so students can photograph their creation for evidence in case you are busy working with other groups.

- Place smartphones or tablets at another station so students can record video or audio of themselves or other students as they perform a lab or present information as experts.

Station 1: Group Reading Station	Station 2: Writing Station	Station 3: Word Study Station	Station 4: Research Station	Station 5: Independent Reading Station
Learning target: I can read a nonfiction article and annotate it based on the thinking job.	**Learning target:** I can write a response to what I read.	**Learning target:** I can create a description for each vocabulary word and elaborate at least two ways on each word.	**Learning target:** I can research two other ways that weathering and erosion can occur on our earth.	**Learning target:** I can read a book of interest at my independent reading level.
Steps to take: Read the article about weathering and erosion. Thinking job (purpose for reading): While reading, determine the three causes and the two effects. Highlight three facts that you learned about.	**Steps to take:** Read the article from previous station. (If starting here, rehearse what you read yesterday and respond to that article.). Read the prompt on the table.	**Steps to take:** Complete the graphic organizer for each word.	**Steps to take:** Use the internet sites listed for your group to research other ways that weathering and erosion are occurring on our earth. Complete the matrix.	**Steps to take:** Make sure book is ready to go at your desk.

Figure 4.12: *Rotation station planning template example.*

continued on next page ⇒

*Visit **go.SolutionTree.com/instruction** for a free reproducible version of this figure.*

Station 1: Group Reading Station	Station 2: Writing Station	Station 3: Word Study Station	Station 4: Research Station	Station 5: Independent Reading Station
Criteria for success for this station (check one): *rubric, checklist, or exemplar*	**Criteria for success for this station (check one):** *rubric, checklist, or exemplar*	**Criteria for success for this station (check one):** *rubric, checklist, or exemplar*	**Criteria for success for this station (check one):** *rubric, checklist, or exemplar*	**Criteria for success for this station (check one):** *rubric, checklist, or exemplar*
I can read the article with the thinking jobs in mind. I can highlight three new facts that I learned. I can mark three causes and two effects.	I can answer the question thoroughly by using two text evidences. I will use evidence and document where I found it. I will have an introduction and conclusion. I will use one or two vocabulary words correctly (bolded) in my writing to convey my points.	I can write a description for each vocabulary word. I can elaborate on each word by creating a synonym or antonym. I can write a meaningful sentence using the word and connect it to my life.	I can complete the matrix about other ways that erosion is occurring on our earth (location, example of real occurrence, effects on the people).	I can enjoy reading the book of my choice.
Student names: McKenzie, Keaton, Jess	**Student names:** Ramona, Sherise, C.G.	**Student names:** Josh, Sean, Tamika	**Student names:** Bo, Jordan, Raoul	**Student names:** Mary, Becky, Eddie

Summary

Just as a professional dancer needs to know the moves to master the dance, teachers need to know how to help students receive the chunks in a way they can digest, own, and manipulate in their minds so the content becomes more meaningful and memorable. Dancers learn their moves by learning a small chunk, a section, and eventually blending all of those sections together to form a beautiful, fluent dance that is seamless to the viewer. Teachers must expertly do the same with their content. Deliver information in small chunks so that students' brains can bring the pieces together to understand the big picture. The dancer knows the chunks that were learned but eventually the body and brain bring the pieces together. Students digest each section through the next chapter, the *chew*.

Text Chunking

	Chunk	The Plan (Book or pages to read, words to preteach, student groupings, and processing students will engage in)
Before Reading	❑ Activate prior knowledge with questions such as, What do you already know about this subject? What experiences have you had in this area? ❑ Give the gist of the text and preview it (for example, do a picture walk or focus on text features). ❑ Preteach vocabulary words. ❑ Create a purpose for reading based on the learning target (the thinking job). ❑ Design some before reading prediction questions and have students partner to share their predictions.	Book: Activate prior knowledge: Grouping: Activate prior knowledge: Words to preteach: Thinking job: Predict:
During Reading	❑ Students read the section and work on their thinking job during the reading. ❑ Thinking job ideas: graphic organizers filled in; tagging text with sticky notes based on what they need to look for; writing answers to questions; finding the main problem, solution, character, cause, effect, and so on. ❑ Design questions while reading: question for author, question for teacher, question for self (something interesting to research further), question for a friend. ❑ Discuss in small groups or whole group the questions that were created for these sections of reading.	
After Reading	❑ Share the results of the thinking job in small groups or whole group. ❑ Summarize, bringing all the chunks together. ❑ Reread anything confusing. ❑ Write a response to what was read. Start with a teacher-created prompt. ❑ Discuss teacher-created after reading questions.	

Partner Reading Checklist—Fiction Strategies

Reader's name: _____ **Partner's name:** _____

Date: _____ **Reading material:** _____

Directions: Take turns reading the text and thinking aloud while reading. While one student is reading and thinking aloud, the other student places a mark next to each comprehension strategy the reader is modeling.

Before Reading
_____ Reads the title
_____ Previews the text by taking a picture walk through the book
_____ Predicts what the text will be about
_____ States the purpose for reading this text
_____ Asks questions about the text
_____ Establishes the purpose for reading
_____ Reviews the list of possible strategies that he or she might use during the reading

During Reading
_____ Reads, stops, and retells
_____ Finds answers to previous questions and forms new questions
_____ Relates what is being read to what he or she knows or experiences
_____ Rereads parts that are hard to understand
_____ Corrects miscues
_____ Revises predictions
_____ Explains or draws what he or she visualizes

After Reading
_____ Explains if predictions are right or wrong
_____ Summarizes the story
_____ Discusses author's purpose
_____ Explains the strategies that he or she uses during reading
_____ Makes connections (text-to-self, text-to-text, text-to-world)
_____ Explains the after-reading writing assignment

Partner Reading Checklist—Nonfiction Strategies

Reader's name: _____   **Partner's name:** _____

Date: _____   **Reading material:** _____

Directions: Take turns reading the text and thinking aloud while reading. While one student is reading and thinking aloud, the other student places a mark next to each comprehension strategy the reader is modeling.

📚 Before Reading
_____ Discusses what he or she knows about the topic
_____ Previews the text's pictures, graphs, captions, and boldface words
_____ Predicts what the text will be about
_____ States the purpose for reading this text
_____ Asks questions about the text
_____ Establishes the purpose for reading and requirements for using the information
_____ Reviews the list of possible strategies that he or she might use

📖 During Reading
_____ Uses headings and topic sentences to form questions
_____ Looks for answers to questions
_____ Discusses and explains vocabulary words, graphs, and charts
_____ Relates what he or she is reading to what he or she knows or experiences
_____ Rereads parts that are hard to understand
_____ Revises predictions
_____ Explains or draws what he or she visualizes
_____ Completes graphic organizer

💭 After Reading
_____ Tries to answer questions that he or she has
_____ Tells the main idea and summarizes the text
_____ Explains if predictions were right or wrong
_____ Explains what vocabulary words mean in own words
_____ Relates the text to prior knowledge and discusses new learning
_____ Explains the strategies that he or she uses during reading
_____ Explains how the after-reading assignment relates to the text

Big Picture Note-Taking Method

Name: _____ Date: _____

The Big Picture It can be questions, a concept, or a main idea statement.	Supporting Details List details about the main idea, question, or concept.	Questions and Reflections While note-taking, jot down questions that pop into your mind or reflections you have about the content.
Chunk one big picture: _____ _____ **Picture or symbol:**		
Chunk two big picture: _____ _____ **Picture or symbol:**		
Chunk three big picture: _____ _____ **Picture or symbol:**		
Summarize all the chunks:		

Mind Map Assessment Rubric

Name: _____ Date: _____

Rating scale: 0 = Not yet; 1 = Somewhat; 2 = Approaching; 3 = Mastery				
Criteria for Success	**Student Rating**	**Peer Rating**	**Teacher Rating**	**Comments**
Main idea is in the middle. Extensions of the key ideas or supporting chunks show a deep understanding of the content.				
Four to five accurate details support the connecting chunks or subheadings.				
Mind mapping format has been followed: color, symbols, highlights, printed words or phrases, lines showing connections, citations simplified if student uses multiple resources.				
Symbols and pictures support the text and are accurate: student draws or pastes five or more images to the mind map.				
Mind map shows that student understands the most important chunks that support the main idea.				
Bonus: Mind map shows interrelated connections among some of the chunks.				

What? So What? Now What?

1. What? (What do we want to know about _____?)

Now, search online for answers.

Question:	Answer:	Resource:
Question:	Answer:	Resource:
Question:	Answer:	Resource:

2. So what?

❑ Why is this information important to know?

❑ How can we use this information to improve our life, school, town, state (or province), county, or world?

❑ How does it connect with me?

3. Now what? (What should we explore next?)

CHAPTER 5

Take Step Two: Chew (Learn)

In step one of the instructional cha-chas, you plan your chunks and consider ways to differentiate your content delivery. You also fully model and guide your students through a chunk, just like you would if you were teaching someone a dance routine. It is now time for the next step. Consider, again, the dance teacher. After teaching the first eight counts, he or she lets dancers practice the steps again and again until their muscle memory can retain the information.

In step two of the instructional cha-chas, you further release the responsibility for learning to students as they process—*chew*—the chunked content, first with a partner or small group and eventually on their own. You're letting them discuss and practice the content to enhance memory before performing a solo.

The following questions will help you understand this step.

- What is *processing*?
- Why does the brain need to process?
- What are the benefits of processing?
- How can you differentiate the content processing?
- What strategies can you use during chewing?

What Is *Processing*?

In our instructional cha-chas cycle, we refer to processing as *chewing*, which in this case you could describe

as "consolidation, transformation and internalization of information by the learner" (Caine, Caine, & Crowell, 1994). Processing is where learning takes place. Quality processing activities engage students at high levels of thinking and will produce deeper understanding of key concepts and skills. Educator Eric Jensen (2005), listed as the number-one educational guru at Global Gurus (www.globalgurus.org), suggests that "teaching heavy, new content to novice learners may require two to five minutes of processing for every ten to fifteen minutes of instruction" (p. 44).

Students can process independently, with a partner, in small groups, or in a whole-group setting in a variety of ways. For example, while reading, students can do the chew activity text tagging (tagging thoughts with sticky notes or annotating on paper the thinking while reading) and then answer questions or discuss with each other before, during, and after the reading. During a lesson, students can do a quick write after a chunk (to summarize what was learned); complete a graphic organizer while reading or during note-taking; answer a question with a short essay; or write an argumentative writing piece (writing process). Socratic seminars (a structured discussion that involves answering or asking questions about a text) or philosophical chairs (using a debate format to discuss two opposing sides of a controversial issue) are powerful forms to assess thinking, speaking, and listening skills. Academic discussions with statement stems engage students and help them communicate their thinking. Processing the content by sorting words, sounds, pictures, and objects helps students see the similarities and differences among the items they're sorting. These examples are just a few of the many ways students can process. In this chapter, we will share more of our favorites.

Why Does the Brain Need to Process?

Learning doesn't happen in the acquisition of content, but rather, during the processing of the content. The students must do the thinking, doing, sharing, writing, or reading to learn it. Whoever retrieves the information is doing the learning. Frequent opportunities to recall information (chew), along with effective feedback (after checking), has an effect size of more than .80 on student achievement (Agarwal et al., 2013). Retrieving, or chewing, looks like thinking, speaking, writing, planning, making, and sorting—and the list goes on. It's when students are doing something with the content that learning can take place.

In their highly practical book titled *Academic Conversations: Classroom Talk That Fosters Critical Thinking and Content Understandings*, researchers Jeff Zweirs and Marie Crawford (2011) illustrate the power of academic talk and conversation to engage students and lead to long-term learning. The bottom line is this: when students spend time talking about their knowledge, comprehension and long-term memory improve. The person in the classroom who is doing the most talking is making the most connections, so it stands to reason that too much teacher talk in the classroom limits student learning.

Processing gives students opportunities to turn the learned content into meaningful, highly connected neural networks within the brain that are stored in the memory sites. All new sensory information (except for olfactory data), enters the thalamus first. Simultaneously, this same information is sent to the amygdala, so that any perceived uncertainty or threat gets top priority. This routing happens in one hundred milliseconds (Davis & Whalen, 2001) and typically helps us survive. The amygdala determines if an emotional or cognitive response is necessary. The rest of the data go to different processing centers in the brain. For example, visual information gets processed in the occipital lobe, sounds in the auditory cortex, touch in the sensory cortex, and spatial representations in the parietal lobe. For students to achieve stronger, lasting learning, provide strategies that allow for processing through as many senses as possible.

What Are the Benefits of Processing?

After presenting content, the processing opportunities that we plan for our students allow them to reflect, study, evaluate, and create meaning to internalize ideas and concepts. In the book *Deeper Learning* (Jensen & Nickelsen, 2008), we discover the benefits of student processing that includes more opportunities.

- For information to become meaningful and, therefore, memorable

- For students to think about the learning, pose questions for clarity, and discover answers (Questions lead to some of the most powerful learning opportunities.)

- For elaboration, which allows for stronger and fuller connections between the neurons (The chunks of information become deeper, allowing for better application and connections in other subject areas.)

- To consider and explore different viewpoints

- To strengthen working memory and attach emotion to the content

- For the teacher to reflect on the lesson's effectiveness and thereby make quick changes or rethink how he or she teaches something

The bottom line: processing is thinking. Thinking is learning. Learning is consolidation into the neural network of memory.

How Can You Differentiate the Content Processing?

Effective teachers, staying current with neuroscience, recognize the value in having students talk about content with their fellow students. Providing students with a variety of purposeful, flexible groups allows for discourse while leaving room for a wide range of student interests, learning preferences, and readiness levels. The following sections will take a closer look at processing in homogeneous groups and processing in heterogeneous, cooperative learning groups.

Processing in Homogeneous Groups

After processing individually, students should also process with others what they learn. New perspectives arise, paradigms change, opinions are challenged, aha moments emerge, and accuracy of our thinking clarifies when we see from another person's perspective.

Effective teachers are purposeful *and* flexible when it comes to placing their students with learning partners or groups. We know that when we place our students in homogeneous *interest* groups, they are often more motivated and attentive. In addition, interest groups help students make analogies between the content and their interests, thus making the content more relevant for them. When we place our students in homogeneous *learning preferences groups*, we notice an increase in the students' retention of the learning since they acquire the information in their strongest modality.

When we place our students in groups homogeneously based on their current content understanding, we are using *readiness groups*, which allows us to:

- Enrich and advance those students who have met the learning target and would benefit from more rigor

- Provide instruction and practice for the students on level

- Close achievement gaps for students who are struggling

Although this outcome *seems* ideal, use readiness grouping sparingly. Education researchers Robert J. Marzano, Debra J. Pickering, and Jane E. Pollock (2001) share that while readiness grouping yields better results than no grouping at all, "students of low ability actually perform worse when they are placed in homogeneous groups with students of low ability—as opposed to students of low ability placed in heterogeneous groups" (p. 87).

The key is to flexibly group and regroup students based on the outcomes you hope to achieve.

Processing in Heterogeneous Cooperative Learning Groups

Marzano, Pickering, and Pollock (2001) show that:

> Cooperative learning has an effect size of .78 when compared with strategies in which students compete with each other (individual competition) . . . and instructional strategies in which students work on tasks individually without competing with each other (individual student tasks). (pp. 86–87)

For these reasons, we consider cooperative grouping the go-to grouping method in our classrooms.

Cooperative learning is the instructional use of small heterogeneous groups so that students work together to maximize their own learning as well as the group's. Allowing students to work in cooperative learning groups helps "develop cognitive abilities, improve working memory and everyday decision-making ability and improve emotional intelligence status and self-esteem" (Jensen & Nickelsen, 2008, p. 40). David W. Johnson, Roger T. Johnson, and Edythe J. Holubec (1994), leaders in the field of cooperative learning, state there are five essential components of cooperative learning.

1. **Positive interdependence:** There is a sense of sink or swim together.

2. **Individual accountability and group accountability:** Each member must contribute to the group to achieve its goals.

3. **Face-to-face interaction:** They help one another learn and celebrate group success and efforts.

4. **Interpersonal and small-group skills:** Those skills include communication, leadership decision making, trust, and conflict resolution.

5. **Group processing:** This means reflecting on how well the team works together and how to help it to function more effectively.

We recognize the importance of these five components not just in our schools, but in our lives outside of the classroom. Therefore, we recommend that students have time daily to process the content in heterogeneous groups and participate in a cooperative learning lesson one day each week. To achieve this, our students typically work with their heterogeneous base group for the initial part of the lesson, processing each small chunk of information. Later in the lesson, or the following day, based on student data, we might choose to make grouping changes.

Lesson Plan With Chew Points

The lesson plan with chew points shows you how to incorporate processing into your lesson plan for students, individually, with partners, or in small groups. Here, we'll provide directions for implementation, an example, and suggestions for differentiating instruction and incorporating technology.

Directions

Since you chose a learning target and designed chunks, it's time to focus your thinking on the best way for students to process the chunk that you just planned, consider how to help them get it into their brain, prepare them for the next chunk, and determine if they understand this chunk. This question will help you determine which type of processing or chewing should occur after each chunk. Place this chew idea in the right column next to that particular chunk. Some chews will be short and sweet, while others may be long and deep. Place the main formative assessment that is the main chew in the appropriate right column. Finally, check the appropriate box to show if it's an independent, partner, or small-group chew. If it's a small-group chew, write the number of students that will be in that group on the given line.

Example

Figure 5.1 builds onto the lesson plan in figure 4.1 (page 54) by adding chews (shaded gray) next to each chunk. Figure 5.2 (page 86) is an example of the main formative assessment for this lesson plan. See "The Main Idea and Detail Tabletop Graphic Organizer" reproducible on page 104.

Daily Lesson Plan

Subject or unit: Reading: Main Idea—Details **Grade:** 5

Standard: Determine two or more main ideas of a text and explain how they are supported by key details; summarize the text (RI.5.2).

Learning target (do and know): I can describe or graphically represent the relationship between main idea and details.

Main formative assessment (show): Students complete "The Main Idea and Detail Tabletop Graphic Organizer" (page 104) to show how the details (table legs) support the main idea (tabletop) based on a given paragraph.

Criteria for success (check type):	**Criteria for success (explain details):** Students self-assess their work and complete a checklist with the following criteria for success.
☐ Rubric	
☑ Self-assessment	☐ I can write accurate details on the legs.
☑ Checklist	☐ I can write the accurate main idea on the tabletop.
☐ Peer assessment	☐ I can write an explanation, in complete sentences, of how the details and main idea are connected.
☐ Exemplars	
☐ Nonexemplars	
☐ Verbal	
☐ Other: _____	

The Chunk Explained: What Teacher Will Do	**The Chew Explained: What Students Will Do***
Beginning chunks (I do): Review the definition of *main idea*. Move your arms as large as possible, creating an invisible square in the air, or frame, to represent the big picture. Define details and make little circles with your hands, going into the invisible square you just motioned. Explain that the little details create the big picture; they help you visualize what the picture looks like.	Students show the body movement that represents the definition of the main idea (arms folded on top of each other to represent a strong tabletop). Students practice showing the details (table legs). Students create the tabletop and then take one arm to represent the table legs. ☑ Individual ☐ Partners ☐ Small-group total: _____

Middle chunks (we do, two do):	Students create a kinesthetic table on the floor after receiving sentence strips with details and one main idea. Students determine who is the main idea. The rest of the students are details that support it. Their bodies create a table on the floor with the sentence strip on their bellies. Teacher checks and gives feedback before they rotate sentence strips.
Say, "There are many visuals that we can create to help us understand the relationship between main idea and details. I have used the visual of an imaginary frame to represent main idea. The circles inside it represent details. Today, we are going to show another visual: a tabletop with legs supporting it."	
Show an anchor chart (a large visual, usually on chart paper) of a tabletop that shows the top of the table labeled Main Idea and the table legs labeled Details. Then, show a paragraph from any of your texts and how the main idea of the paragraph gets written on the tabletop and the details from the paragraph are written on the individual legs supporting the tabletop. Make sure all students can explain that details are the legs of the table that support the tabletop, which represents the main idea.	❑ Individual ❑ Partners ☑ Small-group total: _5_
Share many anchor chart examples: paragraph being separated on the tabletop graphic organizer with main idea on top and details written on the legs.	
Ending chunk (you do):	Students read a paragraph that is under the document camera. You can read it to them.
Summarize the day's learning by pointing out what each group does during the lesson and giving positive feedback to each group. (Group work is explained in this chapter on page 83.)	Main formative assessment: Students complete the drawing by writing the main idea on the top of the table and writing three or four details on the legs. Then, they describe the relationship between the main idea and details on the lines at the bottom of the paper. Each student turns one in.
Explain the exit ticket by modeling how to bring the pieces together with a different paragraph (not the one you use to assess students).	❑ Individual ❑ Partners ☑ Small-group total: _4_

*Note: Place the main formative assessment, indicated earlier in the plan, in the appropriate chunk.

Source for standard: NGA & CCSSO, 2010a.

Figure 5.1: *Sample lesson plan for learning chews.*

Suggestions for Differentiation

The following suggestions can help you differentiate this strategy.

- **Bumping it up:** Provide higher-level-thinking questions by combining other chunks, by comparing or contrasting the content to other topics taught, or by designing and asking open-ended questions.

- **Breaking it down:** Really listen or watch their chew moments so you can determine if they understand the content. Provide feedback or

instruction to help them understand better. Feedback questions like these can help a student close the gap with this activity: How does this detail on this leg of the graphic organizer support the main idea on this tabletop? How do you know? Where did you find it in the text?

- **Specializing for students with working memory challenges:** Ask students to retrieve more often during your lesson plan. In other words, shorten chunk times and decrease the amount of content in each one, then provide a chew moment right after that smaller chunk.

The Main Idea and Detail Tabletop Graphic Organizer

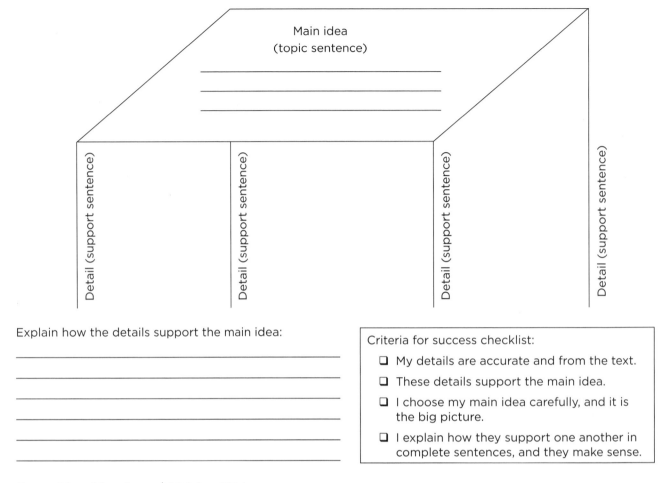

Explain how the details support the main idea:

Criteria for success checklist:
- ❑ My details are accurate and from the text.
- ❑ These details support the main idea.
- ❑ I choose my main idea carefully, and it is the big picture.
- ❑ I explain how they support one another in complete sentences, and they make sense.

Source: Adapted from Jensen & Nickelsen, 2014.

Figure 5.2: *The main idea and detail tabletop graphic organizer.*

Suggestions to Incorporate Technology

The following resources will help you create, share, and manage your lesson plans. (Visit **go.SolutionTree .com/instruction** to access live links to the websites mentioned in this book.)

- Nearpod (https://nearpod.com) helps teachers engage students with interactive lessons.

- Planboard (www.chalk.com/planboard) helps teachers streamline lesson plans, find resources, and collaborate with others.

- Educreations (www.educreations.com) is a community where anyone can teach what they know and learn what they don't. The software turns any iPad or web browser into a recordable, interactive whiteboard, making it easy to create engaging video lessons and share them online.

- Evernote (https://evernote.com) keeps your notes organized. Memos are synced so they're accessible anywhere and searchable.

- ShowMe (www.showme.com) is an open online learning community where anyone can learn and teach any topic. The iPad app lets you easily create and share video lessons.

What Strategies Can You Use During Chewing?

You can use many of this chapter's strategies for short-term processing of two to five minutes (short and sweet) or as a full day or longer (long and deep) team-processing activity, and some you can modify to be either. While we recommend having students chew on the content heterogeneously with a partner or in groups of three to four, we recognize that you may choose to use these strategies independently or with a homogeneous group.

You can place these chew strategies strategically into a daily lesson plan. We show you how to do this in our first strategy designed for you, the teacher. The other strategies are processing tools that your students can engage in throughout the lesson plans that you design based on your unique learning targets.

Question Stars From Bloom's Taxonomy Levels

Question stars from Bloom's taxonomy levels is a processing strategy for individual students, partners, small groups, or whole class. The benefit to this strategy is seeing what vocabulary and key concepts your students already know; from there, you can determine what content you need to teach.

Directions

Print and cut out the "Question Stars for Bloom's Taxonomy" reproducibles (page 105–110), which are based on Bloom's (1956; Anderson & Krathwohl, 2001) revised taxonomy levels one to six. (Many teachers prefer to print each of the question levels on different colored paper.) After reading a text, place students in groups of three or four. Have students turn the stars face down and mix them up. Student one selects a star, turns it over, and asks a question using the question stem on the star. Student two answers the question. Student three shares the evidence that supports the answer. Now, student two selects a star, and students continue rotating roles until they answer all stars or the teacher calls time.

Example

Questions created by the students will be original to them and the text they are reading, but some examples of possible questions follow. The first two examples are based on the fiction text *Lilly's Purple Plastic Purse* by Kevin Henkes (1996), and the last two examples are based on the graphic biography *Martin Luther King Jr.: The Life of a Civil Rights Leader* by Gary Jeffrey (2007).

Questions for Bloom's taxonomy level one (remember) follow.

- Who is Lilly's teacher?
- Can you list three things Lilly loved about school?
- Can you recall where King was born?
- Where or when did King deliver his "I Have a Dream" speech?

Questions for Bloom's taxonomy level two (understand) follow.

- What fact or ideas show that Lilly loved her teacher?
- How would you summarize *Lilly's Purple Plastic Purse*?
- How would you compare or contrast King with Gandhi?
- What is the main idea of the section titled "Freedom's Promise" on pages 4 and 5?

Questions for Bloom's taxonomy level three (apply) follow.

- What might have resulted had Lilly not redrawn her picture of Mr. Slinger?
- What elements would you change to make the Lightbulb Lab better?
- If you saw someone being treated differently because of his or her race, what would you do or say?
- What examples can you find to show that not everyone agreed with King?

Questions for Bloom's taxonomy level four (analyze) follow.

- What is the theme of *Lilly's Purple Plastic Purse?*
- How is Mr. Slinger related to our teacher?
- What is the function of a leader?
- What evidence supports that King was a leader?

Questions for Bloom's taxonomy level five (evaluate) follow.

- Do you believe Lilly is basically good or bad? How will you prove or disprove your response?
- Why is Lilly's purse so important to the story?

- Do you agree with the actions or outcome of the 1963 march on Washington?
- What will you cite to defend allowing children to join in the march in Birmingham?

Questions for Bloom's taxonomy level six (synthesize) follow.

- Why do you think the author repeats the word, "Wow"?
- What might happen if Mr. Slinger brings in a guest musician?
- Can you propose an alternative for "taking a knee" during the national anthem, which is a current common protest against inequality?
- What could you do to minimize or maximize the racial differences being expressed today?

Suggestions for Differentiation

The following suggestions can help you differentiate this strategy.

- **Bumping it up:** Use only question stars from levels four to six (analyze, evaluate, and synthesize). Provide text at a higher readability level.
- **Breaking it down:** Use only question stars from levels one to three (remember, understand,

apply). Provide a page number where they can find evidence to support their thinking. Provide text at a lower readability level.

- **Specializing for kinesthetic learners:** Create a hopscotch board. Place a question star in or beside each box in the board. Students toss an object onto the board, then hop to the object. To retrieve the object, they must correctly answer the corresponding question star. If they are incorrect, they must leave the object in the box and return to home base, where they can consult their resources for the answer. On their next turn, they must hop to the same box to attempt to retrieve their object.

Suggestions to Incorporate Technology

The following apps can help you implement Bloom's taxonomy.

- Edutopia (www.edutopia.org/ipad-apps -elementary-blooms-taxonomy-diane-darrow) offers iPad apps specific to Bloom's taxonomy for grades K–5.
- Plickers (www.plickers.com) allows you to design questions in a multiple-choice format, then have students respond by holding up their Plicker card. Scan the cards using your phone or computer and watch it calculate student results.

Think Notes

Think notes is a processing strategy for individual students, followed by partners or small-group discussion. The benefit of this strategy is that you or your students can determine the important information and it allows for a variety of ways to record student thinking.

Directions

Give students the "Think Notes" reproducible (page 111) or have them fold a blank sheet of paper vertically creating two columns. Students write a heading at the top of each column. The left column, for example, might be labeled *Main idea* and the right column might be labeled *Supporting details*. Table 5.1 has other suggestions. As they are learning (via lecture, video, discussion, or the like), they record their thinking in the columns. Note that there can be a variety of teacher inputs on one

page and a variety of student thinking as well. After students complete their individual responses, allow them to partner or form small groups to compare and extend their responses.

Example

See figure 5.3 for an example of think notes.

Suggestions for Differentiation

The following suggestions can help you differentiate this strategy.

- **Bumping it up:** Students take notes during the learning. Afterward, they organize the notes and develop their own headings.

Table 5.1: *Possible Headings for Think Notes*

Teacher and Other Resources Ideas	Student-Thinking Ideas
Key idea	My response
Fact	Opinion
Vocabulary word	How I will remember it (Examples: image, definition, and sentence)
Important quote	Meaning
Pros	Cons
Main idea	Supporting details
Argument	Supporting evidence
Teacher's questions	My answers
What's important	What's interesting

Name: Pamela		Date: 2/1

The Day MLK Jr., Was Shot by Jim Haskins (1992)	Student-Thinking Ideas Student Response to Left Column
Examples: Key ideas, facts, vocabulary words, quote, pros, main idea, argument, teacher questions, what's important	**Examples:** Opinions, memory cues, inferencing or meaning-making responses, agree or disagree, supporting details or evidence, student questions or answers, *I wonder* statements, and connections
Page 6; MLK was late for dinner on April 4, 1968 and often changed his schedule for the past couple of weeks.	The book said that he told others about the threats on his life. I wonder if he was trying to be less predictable.
Page 6; "But it really doesn't matter to me now. Because I've been to the mountaintop."	He meant that he already hit the goal in a big way. He made a huge difference already.
Page 8; When Dr. King was looking over the railing of a balcony, a shot hit his forehead w/ such force that he fell flat on his back. Chaos broke—moaning and screaming. He died at 7:05pm—Bullet cut through his spinal cord. St. Joseph's Hospital in Memphis could not save him.	At this point in the book, my questions are: o Where was his wife Coretta when this happened? o Who shot him and why? o Did he get caught right away? o Who took over for him as the voice for civil rights?

Figure 5.3: *Student example of think notes.*

- **Breaking it down:** Students complete only the left column during the learning. Afterwards, they discuss with their peers and add to the right column.

- **Specializing for students with auditory processing challenges:** Break the instruction time into significantly smaller chunks and give students the think notes form with the left column already filled in.

Suggestions to Incorporate Technology

The following apps will help with note-taking.

- Evernote (https://evernote.com) keeps your notes organized. Memos are synced so they're accessible anywhere, and searchable so you always find what you need.

- OneNote (www.onenote.com/notebooks) acts as your very own digital notebook.
- Simplenote (https://simplenote.com) is a note-taking app that you can access on different platforms (Android, Apple, and others) and on most web browsers.

- Google Keep (https://keep.google.com) lets you take notes that include text, lists, images, and audio.
- Zoho Notebook (www.zoho.com/notebook) lets you take notes, make checklists, and record audio. Once your notes are created, they go on the cloud so no one loses any work.

 Framing Opinions With SOS

Framing opinions with SOS is a processing strategy for individual students, partners, small groups, or whole group. Forming opinions and supporting them with the framework graphic scaffolds thinking.

Directions

Write an opinion statement (S) on the SOS template in figure 5.4 and give a copy to each student. Students read the statement and form their own opinion (O) about the statement. Then, they explain their reasoning by providing support (S). Once students are familiar with the framework, have them develop their own SOS in small groups or individually.

Example

See figure 5.4 for an example of framing an opinion with SOS.

SOS	
Statement	Dogs make the best pets.
Opinion	☑ I agree
	☐ I disagree
Support	The following are support statements.
	o Dogs can guard your house and bark to scare off people.
	o You can train them to fetch your paper.
	o They like to be with people. You can tell them things that you wouldn't tell anyone else.

Figure 5.4: *Example of framing an opinion with SOS.*

*Visit **go.SolutionTree.com/instruction** for a free reproducible version of this figure.*

Suggestions for Differentiation

The following suggestions can help you differentiate this strategy.

- **Bumping it up:** Have students complete independent research to provide evidence and reasoning to support their opinion. If you provide the texts or online resources, include more challenging articles.

- **Breaking it down:** Provide the text or online resources for students to use to find evidence for their opinion. Ensure that the materials are accessible to students.

- **Specializing for students with processing challenges:** Provide the text. Partner students and assign each partner a different position. Allow time to read the article and highlight anything that supports their position. They can write notes in the margins explaining anything they highlight. Have them use the "Think Notes" reproducible (page 111) for notes. Have them present their opinions orally, rather than written, until they fully understand the process.

Suggestions to Incorporate Technology

The following apps will help with note-taking.

- Think CERCA (www.thinkcerca.com) is a literacy platform for English language arts, science, social studies, and mathematics for students in grade 4 and up.

- Google Forms (www.google.com/forms/about) allows students to write and send responses to the teacher and peers to determine if other agree or disagree with their opinion. Students can create their own surveys to help them form their opinions.

- ProCon.org (www.procon.org) gives brief pros and cons about controversial issues.

It was designed to help EL students easily comprehend the text. This site is easy to use and perfect for preparing claims and evidence.

Framing Arguments

Framing arguments is a processing strategy for individual students, partners, small groups, or whole group. The benefit is scaffolding student thinking through each step of a solid argument.

Directions

Give students the "Framing-an-Argument Organizer" reproducible (page 112), and make sure you explain the domain-specific vocabulary (italicized in this paragraph). Model how to state your position on an issue, explaining that that is making a *claim*. Support your claim with *evidence*. Explain your *reasoning* for each piece of evidence.

Acknowledge the *counterclaims*—the other side of the argument. Provide facts or examples to refute it—make your *rebuttal*. You write a *conclusion* for your argument with a strong statement that calls the audience to act. Once students are familiar with the framework, have them develop their own arguments in small groups or individually.

Example

See figure 5.5 for an example of a framing-an-argument organizer.

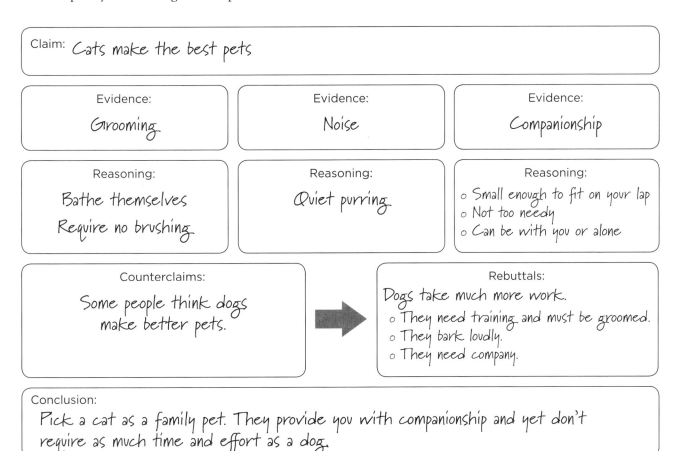

Figure 5.5: *Example of framing-an-argument organizer.*

Suggestions for Differentiation

The following suggestions can help you differentiate this strategy.

- **Bumping it up:** Have students complete independent research to provide evidence and reasoning for their argument. If you provide the text or websites for the students, make sure to include more challenging articles.

- **Breaking it down:** Provide text that is shorter or at each student's independent reading level, for students to use to find evidence for their claim. Ensure that the text or websites you provide are accessible to your students.

- **Specializing for students with processing challenges:** Provide students with the text. Partner the students and assign each partner a different position. Allow them time to read the article and highlight anything that supports their position. They can take notes out to the side explaining anything they highlight. Have them use the organizer for notes and present their argument orally, rather than written until they fully understand the process.

Suggestions to Incorporate Technology

- Think CERCA (www.thinkcerca.com) is a literacy platform for English language arts, science, social studies, and mathematics for students in grade 4 and up.

- ProCon.org (www.procon.org) gives brief pros and cons about controversial issues. It was designed to help EL students easily comprehend the text. This site is easy to use and perfect for preparing claims and evidence.

- Time Edge (www.timeedge.com) is a digital literacy platform with current events information and primary sources for grade 6 and up.

Talking Chips

Talking chips is a processing strategy for partners, small groups, or whole group. During talking chips, students take on various roles as they discuss the previously read text. The benefit is the opportunity for deeper discussions and learning. In grade 4 and earlier, the teacher should model one talking chip at a time so students can practice and understand each role's expectations.

Directions

Place students in partners or in teams of no more than four. Give each team one copy of "Talking Chips Explanation" (page113) and one copy of the "Talking Chips Pieces" (page 114) reproducibles. Have students cut out the talking chips. Before reading the chosen text (you can let individuals read different texts, or have the entire class read the same one), each student chooses one chip and reads the explanation for his or her chip. This sets the student's purpose for reading. After reading the chosen text, either orally or silently, the students roll a die to determine who leads the conversation. The student who rolls highest leads round one. As student one speaks, he or she places his or her talking chip back into the center of the desk. It is now available for another student to use in subsequent rounds. Round one discussion continues clockwise until each person shares. Each student now chooses a new talking chip to begin round two. Students continue their discussion rounds until you call time. As an option to wrap up the learning, you can provide a couple of choices (paragraph, poem, or comic strip, for example) and have students write in that genre about what they learn.

Example

Check out the "Talking Chips Pieces" reproducible (page 114) to see what the pieces look like.

Suggestions for Differentiation

The following suggestions can help you differentiate this strategy.

- **Bumping it up:** Provide more challenging text. Require students to offer multiple explanations for their thinking. Ask students to design their own talking chips icons to represent a type of thinking that is different.

- **Breaking it down:** Provide less challenging text. Provide fewer talking chips and select those that reinforce the skills the students need to develop. Provide prompts to get the talking started. For instance, *An example of _____ is _____.*

- **Specializing for nonreaders or students with speaking challenges:** Read the selection aloud and then allow students to break into groups to discuss. Or, allow a student who is uncomfortable speaking with the group to be the questioner. That student must develop three questions for team members to discuss using the talking chips and record the team's answers.

Suggestions to Incorporate Technology

Rewordify (https://rewordify.com) is a text compactor that simplifies and shortens readings so all students can discuss the same text.

Alternatively, to find readings that are adjusted for high, medium, or low Lexile levels, use the informational text in one of the following websites.

- Newsela (https://newsela.com) delivers daily news articles at five reading levels from grades 3–12. Articles are accompanied by Common Core–aligned quizzes to provide quick and powerful feedback.

- Smithsonian's TweenTribune (www.tweentribune .com) has articles about science, history, and current events for grades 5–8. You also can create an account and use the content in the classroom.

- News in Levels (www.newsinlevels.com) is good for English learners and will help you practice important words in English.

Swap-a-Question

Swap-a-question is a processing strategy for small groups of five students. Students benefit by learning how to use question stems to ask and answer a variety of questions.

Directions

Give students a copy of the "Swap-a-Question Template" reproducible (page 115) and tell them to write their name on each of the four boxes labeled *Question author's name.* Also give them a copy of Webb's Depth of Knowledge question stems (figure 5.6, page 94) to help them create questions for this activity. After presenting material to the class (through reading, video, minilesson, or other method), tell students to write a different question in each of the four boxes on their swap-a-question template. Students then cut apart their boxes and give one to each remaining member of their team. They answer each question they receive and record their name as answer author. (When all five students do this, each student will create and answer four different questions.) When students finish, they return all the cards to the question authors, who read the answers, silently, and determine whether they are correct.

If you have a small class or just prefer to have students write and answer fewer questions, reduce the number of students in each group and have them write one fewer question than the number of students in their group.

Example

See figure 5.7 (page 94) for an abbreviated example of the strategy swap-a-question.

Suggestions for Differentiation

The following suggestions can help you differentiate this strategy.

- **Bumping it up:** Group these students and provide more challenging text or require them to design and answer questions only from Webb's levels three (strategic thinking and reasoning) and four (critical and creative thinking).

- **Breaking it down:** Group these students and provide less challenging text, read it to them, or require them to design and answer questions only from Webb's levels one (routine thinking via recall and reproduction) and two (conceptual thinking via skill and concept).

- **Specializing for students with processing and problems with working memory:** Break the lesson into smaller chunks, having students stop and develop questions after each small section of text or video.

Suggestions to Incorporate Technology

The following apps will help you or your students develop multiple-choice quiz questions.

- Quizworks (www.quizworksinternational.com) lets you create online quizzes and education technology.

- Quizizz (https://quizizz.com) has free gamified quizzes on history, science, mathematics, English language arts, geography, and world languages. Pick an existing quiz or create your own for review, formative assessment, and more.

Level One: Routine Thinking (Recall and reproduction)	Level Two: Conceptual Thinking (Skill and concept)
Question: • Who? What? When? Where? Why? • What do you know about _____? • Can you define, identify, list, or recall _____? • Can you highlight key words? • Can you recall new facts or ideas or retell the story? • How did you represent mathematics in words, pictures, or symbols? • What map or diagram would you reproduce?	Question: • How or why would you use _____? • How would you organize _____ to show _____? • How could you show your understanding of _____? • What other way could you solve or find out _____? • What facts are relevant to show _____? • What is your prediction and why? • What question is this problem asking? • How would you organize these facts or observations?
Level Three: Strategic Thinking (Strategic thinking and reasoning)	Level Four: Extended Thinking (Critical and creative thinking)
Question: • What is the theme or the lesson learned from _____? • What underlying bias is there in _____? • What inferences will these facts support? • What is the impact of the writer's (figurative language, analogy, image) _____? • What ideas justify this position? • What evidence can you find to support _____? • How can you prove your solution is reasonable?	Question: • What changes would you make to solve or address the major issue or problem? • Can you propose an alternative solution to _____? • How would you prove or disprove _____? • How would you justify and present the importance of _____? • Do you agree with the actions, outcomes, or decisions to _____? Why or why not? What is your evidence? • Can you construct a model that would change _____?

Source: Webb, 1997, 1999.

Figure 5.6: *Webb's Depth of Knowledge question stems.*

*Visit **go.SolutionTree.com/instruction** for a free reproducible version of this figure.*

Question author's name: _____Spencer_____

Question: How are the pueblo homes different than your home?

Answer: A pueblo home is in the desert and made of clay. It is several stories high and built on cliffs. My house is not built out of clay, but it is in the desert and on a couple of high cliffs.

Answer author's name: _____Katie_____

Figure: 5.7: *Example of swap-a-question.*

*Visit **go.SolutionTree.com/instruction** for a free reproducible version of this figure.*

Stop-Think-Write

Source: Adapted from Jensen & Nickelsen, 2014.

Stop-think-write is a processing strategy for individual students, partners, or small groups. The benefit is that in addition to content being broken into manageable chunks and having processing time, students discuss their thinking with peers and then synthesize their learning.

Directions

Find four stopping points in the day's lesson. (This could mean breaking a reading text into four sections or finding four stopping points in a video clip or lecture, for example.) Create four specific questions or activities for students to complete at each stopping point. Write these on the stop-think-write template and make one copy for each student. After completing their four boxes, have students meet with a partner or small group of no more than four to discuss and share their thinking. Students may continue adding to their boxes based on their conversation with their classmates. When the discussion time is over, provide students a list of choices (such as poem, song, blog, tweet, comic strip, or graphic) to independently synthesize their learning in the fifth box.

Before reading aloud to elementary students, the teacher decides on a first stopping point and calls it *the beginning of the story*. Students stop and draw at that point. This occurs two more times, in the middle and end of the book. At the end of the book, students return to their seats and write about their drawings.

Example

See figure 5.8 for two first-grade examples.

Figure 5.9 (page 96) shows a fifth-grade example of stop-think-write done while reading a text.

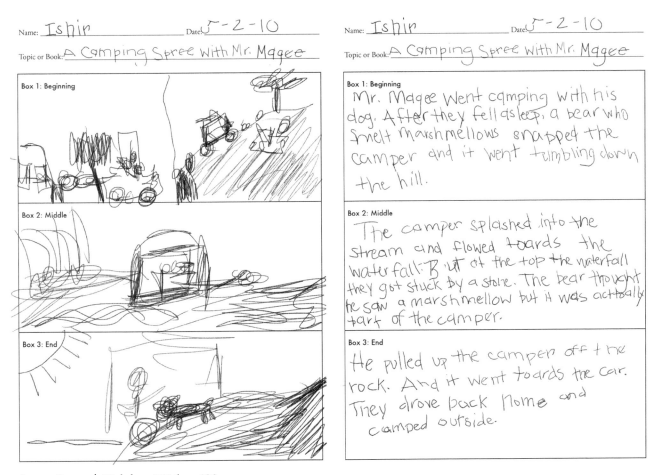

Source: Jensen & Nickelsen, 2014, p. 139.

Figure 5.8: *First-grade examples of stop-think-write.*

Name: _____Scott_____   Date: _____2/18_____

Book: _____Water—Shaping the Earth's Surface (nonfiction)_____

Box 1: pp. 1–2 Define the difference between weathering and erosion in your own words.

Weathering happens when rock slowly wears away. Water is one cause of weathering. Chemicals in rain, ocean waves, and fast-flowing rivers slowly wear rock away. Erosion occurs after weathering. It occurs when water picks up worn-down rock particles and deposits them in other places.

Box 2: pp. 3–4 How does water specifically cause erosion?

Water can change earth by carving out canyons, valleys, and holes. Ocean waves and powerful rivers strike against rocks and soil, changing their space (weathering). Erosion occurs when water picks up the loose rocks.

Box 3: pp. 5–6 Compare and contrast a levee with a dam.

A levee is like a dam but is made of earth, rocks, stones, or sand. They both stop water flow after heavy rainfalls.

Box 4: pp. 7–8 What are some solutions to the massive amounts of flooding that occurs on Earth?

Building dams and flood control channels are two ways of decreasing the chances of flooding.

Synthesis of the boxes:

Weathering and erosion will continually occur on this Earth, but there are some solutions so that the damage is not so devastating to humans.

Source: Jensen & Nickelsen, 2014, p. 140.

Figure 5.9: *Fifth-grade example of stop-think-write.*

Visit **go.SolutionTree.com/instruction** for a free reproducible version of this figure.

Some prompts for processing opportunities follow (Jensen & Nickelsen, 2014, p. 140).

- I have learned these new words: _____.
- I have learned these new facts: _____.
- I still have these questions: _____.
- The most valuable piece of information is _____.
- To summarize, I learned _____.
- The most important things to understand about _____ are _____.
- This concept is related to these other concepts: _____.
- When solving this mathematics problem, remember to _____.
- The main idea of _____ is _____.
- The word _____ means _____.
- One event (use the exact words from text) to elaborate on is _____.
- An illustration of what I learned or visualized while reading is _____.

Suggestions for Differentiation

The following suggestions can help you differentiate this strategy.

- **Bumping it up:** Design open-ended questions that allow for more than one response and require more critical and creative thinking. Use levels three and four of Webb's Depth of Knowledge question stems (page 94). Provide more challenging text.

- **Breaking it down:** Design questions in which the answers appear in the text, video, or lecture. Use levels one and two of Webb's Depth of Knowledge question stems (page 94). Provide less challenging and rigorous text. Break the lesson into four or five chunks. At the end of each, ask questions about the chunk and allow students to respond on that section of the stop-think-write box within the template. By the time you complete your final chunk of instruction, students will have completed their stop-think-write.

- **Specializing for nonwriters or students with fine motor challenges:** Have students use a tablet or smartphone to record their thinking so they can share that way when they arrive in the group.

Suggestions to Incorporate Technology

The following websites will help you work with the stop-think-write strategy.

- Ghostwriter (https://apple.co/2t2I90P) and Skitch (https://evernote.com/products/skitch) let you upload the graphic or take a picture of the graphic for students to annotate directly on it.

- SuperNote Notes Recorder & Photo (https://apple.co/2M7f1wr) helps you quickly take notes and make voice recordings to transcribe later or keep the recordings as audio files. Notes you make are color-coded so it is easy to find them later, and you can change the category and color.

- Google Drawings (https://chrome.google.com/webstore/detail/google-drawings) allows users to create diagrams, charts, and images.

Reciprocal Teaching

Source: Adapted from Jensen & Nickelsen, 2014.

Reciprocal teaching is a processing strategy for small groups of four students, who benefit from the combination of roles, which helps them deepen their comprehension.

Directions

To use this technique, which professor of education at the University of Michigan Annemarie Sullivan Palincsar and her colleague Ann L. Brown (1984) developed, divide a reading text into sections. Explain to students that you will model this strategy for them by thinking aloud and asking them to observe and provide responses to your questions. Afterward, allow them to work in groups to practice the roles of summarizer, questioner, predictor, and clarifier.

Provide each student with copies of the reciprocal teaching role bookmarks (figure 5.10, page 98–99). Introduce each role to students and explain their use. Read aloud the first section of the text. Begin modeling the first two roles (summarizer and questioner) by summarizing the reading and posing questions about the text's main content. Students respond, raise additional questions, and reread the text when they disagree or misunderstand. Synthesize the discussion to agree on the summary. Then, use the third to clarify words or concepts that students might not understand.

You may choose to prompt the students to apply previously learned clarification strategies like using context clues to identify unknown words. Finally, offer or ask for predictions about what might come next in the text. Throughout this discussion, you have been modeling how to use each strategy. Now, move from *I do* to *we do* as students practice the strategies by using (and rotating) the role cards as they discuss the text. During this time, you provide feedback and encouragement.

Suggestions for Differentiation

The following suggestions can help you differentiate this strategy.

- **Bumping it up:** Provide more challenging and complex text and statement stems.

- **Breaking it down:** Provide less challenging text and introduce and practice one role at a time.

- **Specializing for English learners:** Chunk the text into smaller pieces and read the text to them.

Suggestions to Incorporate Technology

Rewordify (https://rewordify.com) is a text compactor that simplifies and shortens readings so all students can discuss the same text.

Summarizer

First, share your summary of the text reading (central idea, theme).

Next, ask others in the group to share their summary or add to your summary.

How to summarize:

- Look for the topic sentence.
- Look for who, what, when, where, why, and how.
- Omit unnecessary information.

Summary stems and sentences:

- This story or section is mostly about _____.
- The topic sentence is _____.
- Some supporting details are _____.
- The author is trying to tell me _____.

Summary frame:

This story or section about_____ begins with _____, discusses (or develops) the idea that _____, and ends with _____.

Self-assessment:

- ❑ My summary is more than one sentence.
- ❑ I asked for contributions to my summary.
- ❑ I listened and piggybacked on others' comments.
- ❑ I looked back in the text to support my thinking with evidence.

Questioner

First, ask your group members to create one or two questions that someone reading this text can answer.

Next, ask your questions first and call on volunteers to answer your questions. Don't allow yes or no answers. Try to ask open-ended questions.

How to question:

- Ask teacher-type questions.
- Ask questions that require returning to the text.

Question stems and sentences:

- Who is _____?
- What is or does _____?
- When or where is _____?
- Why is _____ significant?
- Why does _____ happen?
- What are the parts of _____?
- How do _____ and _____ compare?
- How does _____ happen?
- What if _____?
- What is most important _____?
- What is your opinion of _____?

Self-assessment:

- ❑ I asked more than two questions.
- ❑ I asked for text evidence to support answers from members of my group.
- ❑ I listened and piggybacked on others' comments.
- ❑ I looked back in the text to support my thinking with evidence.

Predictor	Clarifier
First, ask group members to create a prediction based on what they see in the book. Next, share your predictions and explain the evidence for them.	First, share your confusing words, sections, or phrases from the reading with your group and explain why they stumped you. Explain how a clarifying strategy could help all of you. Next, ask your group members what they find confusing in the reading (phrases, words, or even concepts) and why.
How and when to predict: • A title is given. • Headings are provided. • The author poses a question in the text. • The text suggests what it will discuss next.	**How and when to clarify:** • Think about what confuses you or might confuse someone else. • Clarify when anyone is confused during the discussion.
Prediction stems and sentences: • Based on the title, I predict this is going to be about _____. • I already know these things about the topic or story _____. • I think the next chapter or section will be about _____. • Based on _____, I predict _____. • Based on what _____ said or did, I predict _____.	**Clarifying stems and sentences:** • I don't really understand _____. • A question I have is _____. • A question I'd like answered is _____. • One word or phrase I do not understand is _____. • Let's reread section _____.
Self-assessment: ❏ I predicted before, during, and after reading. ❏ I used text features or other text evidence to support my prediction. ❏ I listened and piggybacked on others' comments. ❏ I looked back in the text to support my thinking with evidence.	**Self-assessment:** ❏ I shared something that I find confusing during the reading. ❏ I led our group to deeper understanding by rereading or explaining a piece of the text. ❏ I listened and piggybacked on others' comments. ❏ I looked back in the text to support my thinking with evidence.

Figure 5.10: *Reciprocal teaching role bookmarks.*

Visit go.SolutionTree.com/instruction for a free reproducible version of this figure.

Alternatively, to find readings that are adjusted for high, medium, or low Lexile levels, use the informational text in one of the following websites.

• Newsela (https://newsela.com) delivers daily news articles at five reading levels from grade 3–12. Articles are accompanied by Common Core–aligned quizzes to provide quick and powerful feedback.

• Smithsonian's TweenTribune (www .tweentribune.com) has articles about science, history, and current events for grades 5–8. You also can create an account and use the content in the classroom.

• News in Levels (www.newsinlevels.com) is good for English learners and will help you practice important words in English.

Thirty-Second Expert

Thirty-second expert is a partners processing strategy. Students benefit from the opportunity to get up out of their desks and the speaking and listening practice is good for them too. There is no visual example for this strategy.

Directions

After delivering a chunk of information, have students stand up, find a partner, and decide who will be partner A and who will be partner B. The first to talk is student A and the second to talk is student B. Partner A has thirty seconds to begin sharing everything he or she knows about the chunk of information just learned by saying, "I am an expert on _____ because I know _____." Partner B then has thirty seconds to repeat what he or she hears his or her partner say. Partner B starts with, "According to you, _____." At this point, both partners may access any notes they made during the delivery of information. Partner B has thirty seconds to add to the learning by saying, "In addition to your learning, I know _____." After which, partner A repeats back what he or she hears by saying, "According to you, _____." Students return to their seats for the next chunk.

Suggestions for Differentiation

The following suggestions can help you differentiate this strategy.

- **Bumping it up:** Have students share their learning and provide a real-world example or analogy.

- **Breaking it down:** Provide students with partial notes for each chunk of learning or provide specific guidelines for annotation and note-taking.

- **Specializing for students with low self-esteem, motivation, or engagement:** Have these students be your partner B. This allows you to provide up-front, quality information for them to repeat. Allow them to use your notes as a reference tool. As they gain confidence, pair each with a strong and supportive partner, until they are ready to pair with any student.

Suggestions to Incorporate Technology

The following websites will help you work with the thirty-second expert strategy.

- Popplet (http://popplet.com) allows mini mind map design for students who prefer visual learning.

- Dragon Dictation (https://nuance.com/dragon) provides automatic speech-to-text capabilities.

Chalk Talk, Wisdom Walk

Chalk talk, wisdom walk is a processing strategy for individuals, partners, small groups, or whole group. Students benefit from collaborating and consolidating information, as well as the opportunity to move around the room, glean learning, and provide feedback to each other.

Directions

After delivering a chunk of information, have students work in small groups to write a question or problem on a piece of chart paper and post it on the wall. Groups rotate clockwise to the closest chart paper, answer the

question or solve the problem, and add another question or problem. Continue rotations until all groups write on all the papers. When students return to their own paper, they check their classmates' responses for accuracy.

Suggestions for Differentiation

The following suggestions can help you differentiate this strategy.

- **Bumping it up:** Have more complex questions or problems ready on the chart paper.

- **Breaking it down:** Have less complex questions whose answers are within the text or problems with fewer steps.

- **Specializing for students far below grade level:** Provide exemplars for reference or provide a create-a-cloze response, where some of the answer is present, allowing students to complete the answer by filling in the blanks. This provides a scaffold for the students. Provide fewer and fewer answers as they develop more content knowledge.

Suggestions to Incorporate Technology

The following websites will help you work with the chalk talk, wisdom walk strategy.

- ABCYya! (www.abcya.com) has many activities for students, including word clouds where they can develop a list of words associated with a theme or topic.

- TagCrowd (https://tagcrowd.com) lets you create your own word cloud from any text to visualize word frequency.

Conversation Starters

Conversation starters is a processing strategy for partners, small groups, or whole group. If you have students who are nonreaders, choose the questions, ask them orally, and have the students partner up to discuss.

Directions

Choose questions from the conversation starters for nonfiction (figure 5.11) or fiction (figure 5.12, page 102) that you would like students to answer after reading a chunk of text. You determine how many and which questions for your students, although we recommend four for students in grades K–2 and six for grades 3 and up. Write the questions on the board or on cards and distribute to students. After reading, have students take turns asking and answering the questions. Students should support each answer with reasoning and textual support, if available.

For text questions organized by before, during, and after reading, see figure 4.3 (page 57).

Suggestions for Differentiation

The following suggestions can help you differentiate this strategy.

- **Bumping it up:** Ask questions from the challenging list.

- **Breaking it down:** Ask questions only from the simple list.

- **Specializing for kinesthetic learners:** Put questions on cubes, spinners, cards, or fortune tellers (like the one shown in figure 5.13 on page 103).

Simple:
- What new fact did you learn?
- What is the title, and who is the author?
- What new vocabulary words did you run into?
- Can you retell the facts in order?
- What questions did you have about this topic before reading? Were any questions answered?

continued on next page ⇒

Figure 5.11: Conversation starters for nonfiction.

More challenging:

- What did this book make you think about? How can you relate this book to your life?
- How would you explain _____?
- How would you compare or contrast _____?
- What facts or ideas show _____?
- What would the result be if _____?
- What other way could you _____?
- How would you use _____?
- What are the parts or features of _____?
- What evidence can you find _____?
- What is the relationship between _____?
- Suppose you could _____. What would you do?
- What would happen if _____?
- What is your opinion of _____?
- Would it be better if _____?
- How would you prioritize the facts _____?

*Visit **go.SolutionTree.com/instruction** for a free reproducible version of this figure.*

Simple:

- Who are the characters in the story?
- Who is the main character?
- What is the title of the story?
- Who is the author, and who is the illustrator of the story?
- What is the setting of the story? Where and in what time period does it occur?
- How does the story begin? What happened next?
- How did the story end?
- Which strategies do you use while reading today? Which ones could you use more often next time?

More challenging:

- Is there a problem in the story? If so, how was it solved?
- What is the sequence of the main events?
- What does this book make you think about in your own life?
- How does this book compare to another book you have read?
- How does this book compare to world events?
- How does the main character usually feel in this book? Have you ever felt that way? Explain.
- What do you think the author is trying to say? Do you agree with the author? Why or why not?
- Is this an author whose other book you would like to read? Why or why not?
- Which words are hard to read? How can you remember them better for the next encounter?
- How did the book touch your heart?

Figure 5.12: *Conversation starters for fiction.*

*Visit **go.SolutionTree.com/instruction** for a free reproducible version of this figure.*

Figure 5.13: Fortune teller, also known as finger square *or* cootie catcher.

Suggestions to Incorporate Technology

The following apps will support the conversation starter strategy.

- Flipgrid (https://flipgrid.com) is a social media platform that allows students to respond to discussions in writing or in video form.

- VoiceThread (https://voicethread.com) lets you and your students communicate about content via audio and video.

Summary

Just as a dancer needs lots of practice to master a routine, students need lots of practice processing the content to master the standards. While no single step in the instructional cha-chas is more important than another, step two, chewing, requires more time. This is when learning happens. Providing students the opportunity to engage with content in a variety of ways will deepen their learning and increase retention.

The Main Idea and Detail Tabletop Graphic Organizer

Main idea
(topic sentence)

_____

_____

_____

_____

Detail (support sentence)

Detail (support sentence)

Detail (support sentence)

Detail (support sentence)

Criteria for success checklist:

❑ My details are accurate and from the text.

❑ These details support the main idea.

❑ I choose my main idea carefully, and it is the big picture.

❑ I explain how they support one another in complete sentences, and they make sense.

Explain how the details support the main idea:

_____

_____

_____

_____

_____

_____

_____

_____

_____

Source: Adapted from Jensen, E., & Nickelsen, L. (2014). Bringing the Common Core to life in K–8 classrooms: Thirty strategies to build literacy skills. *Bloomington, IN: Solution Tree Press.*

Question Stars for Bloom's Taxonomy
Level One—Knowledge

Who or what is _____?

Can you list three _____?

Can you recall _____?

How would you explain _____?

Where or when did _____?

Question Stars for Bloom's Taxonomy
Level Two—Comprehension

What fact or ideas show _____?

How would you compare or contrast _____ and _____?

Which statements support _____?

How would you summarize _____?

What is the main idea of _____?

Question Stars for Bloom's Taxonomy
Level Three—Application

What will result if _____?

How will you solve _____?

What elements will you change to _____?

What examples can you find to _____?

How will you organize _____ to show _____?

Question Stars for Bloom's Taxonomy
Level Four—Analysis

How is _____ related to _____?

What is the function of _____?

What conclusions can you draw about _____?

What evidence supports _____?

What is the theme?

Question Stars for Bloom's Taxonomy
Level Five—Evaluation

How will you prove or disprove _____?

How will you prioritize _____?

Why is it better that _____?

Do you agree with the actions or outcome?

What will you cite to defend the actions of _____?

Question Stars for Bloom's Taxonomy
Level Six—Synthesis

What will happen if _____?

How can you change _____?

Can you propose an alternative for _____?

Why do you think _____?

What could be done to minimize or maximize _____?

Think Notes

Name: _____ Date: _____

Directions: In the left column, students cite something from a resource, including the page number. In the right column, they will write their responses.

	Student-Thinking Ideas Student Response to Left Column
Examples: Key ideas, facts, vocabulary words, quote, pros, main idea, argument, teacher questions, what's important	**Examples:** Opinions, memory cues, inferencing or meaning-making responses, agree or disagree, supporting details or evidence, student questions or answers, *I wonder* statements, and connections

Framing-an-Argument Organizer

Claim:

Evidence:

Evidence:

Evidence:

Reasoning:

Reasoning:

Reasoning:

Counterclaims:

Rebuttals:

Conclusion:

Talking Chips Explanation

Directions: Cut out the talking chips on the other sheet of paper. Choose one chip and read what matches your chip on this page. After reading, everyone in your group should roll a die. The person with the highest number starts round one. Place your talking chip back into the center of the desk when you're done talking.

	Predict: Predict what the selection will be about prior to reading or predict how someone else in your group will respond to the selection after the reading.
	Summarize: Sum up part or all of the selection or summarize someone else's thinking about the selection.
	Clarify: State something that was clarified for you after the reading or clarify something for someone else in your group.
	Connect: Make a text-to-self, text-to-text, or text-to-world connection.
	Feeling: Share your feelings about the selection or other people's viewpoints about the reading.
	Visualize: Share something that the selection was able to help you to visualize.
	Vocabulary: Share some vocabulary that draws your attention to the selection or that is new or unusual to you.
	Question: Share a question that you have after reading the selection or ask a question of one of your group members about the selection.
	Piggyback: Piggyback onto someone else's thinking by sharing your own.

Talking Chips Pieces

Directions: Cut out each talking chip.

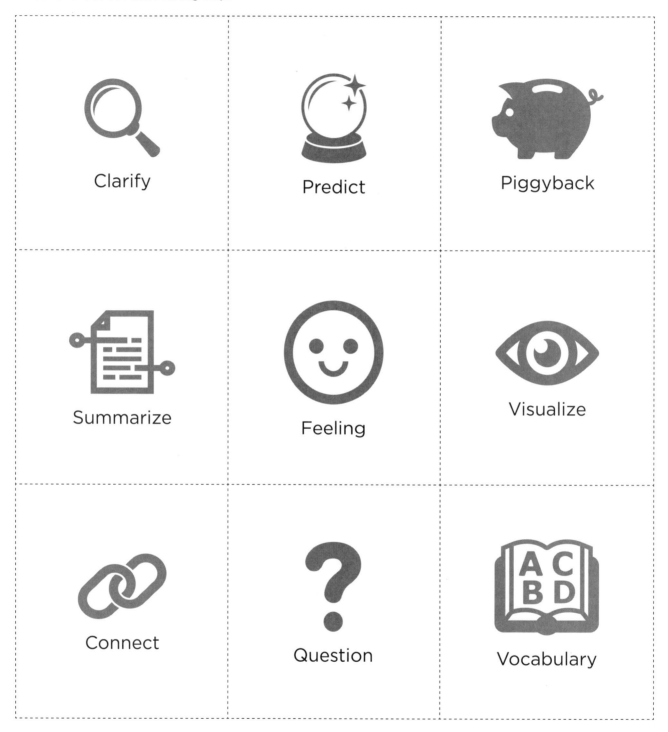

Clarify

Predict

Piggyback

Summarize

Feeling

Visualize

Connect

Question

Vocabulary

Swap-a-Question Template

Question author's name: **Question:** **Answer:** **Answer author's name:**	**Question author's name:** **Question:** **Answer:** **Answer author's name:**
Question author's name: **Question:** **Answer:** **Answer author's name:**	**Question author's name:** **Question:** **Answer:** **Answer author's name:**

Take Step Three: Check (Evaluate)

Imagine a dance studio. The dance instructor has taught the first eight counts and then gives the dancers time to practice. As they practice, the instructor observes the students and provides feedback (extend your arm, point your toe) to help them perfect that part of the dance. Just like the dance instructor, you plan and teach your chunks using a gradual release of responsibility (in step one) before allowing students to chew the content at different times during the lesson and in different ways (step two). While the students are chewing the content, you simultaneously check for understanding. You do this in a variety of ways depending on what you want students to learn or what data you want to gather. For example, if you want to determine whether they comprehend certain vocabulary, you could ask them to write, on a whiteboard, an example of that word in a sentence or to give their own definition. You can quickly check each student's work as they hold up their whiteboards.

To coordinate chunk, chew, and check so that it moves in motion with the gradual release of responsibility, remember this: after you model and explicitly teach a chunk of information (*I do*), guide your students through practicing what you just taught (*we do*). While guiding them, you are giving them opportunities to respond and show what they know so you can check for understanding. While you check your students' work or discussions, you examine how the learning is going.

Consider the following questions to guide your understanding of this step.

- Why is checking for understanding worthwhile?
- How do you differentiate the product with checkpoints and feedback?
- What evidence are you checking?
- How can you respond to the many checkpoints?
- How can you give more powerful verbal feedback?
- What strategies can you use during checking?

Why Is Checking for Understanding Worthwhile?

Logically, someone could say that if we don't check, we won't know how the learning is going, but research also supports this process. First, Paul Black and Dylan Wiliam's (1998) research, detailed in "Inside the Black Box," shows that checking for understanding is one of the vital steps in the formative assessment process to double the speed of learning.

Other research reveals the results in a physics classroom with students who had formative checkpoints versus the students who did not receive the pause and feedback (Vosniadou, Ioannides, Dimitrakopoulou, & Papademetriou, 2001). Both groups received a preassessment to determine content knowledge. In the test group, the researchers checked for understanding before moving onto the next chunk. They presented a scenario related to the content just taught and asked students a question requiring them to use the newly learned information to predict the outcome and explain their reasoning. The control group had the exact same lesson with no checkpoint or scenario—no chew time. The test group had a significantly greater increase on the post-test.

We learn from neuroscientists that memory increases when students participate in free recall of what they learned, or to do a so-called brain dump, to show what they know (McDermott et al., 2014). These researchers say this quick retrieval practice doesn't have to take long—five minutes or less—and it solidifies the memories of the concepts and allows the teacher to determine if students' memories are starting to process. This free recall should have a specific prompt and deliberate feedback from other students or from you. The research also notes that quick retrieval not only improves the chances of memory being formed but also enhances subsequent learning (Arnold & McDermott, 2013).

Barak Rosenshine (2012), professor of educational psychology in the College of Education at the University of Illinois, summarizes more information. He shares that the most effective teachers stop to check for student understanding by doing the following.

- Asking questions
- Asking for summaries
- Asking if students agree or disagree with other students' answers
- Asking for think-alouds through a multistep word problem
- Requiring verbal essay planning, position defense, or main idea identification

Overall, teachers should deliberately pause during instruction and ask students to retrieve what they have learned. Rosenshine's (2012) research shows that pausing instruction to have students answer questions results in their elaborating on the new learning in a way that creates connections to other learning; alerts the teacher to misconceptions or material that needs reteaching; and gives the brain time to connect the new information to existing information, so meaning making can occur.

How Do You Differentiate the Product With Checkpoints and Feedback?

A lesson's main formative assessment, a *product*, is what the students are working on that will show you what they know about the learning target. A product can be many things, including writing, a poster, an electronic tool (such as a blog, book trailer, or mind map created on a website), a Socratic seminar discussion, a lab summary, or the like. This bigger formative assessment brings many chew points together.

When you check for understanding, you get to examine that product in front of the student. Better yet, ask the student to evaluate the product using the criteria for success; it's student self-assessment. That way, you and the student can move the work and thinking closer to the learning target. Remember to always give feedback while the student is working on this main formative assessment, so you can correct misconceptions. This chapter will give you several ways to check for understanding and give feedback to move the student forward faster.

Both of us have experienced the post-observation conference in which we were asked how we thought our lessons went. We both replied enthusiastically, "Very well! All the students were so excited to learn and were engaged the whole time." Then, we were asked, "How many of your students were successful with the learning target?" To which we both responded positively, "Well, all of them." And then we were asked how we knew all the students were successful, and we were silent. We had not collected any evidence during that lesson. We had designed one fun activity after another that may or may not have led them to the learning target. While we asked students questions, we didn't document any results, and we didn't have any hard evidence about the lesson's effectiveness. Gulp. We never wanted to be in that situation again.

This is where our mantra, the *four Es*, comes into play: *examine evidence every day from every* student. In essence, that mantra summarizes the instructional cha-chas cycle. When we teach a chunk and our students chew, we use formative assessments to check (examine) what they say and do (the evidence) to determine whether they are getting closer to mastering the learning target.

We use both the main formative and smaller formative assessments to perform such checks. They are all checkpoints. Every student chew is a checkpoint, though some are formal (every whiteboard work you assess as you walk around the room, for example) and some are informal (turn-and-talk, for example).

What Evidence Are You Checking?

We are checking the student chewing whether it be their writing, their discussions, their thinking, their reading comprehension, or their product. We check their work and analyze how the learning is going. To *analyze* means to break something into parts, and to examine, study, or explore. Since it's a verb, there needs to be action involved. We analyze after we check for understanding.

With summative assessments, we usually check the work and place a grade on the work, but with formative assessments, we are not grading the chewing but rather analyzing how the learning is going. Therefore, the checkpoints must inform our instruction from chunk to chunk during the lesson and help us make decisions after the lesson as to what to do the next day. Every check will include some type of feedback to students, changing instruction based on data collected, or both. We will focus primarily on checking for understanding and providing feedback in this chapter and address the many ways to change instruction in the next chapter.

Table 6.1 gives basic information about checking for understanding.

Table 6.2 (page 120) distinguishes between short-and-sweet checkpoints and long-and-deep checkpoints. This book has directions for text chunking (page 56), exit tickets (page 132), stop-think-write (page 95), and reciprocal teaching (page 97).

Table 6.1: Checking for Understanding

Who does the checking?	Teacher, students, or peers, depending on the current need

What are you checking?	• Student work
	• The product, or show (main formative or small formative assessments)
	  • How the students are using the criteria for success for their checking (even just one criterion from the checklist at a particular checkpoint)
	  • Students' progress toward the learning target
	• Student body language, which might show frustration or ease
	• Short-and-sweet formative assessments and long and deep checkpoints

Why are you checking?	• To determine where students are with the daily learning target at crucial moments before, during, and after learning chunks • To determine any misconceptions or errors in thinking that are occurring at that moment so that students aren't practicing something incorrectly • To help us determine what do next in that day's lesson or the following day • To determine the effectiveness of our instruction • To model how to study so that students can self-monitor their learning and ask clarifying statements or questions for understanding
How often are you checking?	• Before, during, and after the learning (including when you see confused faces, nobody getting started, hands going up for questions) • After each chunk and chew
How are you checking?	• Informally, by bouncing from one student to another to glance at work or to hear the gist of what is being said • Formally, by looking at every student's work or hearing every student's comment to determine where each student is with the learning target; you need many informal checkpoints during the lesson and at least one formal checkpoint during the lesson or after the lesson

Visit go.SolutionTree.com/instruction for a free reproducible version of this table.

Table 6.2: *Checkpoint Types*

Short-and-Sweet Checkpoints	Long-and-Deep Checkpoints
• Exit tickets • Quick written responses via markers and whiteboards or paper in slip covers • Turn-and-talks • Questions (prepared ahead of time by the teacher or designed by student) and answers	• Stop-think-write • Essay writing • Multistep word problems • Before, during, and after reading responses • Projects and products • Reciprocal teaching • Socratic seminars

*Visit **go.SolutionTree.com/instruction** for a free reproducible version of this table.*

It's important to document at least one of your checkpoints in a lesson. You can circle students' names on the cruisin' clipboard forms to remember to check on indicated students after providing feedback. On the form, document your observations, including their level of mastery toward the learning target, what they've mastered, their preferred learning modality, and any notes for teaching the lesson. Visit **go.SolutionTree.com/instruction** for those forms. Other teachers like to use Google Forms on their tablets to document the data.

How Can You Respond to the Many Checkpoints?

Checking for understanding goes hand in hand with feedback. We always respond with actionable feedback to move students forward with some form of changing instruction: change your instruction and students move forward because of it, or we provide feedback that helps students change their work or approach based on the checkpoint data.

First and foremost, there must be a positive relationship between the person receiving the feedback for it to be powerful and well received. Wiliam (2016) adds:

> In the end, it all comes down to the relationship between the teacher and the student. To give effective feedback, the teacher needs *to know the student*—to understand what feedback the student needs *right now*. And to receive feedback in

a meaningful way, the student needs to trust the teacher—to believe the teacher knows what he or she is talking about and has the student's best interests at heart. Without this trust, the student is unlikely to invest the time and effort needed to absorb and use the feedback. (p. 15, emphasis added)

Chapter 3 (page 21) explains the importance of and methods for getting to know your students. One of the *least* effective types of feedback is a grade accompanied by comments (Lipnevich & Smith, 2008). When students receive this type of feedback, they tend to only look at the grade (which tends to be the final feedback) and think, "Why read the comments?" This research shows that when students receive a grade, they might believe the learning is over and the grade is as it is. Changing our approach will help students look at this moment (and all others before) as a learning opportunity. For more about redoing work and retaking tests and quizzes, we highly recommend Wormeli's (2018) updated book, *Fair Isn't Always Equal*.

The most powerful type of feedback is verbal, timely, and individualized for that student—an effective form of differentiation. See table 6.3 for guidelines.

How Can You Give More Powerful Verbal Feedback?

In their famous research, Black and Wiliam (1998) designed three questions that must be part of the feedback cycle. These questions are the foundation of the instructional cha-chas. We use this three-step process to teach and to give feedback.

1. Where am I going?
2. Where am I now?
3. How do I get closer to the goal? How do I close the gap?

While using these questions to design lessons, we also use these three questions to help students close the gaps between what they know and their learning target. Initially the teacher guides feedback, but the goal is for the student to take over the feedback process. It takes students time to own this self-feedback process. When you approach a student to give verbal feedback, keep these three steps in mind.

Table 6.3: *Feedback Guidelines*

What are the feedback types?	• **Verbal**—Interactive back-and-forth talk with student • **Written**—Writing comments around student work, writing, or projects • **Visual**—Showing the student slowly how to do the skill • **Written and grade**—Teacher writes comments and gives a grade • **Grade**—Feedback on summative assessments, not formative assessments
What is the focus of the feedback?	• **The learning target**—Their formative assessments and the criteria for success for the main formative assessment • **The next chunk**—Ensure they have mastered the first chunk and then give feedback to move them toward the next chunk
When do you deliver feedback?	• **When students are chewing**—Practicing, doing, writing, creating, analyzing—any type of thinking • **As soon as needed**—Seconds, minutes, or next day, balancing between providing feedback right away or allowing students to struggle a little bit before intervening • **After a test or quiz**—Summative assessment because learning is never over
How long must the feedback be?	• **Just a few seconds**—Usually • **More explanation or modeling**—Occasionally • **A scheduled three-minute conference time**—With individual students or a small group

Visit **go.SolutionTree.com/instruction** *for a free reproducible version of this table.*

Where Am I Going?

When you are about to start the three-step feedback process, study the student work before talking—side by side at a table, walking around, and bending down to see the work, or other methods with which you are familiar and already use. During step one, determine if the student is going down route one, two, or three before determining what to say.

- Route one students are on the right track, but have a minor misconception to fix.

- Route two students are doing everything correctly.

- Route three students are not doing anything correctly or they are not getting started.

You will see how to handle each case in the following sections.

When you are giving individual feedback, it's imperative to share the learning target or criteria for success that student is working on. That answers the question, Where am I going? Remind the student of the goal at hand. You could ask the student what the goal is, what criterion he or she is working on, or what the formative assessment is. Keep the feedback focused on the learning goals at hand.

Where Am I Now?

Involve your student in the process so both of you are analyzing the work. You could start the process by asking how the student believes his or her work is going, which answers the question, Where am I now? At the same time, examine and analyze the work so that, in addition to getting the student's opinion, you determine how it's going, too. Your second-step approach depends on what you see during this checkpoint.

- The student is taking route one. The student understands some things, and a few things could be going better. State the positives that you see the student is doing that are ensuring success toward the learning target. We highlight the positives by sharing which strategies, efforts, and attitudes are helping the student master the learning target. Share what criterion he or she is meeting, or get the student to name the positives.

- The student is taking route two. He or she has met all criteria and done everything correctly. State specifically what he or she is doing well and what is right. You also can point out the strategies, efforts, and attitudes that the student used to be successful.

- The student is taking route three. This student is not doing anything correctly and will need reteaching. The quick, three-step verbal feedback will not be enough to move him or her closer to the learning target. Instead, you will use the close the gap–reteaching template shown in figure 7.4 (page 169).

How Do I Get Closer to the Goal? How Do I Close the Gap?

This is the last step toward closing the gap with the route one students. You have several choices when helping students ask themselves, "How do I get closer to the goal? How do I close the gap?" Make sure to allow wait time when asking questions.

- Ask the student questions so he or she can determine how to fix the learning misconception or mistake. An example of such a question and follow-up is, "Why did you solve this problem this way? Explain your thinking to me. I wonder, if you thought about it this way, would that help you with this step? What do you think you need to do to continue solving this type of problem?"

- Remind the student of a resource he or she can use. These might include anchor charts, interactive notebooks, books, the internet, exemplars, nonexemplars, and the criteria for success.

- Prompt the student. See the feedback cue cards in figure 6.3 (page 129) for a list of prompts that you could use.

After attempting to help the student close the gap, determine if he or she needs to see you model. You can reteach the missing piece at that moment or pull a small group of students who are making similar mistakes. Following up to ensure they used their own feedback is critical for growth.

Examples of the three-step verbal feedback format follow.

- "What you wrote is a hypothesis because it is a proposed explanation. Something is missing. Can you find it? Looking at the criteria for success on the board, how could you make your statement better? I'll be back to check to see if you found it."

- "Good stories have a beginning, middle, and end. I see that your story has a beginning and middle, just like good stories. What would it take to write a powerful ending? Here's a hint: the anchor chart from yesterday has five ways to end a story. I'll be back to see which one you chose."

Help students understand and own this process by modeling and displaying it, and asking them to respond to these three questions personally with their work and with their peers. Provide questions or stems to help them reflect on their learning. See "The 40 Reflection Questions" (21st Century Learning Academy, 2011; htpps://edut.to/2MCONG8) for ideas.

Lesson Plan With Added Checkpoints

The lesson plan with added checkpoints helps you deliberately plan for the checkpoints while the students are chewing. There is a greater chance you will check student work if you plan for it first. Here, we'll provide directions for implementation, an example, and suggestions for differentiating instruction and incorporating technology.

Directions

Now that you have the chunks and chews in place, it's time to determine where and what your checkpoints will be. Place a check mark on the third column indicating how you will check the chew that is in the middle column. There isn't a place on this template to write in the feedback that you will give to your students after the checkpoint. That is because it should be immediate and based on what you heard or saw. Visualize the errors students can potentially make to prepare better feedback statements or tools. There will be more choices for how to change your tools in chapter 7 (page 159).

Example

This is the next part of the lesson plan, the preceding part of which is in figure 5.1 (page 84). See figure 6.1 for a sample lesson plan with checkpoints shaded gray. A new option, final stretch check, is the last check in a day, often given right before the main assessment; sometimes it is the main assessment.

Daily Lesson Plan

Subject or unit: Reading: Main Idea—Details **Grade:** 5

Standard: Determine two or more main ideas of a text and explain how they are supported by key details; summarize the text (RI.5.2).

Learning target (do and know): I can describe or graphically represent the relationship between main idea and details.

Main formative assessment (show): Students complete "The Main Idea and Detail Tabletop Graphic Organizer" (page 104) to show how the details (table legs) support the main idea (tabletop) based on a given paragraph.

Criteria for success (check type):	**Criteria for success (explain details):** Students self-assess their work and complete a checklist with the following criteria for success.
❏ Rubric	
☑ Self-assessment	❏ I can write accurate details on the legs.
☑ Checklist	❏ I can write the accurate main idea on the tabletop.
❏ Peer assessment	
❏ Exemplars	❏ I can write an explanation, in complete sentences, of how the details and main idea are connected.
❏ Nonexemplars	
❏ Verbal	
❏ Other: _____	

The Chunk Explained: What Teacher Will Do	**The Chew Explained: What Students Will Do** *(Place the main formative assessment from the preceding section in the appropriate chunk.)*	**Check for Understanding** *(Check those that apply.)*
Beginning chunks (I do): Review the definition of *main idea*. Move your arms as large as possible, creating an invisible square in the air, or frame, to represent the big picture. Define details and make little circles with your hands, going into the invisible square you just motioned. Explain that the little details create the big picture; they help you visualize what the picture looks like.	Students show the body movement that represents the definition of the main idea (arms folded on top of each other to show a strong tabletop). Students practice showing the details (table legs). Students create the tabletop and then take one arm to represent the table legs. ❏ Individual ❏ Partners ☑ Small-group total: _____	❏ Exit ticket or final stretch check ❏ Electronic tools ❏ Whiteboards for quick checks ❏ Turn-and-talk ❏ Documented teacher observation ❏ Writing ❏ Self-assessment or peer assessment ❏ Main formative assesment evidence ☑ Other: _Quick view_

Figure 6.1: *Sample lesson plan with checkpoints.*

continued on next page ⇒

The Chunk Explained: What Teacher Will Do	The Chew Explained: What Students Will Do (Place the main formative assessment from the preceding section in the appropriate chunk.)	Check for Understanding (Check those that apply.)
Middle chunks (we do, two do): Say, "There are many visuals that we can create to help us understand the relationship between main idea and details. I the visual of an imaginary frame to represent main idea. The circles inside it represent details. Today, we are going to show another visual: a tabletop with legs supporting it." Show an anchor chart (a large visual, usually on chart paper) of a tabletop that shows the top of the table labeled Main Idea and the table legs labeled Details. Then show a paragraph from any of your texts and how they write its main idea on the tabletop and its details on the individual legs. Make sure all students can explain that details are the legs of the table that support the tabletop which represents the main idea. Share many examples: paragraph being separated out on the tabletop graphic organizer with main idea on top and details written on the legs.	Students create a kinesthetic table on the floor after receiving sentence strips with details and one main idea. Students determine who is the main idea. The rest of the students are details that support it. Their bodies create a table on the floor with the sentence strip on their bellies. Teacher checks and gives feedback before they rotate sentence strips. ❑ Individual ❑ Partners ☑ Small-group total: _5 or 6_	❑ Exit ticket or final stretch check ❑ Electronic tools ❑ Whiteboards for quick checks ❑ Turn-and-talk ❑ Documented teacher observation ❑ Writing ❑ Self-assessment or peer assessment ❑ Main formative assessment evidence ☑ Other: _Quick view_
Ending chunk (you do): Summarize the day's learning by pointing out what each group did during the lesson and giving positive feedback to each group. (Group work is explained in chapter 5 on page 83.) Explain the exit ticket by modeling how to bring the pieces together with a different paragraph (not the one the you use to assess students).	Students read a paragraph that is under the document camera. You can read it to them. Main formative assessment: Students complete the drawing by writing the main idea on the top of the table and writing three or four details on the legs. Then, they describe the relationship between the main idea and details on the lines at the bottom of the paper. Each student turns one in. ☑ Individual ❑ Partners ❑ Small-group total: _____	(Analyze the main formative assessment by determining if the criteria for success are in place.) Hand out exit tickets.

Source for standard: NGA & CCSSO, 2010a.

Suggestions for Differentiation

The following suggestions can help you differentiate this strategy.

- **Bumping it up:** When you do the checkpoint, ask other questions to increase the complexity of their thinking. Think about Bloom's (1956) taxonomy and ask level three to level six questions to help them go deeper. (See chapter 5, page 87, for the Bloom's taxonomy strategy.) You could have them elaborate with prompts like the following.
  - Will you tell me more?
  - Why could that be?
  - What if?

- **Breaking it down:** Break down the thinking further by asking questions that help them see the steps in their thinking. You could have them consider thoughts such as, What do you need to do first? After that, step, then what? Would you do _____ or _____?

- **Specializing for students with working memory challenges:** Refer them to the anchor charts and other visuals in the room to prompt their thinking, including feedback cue cards in figure 6.3 (page 129). Give as many clues and prompts as possible, but don't do the thinking for them. Set them up for self-confidence with some retrieval opportunities.

Suggestions to Incorporate Technology

The following apps will help you create, share, and manage your lesson plans.

- Nearpod (https://nearpod.com) helps teachers engage students with interactive lessons.

- Educreations (www.educreations.com) is a community where anyone can teach what they know and learn what they don't. The software turns any iPad or web browser into a recordable, interactive whiteboard, making it easy to create engaging video lessons and share them online.

- Evernote (https://evernote.com) keeps your notes organized. Memos are synced so they're accessible anywhere and searchable.

- ShowMe (www.showme.com) is an open online learning community where anyone can learn and teach any topic. The iPad app lets you easily create and share video lessons.

What Strategies Can You Use During Checking?

To bring all of these pieces together, the strategies in this chapter will start with the continuation of the lesson-plan template, showing you how to incorporate the checkpoints. Since checking for understanding should happen daily, and often, you will need to use multiple pathways and a variety of formats. We explain in chapter 3 (page 21) the many ways to assess a student's prior knowledge before the learning occurs. Those checkpoints help you determine how to plan your lessons. In the following sections, we will describe specific during-the-learning and after-the-learning checkpoints. We have included strategies that the teacher, students (for self-assessment), and peers can use. Each strategy will help you and the students themselves determine how close they are to the learning target.

 All-Student Response Quick-Check Tools

All-student response quick-check tools is a checking strategy for individual students. The benefit is that learning becomes visible to you, so you can decide what level of mastery students have.

Directions

You administer these quick-check tools during the learning. Review table 6.4 (page 126) to decide which quick-check tool works best for your checkpoint. After choosing, modeling, and practicing it with students, ask them to use that tool to show what they know. That show will be based on a prompt you create ahead of time. All students respond to the teacher's question or prompt.

Table 6.4: *Quick-Check Tools*

Quick-Check Tool	Description	Example
Fist-to-five strategy	This is a student self-assessment. Students give you a fist in the air, then you give a question or statement. They rate their opinion or level of understanding by showing you a fist, one, two, three, four, or five fingers.*	The teacher says: • "Show me with your fingers how well you understand what I just taught you." • "If you keep your fist, that means *I don't get any of it yet.*" • "One finger means *I need help, but I did get started.*" • "Two fingers means *I need more examples.*" • "Three fingers means *I need more practice, but I'm getting it.*" • "Four fingers means *I understand most of it.*" • "And five fingers means *I understand it all and could teach it to someone else.*"
Whiteboard	Students write or draw their response to the teacher's question or statement.	The teacher says: "Show me how you would draw the number twenty-five using your base-ten blocks" or "Show me what type of punctuation mark goes at the end of the following sentence . . ."
Ball toss	Using a cheap, soft ball that fits in the palm of student-size hands, students hold the ball, taking turns verbally sharing their answer to the teacher's prompt or question. Whoever has the ball in his or her hand is the only one allowed to talk at that time.	The teacher says: "The student with the brightest colored shirt on goes first. Answer the following prompt and then toss the ball to someone else in your group to answer." Because this is an open-ended prompt, hopefully there will be a variety of answers. The teacher might prompt students with, "Share one new fact that you learned from the nonfiction book that you just read."
Touch cards	Design cards based on what you need. Each student receives a blank 3 x 5 card and writes the choices on the cards. Ideas follow. • A, B C, D (four boxes) • Four vocabulary or sight words • Fact versus opinion • Agree or disagree • Mathematics symbols	The teacher creates questions about a word's meaning and then four multiple-choice options, then creates cards with four blank boxes and laminates them. Right before a lesson on context clues, the teacher says "Using a dry-erase marker, write the letters A, B, C, and D—one in each box." Students determine what kind of clue was in the book based on the options on the class whiteboard. Students touch the letter on their card to indicate their answer.

* Many students struggle to determine their level of understanding. Make sure you have collected evidence during this checkpoint too.

Visit **go.SolutionTree.com/instruction** *for a free reproducible version of this table.*

Suggestions for Differentiation

The following suggestions can help you differentiate this strategy.

• **Bumping it up:** Homogeneously group these students and increase the prompt's or question's challenge. For example, ask them to compare and contrast the concept to another concept, connect the concept to a bigger theme or different discipline and support it, or elaborate with at least one detail to support their answer.

You can explicitly give them these concepts, themes, or disciplines, or students can choose them based on the curriculum.

• **Breaking it down:** Homogeneously group students to be near you in case you need to give them additional support. When checking for understanding, give prompts, cues, and feedback to their responses.

• **Specializing for students with working memory challenges:** Invite them to use their resources—notebooks, texts, anchor charts, and so on—to retrieve the content from their brain during this time. Give additional time, since it will take them a while to sort through the resources.

Suggestions to Incorporate Technology

The following apps will help you work with multiple-choice formative assessments.

- Kahoot! (https://kahoot.it) helps students retrieve information quickly. Design questions and then give possible answers in multiple-choice format. If your school is one-to-one with computers, all students can type in their answer and the classroom receives a score according to how many answers were correct (providing immediate feedback). You receive computer data revealing specific students' answers.

- Plickers (www.plickers.com) allows you to design questions in a multiple-choice format, then have students respond by holding up their Plicker card. Scan the cards using your phone or tablet and watch it calculate student results.

Seven-Step Feedback

Source: Adapted from Lucy Calkins.

Seven-step feedback is a checking strategy for individual students. Conferring with the teacher and receiving his or her feedback benefits students because then the students knows what is going well, what could improve, and how to improve it to move forward.

Directions

Administer this checkpoint during a reading or writing chunk. Create a weekly or biweekly system for giving feedback to all students. For example, during guided reading in small groups on Mondays, give a certain student one-to-one feedback. During writing workshops on Tuesdays, give five designated students feedback, five others on Wednesdays, and so on.

Follow the seven steps to give students more powerful feedback and move them forward faster.

1. **Determine:** Study the writing, listen to the reading, or ask questions to decide what feedback students need. It could be, for example, reading strategy, fluency, context clues, word choice in writing, or writing organization.

2. **Praise:** Note the positive. Find one or several awesome examples of great work to compliment them on—be specific and make sure it connects with your standards.

3. **Find one growth opportunity:** It should be developmentally appropriate for that student.

Make sure it's an important skill that can transfer to other work in the future and point it out. For example, if it's reading, make sure he or she knows that every time there is a question mark, his or her voice should change.

4. **Teach:** Instruct and model how it is accurately done.

5. **Try:** Ask the student to attempt the new skill or to correct the work.

6. **Ask:** Have the student state what he or she learns from this feedback time and ensure that he or she used your feedback to improve the reading or writing (or the learning in general). This can last from thirty seconds to two minutes, depending on the feedback type and the student's understanding and implementation of the feedback.

7. **Document:** Record the positive and growth opportunity with a date so that the next time you give individual feedback, you and the student can re-examine the previous growth opportunity. If it's mastered, present a new growth opportunity. If it isn't, present additional examples or strategies.

Example

See figure 6.2 (page 128) for an example of guided-reading documentation.

Student name: __Sue Steiner__

Date	Compliment	Teaching Point
9/8	Sue is pointing to words as she reads them; she's reading from left to right.	Sue is not making good guesses at the unknown words that she is trying to figure out. Does that word make sense based on the illustration? She can look at the picture for clues.
9/15	Sue studies illustrations to figure out unknown words and guesses what the word might be.	Sue needs to look at the beginning of that unknown word to see what the beginning sound is accurately. She needs to say the first sound and try to say the word—just try.

Figure 6.2: *Example of guided-reading documentation.*

Visit **go.SolutionTree.com/instruction** *for a free reproducible version of this figure.*

Suggestions for Differentiation

The following suggestions can help you differentiate this strategy.

- **Bumping it up:** Some students can handle two or three growth opportunities if the corrections are smaller. Every student is different. For example, one piece of feedback is more than enough for a perfectionist, but other students can handle several smaller pieces of feedback. For example, you might give the following three pieces of feedback for a writing selection: "There are some words where you need to drop the *e* before adding *ing.* Vary the way you start sentences. Could you add a few Tier 2 words that we have been studying to make some of the trite words more sophisticated?

- **Breaking it down:** Model the skill several times. Check for understanding often during the fifth step (when they are trying). If the seven steps are too much, just do this three-step process.

  a. *Restate* the learning target with the student.

  b. *Examine* where the student is with this learning target. Share what he or she did well.

  c. *Ask* a question to help him or her determine the next steps. If the student doesn't know, give hints and suggestions. The ultimate goal is for the student to do his or her own thinking about how to close the gap.

- **Specializing for students with working memory challenges:** Create visuals about the skill that you will give feedback about. For example, figure 5.2 (page 86) shows a main idea table with legs (details) that support it. This visual can help students remember the relationship of details to support the main idea. Model the skill more than once. Model it in other contexts if possible (with other texts, mathematics problems, and so on). Ask the student to try more than once in different contexts as well. Make sure the student can paraphrase and explain what he or she learns from that chunk.

Suggestions to Incorporate Technology

The following will help you record formative assessment data.

- Google Forms (www.google.com/forms/about) is a great way to store the data you glean from students. With these forms, other teachers who read and write with your students can look at the feedback you have given to the students and add to the documentation with their dates and names. The more data you have about students, the better you can meet their needs.

- Zoho Notebook (www.zoho.com/notebook) has virtual notebooks in which you can store data. In the notebooks, you can create notes in different categories: text, notes, checklists, audio, photos, sketches, and documents.

Feedback Cue Cards

Feedback cue cards is a checking strategy for individual, partners, small groups, or whole group. One of the benefits of this strategy is that you can use it for most any subject or product.

Directions

Administer this checkpoint during the learning. After checking for understanding during a lesson, be prepared to give feedback based on what you see or hear. The feedback cue cards in figure 6.3 will prepare you to move students forward faster and promote metacognition.

There is a time to tell students, step-by-step in different words, how to do the process again, different ways of modeling it, and different checkpoints. There is also a time, which is the case more often than not, to ask students questions or prompt them to get their thinking started so the ideas come from them. When first using the "Feedback Cue Cards" reproducible (page 147), make a copy and keep it nearby so you can see it while you are teaching. Some teachers punch a hole in the corner and loop it on their identification badge so they can glance quickly at it when in need.

When students answer or their work needs redirecting:

"The learning target is _____. I notice that you accomplished _____ with this learning target. What will it take to master this learning target? What else do you need to do, learn, or include?"

"Do you want to phone a friend?"

"Do you want to ask a question to clarify your thinking?"

"Class, would you like to ask this student a question?"

Rephrase the question for better student understanding. Ask the student to explain his or her reasoning. Keep asking questions to get to the root of the error in thinking.

Use symbols, images, words, or letters to help students recall the information. Examples include "Starts with _____" and "Sounds like _____."

Pose the same question to a different student if the student wants to pass, but check back and hold the original student accountable.

"So, I think I heard you say _____. Is that what you meant?"

When you want students to dig deeper:

"Can you give some examples?"

"Tell me more."

"Can you explain the steps you took to solve that problem?"

"What would you compare that with? How does that connect with _____?"

"What if _____ happens. How will that change _____?"

"What are the characteristics of _____?"

"What details can you add to _____?"

"How can you prove _____? What evidence will you need to give?"

"How might _____ view this?"

When you want students to justify their thinking:

"So, I think I heard you say _____. Is that what you meant?"

"What do you mean when you say _____?"

"I'm confused by _____. Can you help me understand?"

"Why do you think that? Have you thought about _____?"

When you want students to show evidence:

"Where did you find that information? What page? What article?"

"How do you know that is a credible resource?"

"What paragraph did you read that in?"

"What website has that information? What other websites could you use?"

"How do you know that?"

Figure 6.3: *Feedback cue cards.*

Suggestions for Differentiation

The following suggestions can help you differentiate this strategy.

- **Bumping it up:** Provide more challenging feedback questions for them to improve their work. Ask them to challenge one another with these statement or question stems. Increase wait time before giving feedback.

- **Breaking it down:** Provide more prompts and cues. Refer to examples, visuals, or text when giving feedback. Keep wait time minimal if you see them feeling defeated and giving up. This wait time depends on the student's age and persistence level.

- **Specializing for students who are introverted and those who are extroverted or for those who don't participate as often:** Give all students two or three discussion disks (bingo chips or other manipulatives) and explain that the chips represent how many times they can contribute to the conversation. If they have two manipulatives, they must contribute or participate two times. As they begin to speak, they place the manipulative in the middle of the discussion group. This ensures that all students participate.

Suggestions to Incorporate Technology

The following apps help you work with the feedback cue cards strategy.

- Swivl (www.swivl.com) records discussions to determine how students can improve their work. The Swivl attaches to an iPad and moves around to focus on the speaker. You can pass a microphone to the speaker as well; the Swivl will follow.

- Zoho Notebook (www.zoho.com/notebook) has virtual notebooks in which you can store data. In the notebooks, you can create notes in different categories: text, notes, checklists, audio, photos, sketches, and documents.

Multiple Intelligence Closure

Lesson closures are a natural spot for checking for understanding. Multiple intelligence closure is a checking strategy for partners or small groups. The benefit is that students summarize their learning in their dominant multiple intelligence, and that type of metacognition helps their general learning. It also helps you understand how they learn best and give feeedback that deepens understanding.

Directions

Administer this checkpoint after the learning. Print each of developmental psychologist Howard Gardner's (1993) multiple intelligences on separate pieces of paper and post them around the room. (See "Suggestions to Incorporate Technology" on page 131 for websites that will help you and your students learn about multiple intelligences.) At the end of a lesson about a new skill or content, ask students to stand in front of the paper representing their strongest intelligence. Remind them that they are more likely to remember the content when they chew it in a preferred, strength-based mode.

While they stand in their places in the room, give each group a copy of the multiple intelligence closure in figure 6.4, so they can choose which closure they will create. Give students about six minutes to create their closure. Finally, have each group share with the whole class and celebrate their new learning. This informal formative assessment is a fun, powerful way to let new information sink into the brain. This activity works best when there are three or four students per group. You may need to ask some students to move to their second- or third-strongest intelligence to ensure that no one is solo or to avoid groups that are too large. You might even need to help elementary students choose

Directions: Choose either option A or option B.

Intelligence	Option A	Option B
Verbal-Linguistic	Write three things you learned.	Write a summary of the lesson or reading.
Logical-Mathematical	Create an outline of today's learning.	Design a time line sequencing the events of today's learning and evaluate them by placing a plus sign with one, two, or three on it. The one means less important information, two means somewhat important information, and three means very important information.
Visual-Spatial	Illustrate or create a diagram about today's learning.	Create a mind map of today's learning.
Musical-Rhythmic	Create a rap song containing the most important facts from today's learning.	Write a poem explaining the key points from today's learning. Make sure there is a distinct rhyming pattern. For example, you might choose a rhyming couplets and A, B, A, B. (Provide examples of the type of pattern you want from your students.)
Bodily-Kinesthetic	Role-play the key event in today's lesson.	Create a cheer or rap with movements that go with words in today's lesson.
Interpersonal	With a partner, conduct an interview of today's learning.	With a partner, debate today's learning.
Intrapersonal	Create a personal goal to implement based on today's learning.	Write a diary entry discussing how you feel about today's lesson.
Naturalist	Explain how today's learning might impact the earth, animals, or human beings.	Make an analogy between today's learning and the world.

Source: Adapted from Gardner, 1993.

Figure 6.4: *Multiple intelligence closure.*

Visit **go.SolutionTree.com/instruction** for a free reproducible version of this figure.

another intelligence based on what you know about those students.

Suggestions for Differentiation

The following suggestions can help you differentiate this strategy.

- **Bumping it up:** Encourage students to use option B activities. Encourage students to choose a multiple intelligence that is a stretch for them rather than one that is their strength or preference.

- **Breaking it down:** Encourage students to use option A activities.

- **Specializing for students who are introverted:** Encourage these students to go to the intrapersonal intelligence group.

Suggestions to Incorporate Technology

The following websites will help students determine their intelligence type.

- Surfaquarium (http://surfaquarium.com/MI/inventory.htm) lets students assess their intelligence strengths.

- Multiple Intelligences Research Study (https://bit.ly/2tbz7Pg) offers multiple-intelligence tests at different grade levels, as well as teacher documentation forms and ideas and suggestions for activities.

Exit Tickets

Source: Jensen & Nickelsen, 2014.

Exit tickets are a checking strategy for individual students. The benefit is that you can examine evidence from every student and determine what to do the next day to close the gaps.

Directions

Administer this learning checkpoint in the final chunk. Decide on a prompt that helps you determine each student's learning target mastery level. (Since you know the lesson's last chunk is the second best remembered section, plan to always have some individual closure via a learning summary of that lesson and accountability at the end of the lesson.) Be sure that your prompt tells students what you need to see to determine their mastery. Display the prompt where students can see it, such as on a whiteboard, a PowerPoint slide, or under the document camera, a digital overhead that displays real-time images to a large audience.

You might also want to create a list of criteria for success for the exit ticket and post it on the whiteboard for more quality thinking. Pass out copies of "Exit Ticket Templates—Version One" reproducible (page 148).

Have students record their name and the daily learning target on the exit ticket, read the prompt, and write a response in the Demonstrate section. Afterward, students self-assess by checking the appropriate box (Got It,

Need More Practice, or Did Not Get It). Students who check Need More Practice or Did Not Get It explain why on the lines provided.

Once students turn in the exit tickets, you can sort them into the piles based on what boxes they checked. Examine the evidence from every student and determine what to do next based on the results of these data. You can help students improve their self-assessment by doing a think-aloud (page 58) while you assess your own work. Then, provide an anonymous student example as a practice assessment. Discuss the process as a whole class so students can determine if their assessment was in line with what others noticed. Then engage students in peer assessment so they evaluate how a student sitting right next to them did. By this time, they might do a better job assessing their own work. Constantly model your thinking aloud while assessing work.

Example

Figure 6.5, figure 6.6, figure 6.7, and figure 6.8 (page 134) are completed exit ticket examples. A new option, final stretch check, is the last check in a day, often given right before the main assessment; sometimes it is the main assessment. See "Exit Ticket Templates—Version Two" (page 149) also. Visit **go.SolutionTree .com/instruction** for more examples you can use.

Name: Raiza   Date: 10/13

Today, I learned about how to look for clues around unknown words with my class.

The tricky part is that some clues are several sentences before or after the unknown word, but it helps when I ask myself questions about what I do know about this word.

It's important that I know this because when I can figure out words' meanings, I don't have to take the time to look them up.

Figure 6.5: *Exit ticket example for elementary students.*

The following are some great phrases to guide their response.

- I don't understand how to _____.
- I don't understand the word _____.
- I don't understand how _____ relates to _____.
- I don't understand how _____ causes _____.
- My question is _____?
- I need you to show me _____.
- I need more practice with _____.

As a variation, try the stoplight, which you also administer after the learning. Create a stoplight and the following labels: *Yes, I Can* (placed by the green light), *I'm Getting It* (placed by the yellow light), and *I Need More Help* (placed by the red light). Design a prompt that measures learning target mastery and post it on the whiteboard or document camera for all to see. Students respond on a sticky note, self-assess on the bottom portion of it, and then place it on the part of the stoplight that corresponds to their self-assessment. Decide whether each students' evidence matches their self-assessment. When they don't match up—a student feels like he or she got it but hasn't—give him or her specific feedback to help them improve their self-assessment skills and the skills they learned in that lesson. See figure 6.7 and figure 6.8 (page 134) for a close-up and broader view of a stoplight exit ticket.

Sample mathematics prompts follow.

- Solve the following equation.
- Draw the representation of the manipulatives to show the number thirty-six.
- Explain to a third grader how to solve this problem using three vocabulary words from the lesson.
- Explain the relationship between a decimal, fraction, and percent.

Sample English language arts prompts follow.

- Write two complex sentences about the topic.
- Define what adjectives do and then write a sentence that has two adjectives. Underline the adjectives.
- Explain the major cause and effect in the reading today in complete sentences.

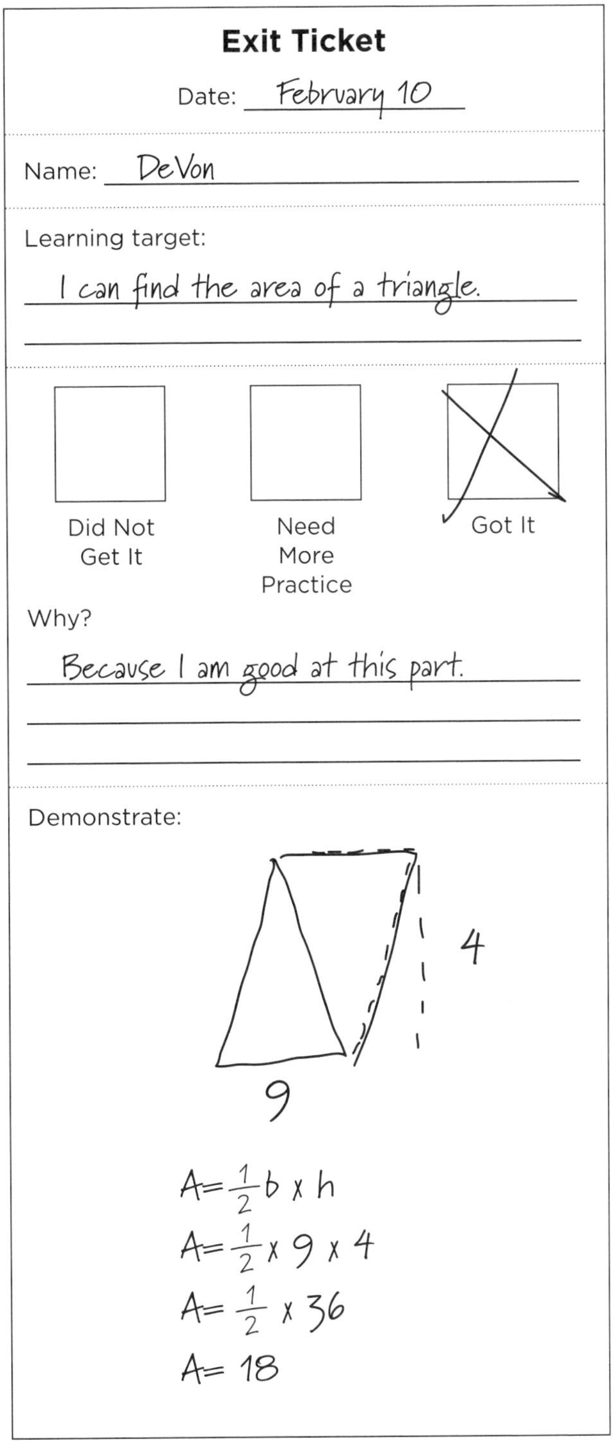

Exit Ticket

Date: _February 10_

Name: _DeVon_

Learning target:

I can find the area of a triangle.

☐ Did Not Get It   ☐ Need More Practice   ☒ Got It

Why?

Because I am good at this part.

Demonstrate:

$A = \frac{1}{2} b \times h$

$A = \frac{1}{2} \times 9 \times 4$

$A = \frac{1}{2} \times 36$

$A = 18$

Figure 6.6: *Exit ticket example for grades 5–8.*

Figure 6.7: *Example of stoplight exit ticket sticky note.*

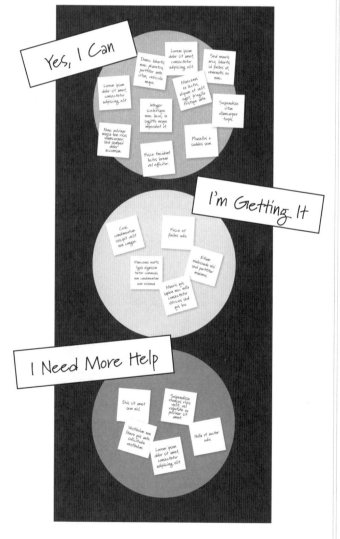

Figure 6.8: *Example of stoplight exit ticket from farther away, with sticky notes.*

- Stump someone by creating a sentence with a nonsense word that you surround with a context clue. We will exchange exit tickets tomorrow to see if anybody can figure out what your nonsense word is based on the clues.

- Explain the relationship between details and main idea.

Sample social studies and science prompts:

- List the three types of rocks and draw a picture of each.

- Explain how solids, liquids, and gasses differ from one another.

- Write two new key details that you learned from today's reading.

- Explain what happened in today's lab and what data surprised you.

Suggestions for Differentiation

The following suggestions can help you differentiate this strategy.

- **Bumping it up:** Give students a more complex prompt. For example, make the prompt open-ended, ask them to compare and contrast with another concept, or ask them to create a prompt and answer it. Add a second prompt incorporating upcoming skills that you haven't yet taught to use as preassessment data.

- **Breaking it down:** If, based on other checkpoints in the lesson, you know a student will not successfully complete the exit ticket, pull him or her into a small group. These students may be stuck in their thinking, unable to start because of a misconception, or truly not possess the skill. You will know what the reason is if you checked for understanding during the lesson. This is a great time to give extra support and more modeling versus setting them up to fail with the independent exit ticket. Reteach, model, and explain one more time. Follow up with the student the next day to see where he or she is with that learning target after receiving the extra support.

- **Specializing for students who process slowly:** Allow extra time or shorten the prompt or problem. You can ask students to give their answers to you verbally, which is faster than writing it. Give them extra time to complete the exit ticket, which may take some clever time manipulation.

Suggestions to Incorporate Technology

The following websites will help you work with exit tickets.

- Google Drive (www.google.com/drive) helps students turn in paperless exit tickets. Design your form and have it ready to complete individually at the end of the lesson.

- Lino (http://en.linoit.com) is a virtual corkboard of sticky notes that could help you see all student responses.

- Socrative (www.socrative.com) allow students to respond digitally both during and after the learning.

- Formative (https://goformative.com) allows teachers to track student performance or partner with their school or other teams to build, distribute, grade, and analyze assessment results.

 Dynamic Duo Feedback

Dynamic duo feedback is a checking strategy for individual students and partners. The benefit is students learn how to support a score by finding what the other student did well and how the student can improve the work. Both students grow from the process, especially if they use the feedback to move their work forward.

Directions

Administer this student self-assessment and peer-assessment checkpoint during or after the learning. Give students a rubric of expectations for a particular project, writing, lab, or other assignment. Be sure to explain and show exemplars for each criterion on the rubric so students know exactly what you expect.

Give students the dynamic duo feedback rubric. Have them determine which score they think they deserve and justify why by retrieving and producing evidence from their work. Students then fold the paper in half, so their peer cannot see how the student self-assessed. Next, the peer goes through the same process to assess his or her partner's work. Papers are returned to their original owner, who lists how he or she will change the work to improve it. Specific feedback plus immediacy equals improved learning.

Example

See figure 6.9 for an example of dynamic duo feedback.

Directions: Use the teacher-provided rubric to determine the score you believe you deserve on this work. List the evidence to support your score in the left column. Have a partner do the same for your work in the right column.

My work deserves the score of: 4/5 Name of author: Chandra	This work deserves the Score of: 3/5 Name of assessor: Jalen
Evidence to Support My Score (Use words from the rubric and share specific examples from your work.)	**Evidence to Support This Score** (Use words from the rubric and share specific examples from your partner's work.)

o I have strong word choice and did not use any taboo words.
 	
o I have the paper organized the way it should be.
 	
o I have evidence and reasons to support them.
 	
   *I took one point off since I didn't include figurative language.
	o The following taboo words were found: nice, fun.
	
	o You have a beginning, middle, and end.
	
	o You have three pieces of evidence, but you forgot a reason for number 2.
	
	   *I don't see the figurative language in this piece.

***Figure 6.9:** Example of dynamic duo feedback.*

continued on next page ⇒

Strengths of the work: *My evidence and reasoning*	Strengths of the work: *Strong evidence—just add the reasoning for middle idea*
Overall areas for growth: *Figurative language*	Overall areas for growth: *Figurative language, reasoning, and maybe use a more creative conclusion*
How I will improve my work after this analysis: *I will add better reasoning for my middle evidence. I will add two figurative language comparisons in this writing somewhere. I didn't see the taboo words. I will replace them with more specific words.*	

*Visit **go.SolutionTree.com/instruction** for a free reproducible version of this figure.*

Suggestions for Differentiation

The following suggestions can help you differentiate this strategy.

- **Bumping it up:** Purposefully pair two students who need and want to challenge each other with more rigorous feedback. Raise the rubric's complexity by changing some criteria. Allow the students to create a rubric or add one or two criteria, to increase their autonomy and creative thinking.

- **Breaking it down:** Help them with their self-assessment by reflecting on the exemplar that you showed at the beginning of the lesson. Provide more support so they understand the rubric. Lower the rubric's complexity by changing some of the criteria.

- **Specializing for students with working memory challenges:** Have them assess just one criterion on the rubric. Highlight the criterion they should evaluate.

Suggestions to Incorporate Technology

The following websites will help you design a rubric for your writing assignment.

- RubiStar (http://rubistar.4teachers.org) allows you to design a rubric for specific classroom purposes, edit an existing rubric, and look at example rubrics.

- EssayTagger (www.essaytagger.com/commoncore) is a great way to give students feedback on their writing. Simply flag the problematic passage or sentence within the digital version and hold students accountable for figuring out the error and submitting the corrected version. You can also build rubrics at this site.

- Teachnology General Rubric Generator (https://bit.ly/2llt9qp) gives K–12 teachers access to reproducibles in all subjects areas, rubrics, teaching tips, and other resources that help you save time.

- iRubric (www.rcampus.com/indexrubric .cfm) is a comprehensive rubric development, assessment, and sharing tool. You can collaborate with other teachers who share their rubrics.

 ## Praise-Question-Polish+

Praise-question-polish+ is a checking strategy for individuals, partners, or small groups of students. The benefit of this strategy is learning how to give others feedback, receiving the feedback to improve the work, and determining which part of the feedback they will use to improve their work.

Directions

Administer this peer-feedback checkpoint after the learning. Prior to releasing this strategy to students, model how to use the PQP+ process with a piece of exemplar writing and the rubric you will be using to assess the writing. Gradually release the responsibility for students by providing guided practice with an anonymous piece of student writing. Then, partner students so they can use the PQP+ process on their own work with a partner.

Purposefully partner the students and distribute your teacher-made rubric and the PQP+ writing feedback ideas form (figure 6.10, page 138). Have students exchange papers and complete a first read. We encourage students to mark minor errors such as spelling, punctuation, and capitalization during this first read. Students then reread the paper to create the praises, questions, and polishes. Each student writes one or two specific praise comments about the paper. The PQP+ form gives students ideas of what kind of feedback to give. The student then creates questions about the writing. They can range from Why did you include this in your writing? to Could you place this paragraph before this one? Finally, each student writes one or two ways to polish, or improve, the paper. Papers go back to the original author, who commits to revising the writing. All students record their plan for revision in the +Plan to Change section of the form.

Example

See figure 6.10 (page 138) for a completed example.

Suggestions for Differentiation

The following suggestions can help you differentiate this strategy.

- **Bumping it up:** Examine the requirements for writing from a higher grade level. Design another cheat sheet and use the rubric from the more advanced grade level. Make sure the assessor understands the new look-fors required with the advanced grade level. Purposefully pair students who need and want to challenge each other with more rigorous feedback.

- **Breaking it down:** Assist students with the PQP+ process when they are in the role of the assessor. Guide students during the plus part of the process. Help the student list one or two ways to change the writing based on the feedback.

- **Specializing for students who are overwhelmed easily:** Highlight the comment on the left side of the form that this student should focus on. Redesign the template so there are only one or two choices for each section on the left.

Suggestions to Incorporate Technology

The following apps and websites support trouble areas in writing.

Ideas:

- Story Wheel (https://apple.co/2tdReE6) lets students create their own stories.

- The Brainstormer (https://apple.co/2tds5JN) includes a visual component for students who combine plot, subject, and setting to create a story.

- A+ Writing Prompts and Creativity Bundle (https://apple.co/2ysdizI) offers prompts that can get students thinking creatively and writing.

Voice:

- Sock Puppets (https://apple.co/1j3J0CE) lets students lip synch with puppets and settings they have chosen.

- Flocabulary (www.flocabulary.com) has text-to-speech capability and incorporates hip hop into several subjects, including mathematics, science, and life skills.

Sentence fluency:

- Talking Tom Cat (https://outfit7.com/apps/talking-tom-cat-1) helps students by getting them reading aloud.

- Sentence Maker (www.teacherswithapps.com/sentence-maker) lets students build sentences by moving letter tiles.

Word choice:

- Mad Libs (www.madlibs.com/apps) is a classic fill-in-the-blank game that helps students identify parts of speech.

- Bluster! (https://apple.co/2M3SosA) is a word-matching game that boosts vocabulary.

- Vocabador (https://apple.co/2K10phC) has fun *lucha libre* (Mexican wrestling) graphics that will appeal to middle schoolers.

Conventions:

- Grammar Flip (www.grammarflip.com) offers video lessons and writing prompts, as well as easy data for teachers.

- Painless Grammar Challenge (https://apple.co/2tptrjQ) lets students take grammar quizzes.

PQP+ Writing Feedback Ideas

Directions: Create praise, questions, and polish suggestions using the following (if pertinent).

- Organization (logical sequence)
- Word choice and figurative language
- Complex sentence arrangement
- Elaborations and details (adjectives, proper nouns, adverbs, quotations, and so on)
- Introductions and conclusions
- Ideas
- Voice
- Clear, coherent, easy to understand the flow

Author of the writing: *Mary Rose*

Author of this feedback: *Ann Stevens*

Date: *2/19*

Praise Start with: • I like the way _____. • I like the part _____. • I noticed that _____. • This reminds me of _____.	*I like the way you grabbed my attention with that startling fact about whales.* *After reading this, I want to learn more about whales. You piqued my interest.*
Question Ask questions about things you want to know more about or don't quite understand: • Why did you _____? • How could you have _____? • Did you think about _____? • What if you did _____?	*Why do you talk about dolphins and plankton in the same paragraph? Why did you mention them in this informational writing about whales being an endangered species?*
Polish Do the following. • Give suggestions to improve the writing. Writer can accept or reject any suggestion. • Explain why and how the suggestion could improve the writing.	*Whales have so many interesting characteristics, but I had a hard time visualizing them from this writing. Can you add more adjectives to describe them physically? Can you explain what noises they make?* *I don't see a conclusion. I wonder if you could end this piece of writing with your "I wonders" about whales?*
+Plan to Change What pieces of feedback will you incorporate into your writing? What is your plan for improving your writing after this process?	*I'm going to add ten more adjectives about whales so the reader can visualize them better. I'm going to add some sound words so the reader can understand what noises whales make. I will also have more paragraphs so the reader can understand why I brought in other topics such as dolphins. It wasn't clear.*

Figure 6.10: Example of PQP+ feedback.

*Visit **go.SolutionTree.com/instruction** for a free reproducible version of this figure.*

Fix-It Activities

Source: Adapted from Jensen & Nickelsen, 2014.

Fix-it activities is a checking strategy for partners that benefits students by modeling metacognition. It also helps hold students accountable for fixing their reading.

Directions

Administer this peer-feedback checkpoint during the learning. Use fix-it activities when students get stuck with words or comprehension during reading. Before giving this activity to partnered students, model and explicitly teach each of the activities during read-aloud time. Choose either the "Fix-It Activity Tally Page for Grades K–3" (page 150) or "Fix-It Activity Tally Page for Grades 4–8"(page 151) reproducible, keeping in mind your student's instructional reading level. Partner students who read at a similar instructional level.

Give each student a copy of the fix-it activities tally page and one text to read aloud to one another. As each student reads aloud, his or her partner places tally marks next to each tool that the student uses while reading. There isn't a set number of tallies one should strive for; the focus is on determining whether students use appropriate tools when they get stuck. The completed tally pages help teachers give feedback during guided or shared reading. When finished, each student completes the Self-Monitoring Reflection section and gives the whole page to the teacher.

Example

See figure 6.11 for an example.

Name of reader: _Upton_   **Name of partner:** _Neveah_

Directions: Partner will place tally marks next to the tool that the reader uses when he or she is stuck.

_____ Reread tricky parts slowly; visualize what you reread; retell what you reread.

_____ Look for clues in the paragraph to figure out a tough word.

___||___ Build up background knowledge on the topic. Learn more about the content before reading further by looking online.

___|_|__ Stop to ask questions about the text; create questions for clarification.

_____ Make a connection between the text and your life, another text, or what you know about the world.

_____ Stop and think about what you just read; paraphrase or summarize it.

____|___ Adjust your reading rate by either slowing down or speeding up.

_____ Look up a word in the dictionary if there aren't context clues.

_____ Stop to highlight, mark, or tag a thought in the confusing area.

____|___ Ask a peer or teacher for help when none of these tools work.

Self-Monitoring Reflection

Directions: Fill in the following.

The reader will complete the following section about what tools helped during the tough times or when he or she was stuck on a word or thinking.

I am confused by _____ on page _____.

I am confused because _____.

I tried the fix-it activity _asking questions. I asked my partner_ _____.

I now understand _what the main theme is_ _____.

I now have questions about _____.

Source: Adapted from Jensen & Nickelsen, 2014, p. 134.

Figure 6.11: *Fix-it activity tally page for grades 4–8.*

*Visit **go.SolutionTree.com/instruction** for a free reproducible version of this figure.*

Suggestions for Differentiation

The following suggestions can help you differentiate these activities.

- **Bumping it up:** Design a special fix-it activities tally page for students. For example, you could add *Looked up affixes and roots to figure out unknown word*. Ask them to come up with one or two strategies that aren't listed and try them. Ask them to reflect on a pattern they notice when they get stuck and explain how they respond.

- **Breaking it down:** Pull together a small group and model the tools, to observe certain students using the tools and to share the power behind the tools. Offer fewer choices on the fix-it activities tally page so it focuses on the activities you want these students to use.

- **Specializing for students who are overwhelmed easily:** After preassessing students, know which activities they can use and one or two they can practice more. Have these students focus only on two or three fix-it activities—one they already know and one they could practice more.

Suggestions to Incorporate Technology

The following websites support trouble areas in writing.

- Target the Problem! (www.readingrockets.org/helping/target) helps you differentiate and respond to the specific needs of students who are struggling.

- Zoho Notebook (www.zoho.com/notebook) has virtual notebooks in which you can store data. In the notebooks, you can create notes in different categories: text, notes, checklists, audio, photos, sketches, and documents.

Daily Learning Target Check

Source: Adapted from Jensen & Nickelsen, 2014.

Daily learning target check is a strategy for individual students. Students benefit by sharing how well they think they are moving toward the learning target and why they may not be at *got it* yet.

Directions

Administer this student self-assessment checkpoint after the learning. You can create others for other subjects after your students get used to this process. Make copies of "Daily Learning Target Self-Assessment—Version One" (page 152) or "Version Two" (page 153). Tell them this tool is a way they can communicate to you how they are doing daily with learning target mastery. Explain the following two steps for self-assessing.

1. After you announce the learning target, ask students to write it in the appropriate day of the week's *I can* box (version two) and place this paper at the corner of their desks.

2. At the end of the lesson, after students complete the main assessment and you provide feedback, ask the students to place an *X* in the appropriate box (figure 6.12) or the target graphic circle (figure 6.13) that reflects their mastery level. If they marked the columns Need More Practice or Not There Yet, have them explain in the Comments column. There, they will use one of the potential comment starters.

Suggestions for Differentiation

The following suggestions can help you differentiate this strategy.

- **Bumping it up:** Ask them to write questions they have about the learning today. Did anything intrigue them? They can write this question in the Comments column.

- **Breaking it down:** Enter the learning targets for the week (version two) ahead of time so students don't have to look at the whiteboard and write them on the paper. You might need to help them determine if they reached the learning target. You can do so by asking them probing questions such as "How do you know you got it?" "What did you do that proved that?" and "Does your example match the exemplar?"

Name: ___Jaden___   Subject: ___English language arts___   Unit: ___Commas___

I Can Learning Target	Not There Yet	Need More Practice	Got It	Comments
1. I can use commas in a series.	X			I get confused with the third comma.
2. I can use commas in a complex sentence.			X	
3. I can use commas to make a sentence more clear.		X		I use them too often and that confuses the reader.

If you need more practice or are not there yet, please explain why in the Comments column. When you do that, use one of these comment starters.

- I don't understand how to ___know when not to use a comma___.
- I don't understand the word _____.
- I don't understand how _____ relates to _____.
- I don't understand how _____ causes _____.
- My question is _____.
- I need you to show me _____.
- I need more practice with _____.

Figure 6.12: *Example of the first version of a daily learning target self-assessment.*

Name: ___Isabella Gamez___   Subject: ___Math___   Unit: ___Multiplication___

Learning Targets	Comments
Monday Learning Target: ___I can show how multiplication is a shortcut for addition.___ 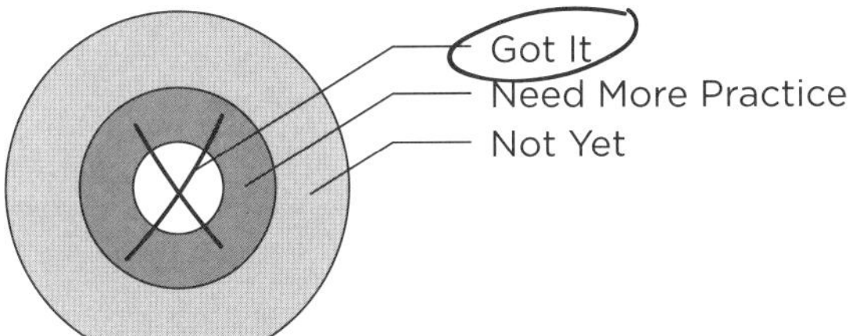 (Got It) / Need More Practice / Not Yet	Explain why you placed the *X* in that spot. Demonstrate your learning today. I did it because I learned about multiplication in 3rd grade. $4 + 4 = 8$ $4 \times 2 = 8$
Tuesday Learning Target: ___Multiply by 0 and multiply by 1___ 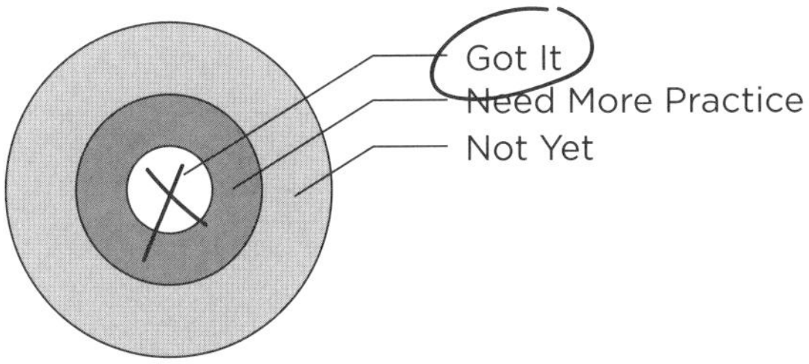 (Got It) / Need More Practice / Not Yet	Explain why you placed the *X* in that spot. Demonstrate your learning today. I did it because I understand how to multiply 1 and 0. $7 \times 0 = 0$ $7 \times 1 = 7$

continued on next page ⇒

Figure 6.13: *Example of second version of a daily learning target self-assessment.*

Learning Targets	Comments
Wednesday Learning Target: _Multiply by 2._ (circle diagram: Got It / Need More Practice / Not Yet — "Got It" circled, X marked in center)	Explain why you placed the X in that spot. Demonstrate your learning today. Because I understand multiplying 2s. 7 x 2 = 14
Thursday Learning Target: _Multiply by 3._ (circle diagram: Got It / Need More Practice / Not Yet — "Got It" circled, X marked in center)	Explain why you placed the X in that spot. Demonstrate your learning today. I know how to multiply by 3. 7 x 3 = 21
Friday Learning Target: _Multiply by 4._ (circle diagram: Got It / Need More Practice / Not Yet — "Need More Practice" circled, X marked near bottom)	Explain why you placed the X in that spot. Demonstrate your learning today. I know how to multiply by 4 but sometimes I get the answer wrong.

If you need more practice or are not there yet, please explain why in the Comments column. When you do that, use one of these sentence starters:

- I don't understand how to _____.
- I don't understand the word _____.
- I don't understand how _____ relates to _____.
- I don't understand how _____ causes _____.
- My question is _____?
- I need you to show me _____.
- I need more practice with _memorizing the 4s_.

Conference with teacher notes (goals for weekend review or for next week):

Isabella will spend some time during our next class working with Desmond, who also is memorizing multiplying by 4. They will quiz each other.

Source: Adapted from Jensen & Nickelsen, 2014.

- **Specializing for students who are overwhelmed easily:** Redesign these forms and cut out each day (version two) so the student sees and completes just one slip of paper for each day. The learning target is isolated, and there is more space for the student to write comments.

Suggestions to Incorporate Technology

Instead of using exit tickets, create a document with Google Docs (www.google.com/docs). It allows students to respond with their self-assessments on a daily basis. This saves paper—but still requires that you look through all the documents, examine the evidence, and determine your next steps. Some teachers find this electronic process easier, while others say they need the paper and evidence in front of them.

Student Self-Assessment and Goal Setting

Student self-assessment and goal setting is a change strategy for individuals, partners, small groups, or the whole group. Student self-assessment helps students take more responsibility for their learning and set goals to become more academically successful. Self-assessment, which they can do solo or with a peer, allows students to identify their own academic strengths and growth areas. Additionally, it allows them to set realistic goals, revise their own work, and track their own growth process. Of course, you must remember to set clear expectations for your students and give them the time and practice (*I do*, *we do*, *two do*, and *you do*) to develop these skills. Be patient. It takes a while for students to learn how to self-assess.

Directions

Follow these six steps, remembering to be patient. This begins with you doing all the modeling and gradually releasing the responsibility to the students.

1. Tell students what you expect of them. This communication can be an exemplar, a rubric, or a checklist, for instance. It is the criteria for success.

2. Use a teacher or student example to model how to assess the work using the criteria for success.

3. With the class, highlight strengths and solicit feedback to help move the work closer to the expected outcome.

4. Have students discuss specific goals for improvement.

5. Be prepared to model multiple times until students can assess their own work and set goals.

6. Continue to facilitate as students become more independent and masterful in their self-assessment.

Examples

Consider the following examples.

- **Exam error breakdown (Wormeli, 2018):** The teacher returns a summative assessment identifying each standard that the lesson or unit addresses. The student examines his responses and identifies whether he answered the question correctly. His answer is wrong, so he researches to see if it was due to carelessness or a lack of content knowledge. After analyzing his responses, he synthesizes his strengths and weaknesses and sets a goal for future success in writing in the bottom box. (See figure 6.14, page 144, and the "Exam Error Breakdown" reproducible on page 155.)

- **Rubric for self-assessment and goal setting:** The student assesses her work using the "Rubric for Self-Assessment and Goal Setting" reproducible (page 156), which she completes with her teacher (example in figure 6.15, page 145).

- **Reading strategy goals bookmark:** During guided-reading time, each student writes a strategy he or she would like to use. Each student writes his or her ideas in one of the boxes on the "Reading Strategy Goals Bookmark" reproducible (page 157; the example is in figure 6.16, page 146) and draws a star in the smaller boxes every time he or she practices that reading strategy. When all three boxes have stars, the student moves on to another reading strategy goal.

Question Number	Standard or Learning Target	Answers Correctly	Answers Incorrectly	Misses Due to Not Being Careful	Misses Due to Lack of Knowledge
1	Multiplying fractions	✓			
2	Multiplying fractions		✓	✓	
3	Reducing fractions	✓			
4	Reducing fractions	✓			
5	Dividing fractions		✓		✓
6	Dividing fractions		✓		✓
7	Reducing fractions	✓			
8	Reducing fractions		✓	✓	
9	Multiplying fractions	✓			
10	Multiplying fractions	✓			
11	Problem solving with multiplying fractions	✓			
12	Problem solving with multiplying fractions	✓			

My error breakdown:

I know how to multiply and reduce fractions. I made mistakes with the numbers five, six, and eight. I do not understand how to divide fractions.

My plan:

　　　Listen carefully and ask questions about dividing fractions in class.

　　　Meet with Sam to double-check our homework on dividing fractions. He knows how to do it.

　　　Use flash cards.

　　　Slow down and check my answers.

Source: © Wormeli, 2018. Used with permission.

Figure 6.14: *Exam error breakdown example.*

*Visit **go.SolutionTree.com/instruction** for a free reproducible version of this figure.*

Name: *Jayden*

Title of writing: *Memoir*

Use the following scale ratings.

0 = There is no evidence

1 = I have done pieces of this, but not everything

2 = I accomplished this

3 = I went above and beyond

Criteria	Rating	Comments and Evidence
I have a main idea (a thesis) statement for my writing.	3	This is a simple claim since I answered the prompt that is the main idea in the first sentence: "What I like doing best is playing football because it's one my best sports."
My introduction has a hook that grabs the reader's attention.	3	I know that people will want to read more because they will want to know what "mental aspects" my writing will be about.
I have at least three different supporting details in the middle of my writing.	1	I have many details, but they don't support the main idea.
All my details support my main idea.	1	Not all of the details support the idea of mental aspect. Ugh! I need to change these paragraphs to focus on the mental aspects.
All my details are in my own words or are quoted correctly.	3	These are my experiences with the game of football. My words.
Each of my paragraphs has a topic sentence, two to three details, and a concluding sentence.	1	My paragraphs are not organized this way. I'm not sure how I organized them.
My conclusion restates the main idea.	3	My conclusion relates right back to the aspect of football being a mental game.
My writing is complete sequentially, in order. I use transition words.	2	I don't think there needs to be a sequence to this type of writing. But I did use words such as: the first time, after a while, during the game, for example.
I include __2__ new vocabulary words that relate to my research.	1	I need to include some of the tier 2 words the teacher encourages us to use. I didn't use any. She said to try to include two to three.
I have the correct punctuation and start every sentence with a capital letter.	2	Yep.
I capitalize proper nouns.	3	Just a few football players.
These are my personal writing goal ideas.	2	I like every idea in the writing. I can probably elaborate on a few of the ideas more.

Changes I plan to make to my writing: I need to reorganize my paragraphs. I need some type of structure to follow since my content is a mess. I need to add better word choice too—the tier 2 vocabulary terms from teacher list.

Changes I plan to make to my writing after peer review: Give more details in my story. Reorganize my writing. Use better words to help reader visualize the game of football.

Figure 6.15: Rubric for self-assessment and goal-setting example.

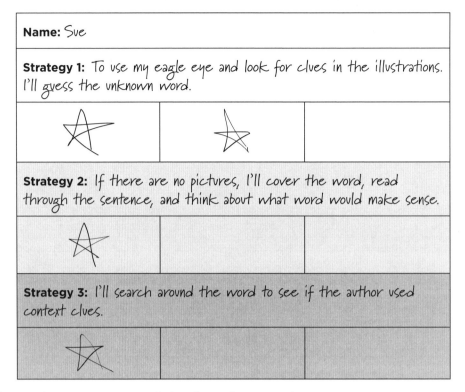

Figure 6.16: *Reading strategy goals bookmark example.*

Summary

During this step in the instructional cha-chas, you observe your students' dance moves as they discuss and practice—chew—the content. You also provide feedback to move them forward in their learning. Here, you collect and analyze data. Now it's time to do something with the results. It's time to change the pace.

Feedback Cue Cards

When students answer or their work needs redirecting:

"The learning target is _____. I notice that you accomplished _____ with this learning target. What will it take to master this learning target? What else do you need to do, learn, or include?"

"Do you want to phone a friend?"

"Do you want to ask a question to clarify your thinking?"

"Class, would you like to ask this student a question?"

Rephrase the question for better student understanding. Ask the student to explain his or her reasoning. Keep asking questions to get to the root of the error in thinking.

Use symbols, images, words, or letters to help students recall the information. Examples include "Starts with _____" and "Sounds like _____."

Pose the same question to a different student if the student wants to pass, but check back and hold the original student accountable.

"So, I think I heard you say _____. Is that what you meant?"

When you want students to dig deeper:

"Can you give some examples?"

"Tell me more."

"Can you explain the steps you took to solve that problem?"

"What would you compare that with? How does that connect with _____?"

"What if _____ happens. How will that change _____?"

"What are the characteristics of _____?"

"What details can you add to _____?"

"How can you prove _____? What evidence will you need to give?"

"How might _____ view this?"

When you want students to justify their thinking:

"So, I think I heard you say _____. Is that what you meant?"

"What do you mean when you say _____?"

"I'm confused by _____. Can you help me understand?"

"Why do you think that? Have you thought about _____?"

When you want students to show evidence:

"Where did you find that information? What page? What article?"

"How do you know that is a credible resource?"

"What paragraph did you read that in?"

"What website has that information? What other websites could you use?"

"How do you know that?"

Exit Ticket Templates—Version One

If students check the boxes Did Not Get It Yet or Need More Practice, they need to explain why on the lines below it.

Exit Ticket	**Exit Ticket**
Date: _____	Date: _____
Name: _____	Name: _____
Learning target:	Learning target:
_____	_____
_____	_____
_____	_____

□	□	□	□	□	□
Did Not Get It	Need More Practice	Got It	Did Not Get It	Need More Practice	Got It

Why?

_____

_____

_____

_____

_____

Why?

_____

_____

_____

_____

_____

Demonstrate:

Demonstrate:

Exit Ticket Templates—Version Two

Name: _____ Date: _____

Today, I learned about _____ with my class.

The tricky part was or is _____

_____

_____ .

It's important that I know this because _____

_____ .

Name: _____ Date: _____

Today, I learned about _____ with my class.

The tricky part was or is _____

_____

_____ .

It's important that I know this because _____

_____ .

Name: _____ Date: _____

Today, I learned about _____ with my class.

The tricky part was or is _____

_____

_____ .

It's important that I know this because _____

_____ .

Fix-It Activity Tally Page for Grades K–3

Name of Reader: _____ Name of Partner: _____

Directions: Your partner will place a check mark next to the tool you used when you got stuck.
☐ Get your lips ready to say the first sound.
☐ Stretch out the word slowly.
☐ Find the chunks in the word. Then blend them together.
☐ Skip the word. Then go back at the end of the sentence.
☐ Flip the vowel sound to a long or short vowel sound.
☐ Try another word until it makes sense. Then check to see if it's right.
☐ Reread tricky parts slowly. See in your mind what you reread, and retell what you reread.
☐ Look for clues in the picture or sentence to figure out a hard word.
☐ Stop to ask questions about the text.
☐ Stop and think about what you just read. Describe it in your own words or sum it up.
☐ Ask another student or teacher for help when none of these tools work.
Directions: Now you, the reader, will fill in these answers.
I did not understand _____ on page _____.
I did not understand because _____.
I now understand _____.
I tried this new fix-it activity today: _____.

Source: Adapted from Jensen, E., & Nickelsen, L. (2014). Bringing the Common Core to life in K–8 classrooms: Thirty strategies to build literacy skills. *Bloomington, IN: Solution Tree Press.*

Fix-It Activity Tally Page for Grades 4–8

Name of Reader: _____ **Name of Partner:** _____

Directions: Partner will place tally marks next to the tool that the reader uses when he or she is stuck.

_____ Reread tricky parts slowly; visualize what you reread; retell what you reread.

_____ Look for clues in the paragraph to figure out a tough word.

_____ Build up background knowledge on the topic. Learn more about the content before reading further by looking online.

_____ Stop to ask questions about the text; create questions for clarification.

_____ Make a connection between the text and your life, another text, or what you know about the world.

_____ Stop and think about what you just read; paraphrase or summarize it.

_____ Adjust your reading rate by either slowing down or speeding up.

_____ Look up a word in the dictionary if there aren't context clues.

_____ Stop to highlight, mark, or tag a thought in the confusing area.

_____ Ask a peer or teacher for help when none of these tools work.

Self-Monitoring Reflection

Directions: The reader will complete the following section about what tools helped during the tough times or when he or she was stuck on a word or thinking.

I am confused by _____

_____

_____ on page _____.

I am confused because _____

_____

_____.

I tried the fix-it activity _____

_____

_____.

I now understand _____

_____

_____.

I now have questions about _____

_____

_____.

Source: Adapted from Jensen, E., & Nickelsen, L. (2014). Bringing the Common Core to life in K–8 classrooms: Thirty strategies to build literacy skills. *Bloomington, IN: Solution Tree Press.*

Daily Learning Target Self-Assessment—Version One

Name: _____ **Subject:** _____ **Unit:** _____

I Can Learning Target	Not There Yet	Need More Practice	Got It	Comments
1.				
2.				
3.				
4.				
5.				

If you need more practice or are not there yet, please explain why in the Comments column. When you do that, use one of these potential comment starters.

- I don't understand how to _____.
- I don't understand the word _____.
- I don't understand how _____ relates to _____.
- I don't understand how _____ causes _____.
- My question is, _____?
- I need you to show me _____.
- I need more practice with _____.

Daily Learning Target Self-Assessment—Version Two

Name: _____ Subject: _____ Unit: _____

Learning Targets	Comments
Monday Learning Target: _____ _____ Got It Need More Practice Not Yet	Explain why you placed the *X* in that spot. Demonstrate your learning today.
Tuesday Learning Target: _____ _____ Got It Need More Practice Not Yet	Explain why you placed the *X* in that spot. Demonstrate your learning today.
Wednesday Learning Target: _____ _____ Got It Need More Practice Not Yet	Explain why you placed the *X* in that spot. Demonstrate your learning today.

Teaching With the Instructional Cha-Chas © 2019 Solution Tree Press • SolutionTree.com
Visit **go.SolutionTree.com/instruction** to download this page.

Thursday Learning Target: _____ _____ Got It / Need More Practice / Not Yet	Explain why you placed the *X* in that spot. Demonstrate your learning today.
Friday Learning Target: _____ _____ Got It / Need More Practice / Not Yet	Explain why you placed the *X* in that spot. Demonstrate your learning today.

If you need more practice or are not there yet, please explain why In the Comments column. When you do that, use one of these potential comment starters:

I don't understand how to _____.

I don't understand the word _____.

I don't understand how _____ relates to _____.

I don't understand how _____ causes _____.

My question is _____?

I need you to show me _____.

I need more practice with _____.

Conference with teacher notes (goals for weekend review or for next week):

Source: Adapted from Jensen, E., & Nickelsen, L. (2014). Bringing the Common Core to life in K–8 classrooms: Thirty strategies to build literacy skills. *Bloomington, IN: Solution Tree Press.*

Exam Error Breakdown

Directions: Write the standard or learning target in the second column. If you answered that question correctly, mark the Answers Correctly column. If you answered it incorrectly, mark the Answers Incorrectly column and mark the column that explains why. At the bottom of the page, please break down what you know, what you don't know, and what your plan is for learning what you don't know.

Question Number	Standard or Learning Target	Answers Correctly	Answers Incorrectly	Misses Due to Not Being Careful	Misses Due to Lack of Knowledge
1					
2					
3					
4					
5					
6					
7					
8					
9					
10					

My error breakdown:

My plan:

Source: Wormeli, R. (2018). Fair isn't always equal: Assessment and grading in the differentiated classroom (2nd ed.). Portland, ME: Stenhouse.

Rubric for Self-Assessment and Goal Setting

Name: _____

Title of writing: _____

Use the following scale ratings.

0 = There is no evidence
1 = I have done pieces of this, but not everything
2 = I accomplished this
3 = I went above and beyond

Criteria	Rating	Comments and Evidence

Changes I plan to make to my writing:

Changes I plan to make to my writing after peer review:

Reading Strategy Goals Bookmark

Name:

Strategy 1:

Strategy 2:

Strategy 3:

Reading Strategy Goals Bookmark

CHAPTER 7

Take Step Four: Change (Differentiate)

You've danced almost full circle with the instructional cha-chas cycle. This is where you use your check results to make changes. While the first three steps allow you to differentiate your chunks, chews, and checks to address different learners, primarily in a whole-class setting, it is time to use your gathered data to differentiate more purposefully with individual or small groups of students in mind. These data help you determine the most effective means of ensuring your students master the learning target (and ultimately the standard). This step is the heart and soul of differentiation.

A dance instructor teaches the dance to the entire troupe, but at this point the instructor selects the principal dancers for solos or duets. Like that, classroom differentiation becomes even more purposeful as you change groupings, instruction, activities, or assessments to create an environment that celebrates diversity, perseverance, and grit. You're allowing students to be more independent learners and facilitating their learning in whatever way they need.

In this chapter, we will answer the following questions before offering strategies for change.

- What common changes exist?
- How can you find the time for change?

- How do you use data to determine what change to make?
- What strategies can you use during change?

What Common Changes Exist?

The instructional cha-chas allow for change to happen in a variety of different ways and places in the lesson. All changes are based on some type of data: preassessment, formative assessments, documented observation, student self-assessment plus raw data, benchmark data, or summative assessment data, for example. Remember that the best type of data response is daily, which means acting quickly. The most common types of change follow.

- **Right-now changes:** Give the students a formative assessment and quickly analyze the data to determine if an immediate change is necessary. You might change the pacing by accelerating or decelerating the lesson or changing a specific strategy or activity.

- **Near-future changes:** Give a formative assessment, usually at the end of a class period, and then analyze the results to determine what changes you can make within the next few class periods to increase student learning. For example, you may decide to change instructional strategies, warm-up activities, or groupings, or design tiered assignments.

- **Last-chance changes:** Give a formative assessment, usually close to the end of a unit, and analyze the results to see if students will successfully master the upcoming unit summative assessment. You may decide to change the actual test date or student grouping, reteach and reassess, or create gap-closing or enrichment stations. When reassessing students, we give them full credit for their new learning. In other words, we change the grade since it represents their mastery level. For more information about how to do these things correctly, please refer to "Rick Wormeli: Redoes, Retakes, and Do-Overs, Part One" (www.youtube.com/watch?v=TM-3PFfIfvI) and "Rick Wormeli: The Right Way to Do Redoes" (https://bit.ly/2jmRYTL).

- **Student-driven learning changes:** This change allows students to take more responsibility for their learning. Allow them to analyze their assessment data so they can determine whether they need to change their learning methods, focus on a specific topic, or redo work.

- **Teacher-driven environmental changes:** This is a big-picture change. Examine academic data (last year's state exam, benchmarks, and so on), as well as student information data (learning preferences, ethnicity, gender, specific academic and behavioral needs, and so on). Determine what changes you might need to make in your classroom's learning climate to ensure all students succeed. That might mean changing your mindset, which recognizes that a traditional one-size-fits-all approach to instruction is not as effective as a differentiated approach.

How Can You Find the Time for Change?

So far in this book, you have learned how to differentiate the content (chunk), the process (chew), and the product (check). But step four (change) requires you to analyze data from your assessment (either formative or summative) and make a very specific and purposeful *change*. This might mean altering groupings, instruction, activities, or assessments, including student reteaching and retesting all or part of the content, a step that yields the greatest results, but many teachers have trouble finding time to enact it. Given the vast amount of content they must teach, when do effective teachers find time to change their lessons and differentiate more fully? The most common times for more purposeful differentiation follow.

- During class:
  - Warm-up
  - Lesson closure
  - Independent practice
  - Review for an upcoming test
  - A tiered assignment (page 171)
  - Rotation stations (page 72)
  - Anchor activities
- Outside class:
  - Homeroom
  - Advisee time
  - Specially created blocks of time designed for an enrichment or intervention
  - Before or after school
  - During lunch
  - During flexible or modified schedules

Another option is academic boot camp—a sort of all-hands-on-deck approach. In this case, every teacher on a team reteaches or extends and enriches the standard based on benchmark results or daily data. Teams might be grade level, vertical, or simply a group of teachers who have volunteered for a specific skill or standard. Options include intense time before a test, two or three times a week, two or three times a month, and rotation stations on the standards for which students need more time.

How Do You Use Data to Determine What Change to Make?

Say that you give an exit ticket at the end of today's lesson, and it measures mastery of the daily learning target. After the students leave, you sort all the exit tickets into groups you label Got It, Need More Practice, and Did Not Get It. You discover that six students got it, eleven students need more practice, and five students do not get it yet.

As the teacher, it is your decision what to do with your results. Some teachers might glance at these data and continue their weekly path of learning, moving to the next day's lesson regardless of the results. The effective teacher recognizes she or he has decisions to make that impact successful student learning. Teachers—you—make a multitude of decisions daily, perhaps none more important than those that match curriculum goals to your students' needs. Figure 7.1 is an example of a teacher's reflection on the described exit ticket results. While the teacher's reflection seems lengthy, this thought process takes only a few minutes once you have analyzed the exit ticket results. Taking this moment to reflect and make the right decisions for your students will save you time in the long run.

How Might I Change Tomorrow's Lesson?	My Thoughts
Should I add a question to the warm-up?	The majority either need more practice or don't know it. Since the warm-up is for review, I don't think this will be a good use of my time.
Should I add a question to the exit ticket?	No point in doing this unless I can teach it and provide practice time to those who need it. The only students who will be successful are those who already proven their success on today's exit ticket.
Should I give a quiz?	I can't see the point of giving a quiz when I already know that most of the students will not do well on it, and it will take up valuable teaching time in my classroom.
Should I continue reviewing the concept the rest of the week as I continue with the upcoming lessons?	Since today's skill is the foundation for tomorrow's lesson, the students really need to grasp this before I can go on. I can't move on until they understand this piece of the content.
Should I compact the curriculum for those who show mastery?	Today's learning target is just one step on the learning ladder toward mastery of the standard. These students haven't mastered the entire standard, so they'll need my instruction. Therefore, I can't compact them to the next step.
Should I design and play a game to review the learning target and then check for mastery?	Although my students love games, most of them don't have enough understanding of the learning target to be successful with the game.
Should I set aside time to teach a new strategy?	Unfortunately, my time is limited since the curriculum has me moving on quickly to the next learning target.
Should I reteach in strongest multiple intelligence or learning preferences?	This will be great if all the students who still need practice learn in the same way, but those that struggle have vast differences in their learning preferences.
Should I reteach differently from original teaching: small group, half the class, or whole group, excluding the few who mastered it?	This is a possibility, but I would need the six students who have it to work independently on an anchor activity (which I will need to create), and I think that some of the students might get it quickly with a little more practice, while some of them are going to need a lot of instruction and practice that might mean I end up with off-task behavior.

continued on next page ⇒

Figure 7.1: A teacher's reflection on an exit ticket.

How Might I Change Tomorrow's Lesson?	My Thoughts
Assign peer tutors.	I might be able to do this, although I would never put those that have it with those that don't because the gap is too large. Plus, I think those that don't have it yet, need me to instruct them. But I might be able to use those that have it as peer tutors to those that just need more practice. Unfortunately, a couple of those who have it don't really have the social skills to be good peer tutors.
Regroup heterogeneously and continue grade-level activities.	This might work, but I'm concerned that I'll end up with one student doing all the work and another just sitting there doing nothing. To avoid hogs and logs, I would need to create very specific roles for each student, and I would need to spend time modeling what strong heterogeneous groups look like and sound like. Do my students know how to use teacher talk when working in groups? Will my students who don't yet know it learn with their peers, or do they need me?
Regroup homogeneously and design a tiered lesson.	I think this might be the best option for tomorrow. Although I'll have to design three different activities, I'll be able to provide more rigor for the students that have it, while providing practice opportunities for the student who need that. I'll also be able to scaffold the lesson, and provide more support for the students who didn't get it. Everyone will stay focused on the learning target and will engage in an activity designed to meet their academic needs.

When the teacher has determined the best choice for the following day's lesson, he or she records it on the lesson plan. (See a completed lesson plan with differentiation points added in figure 8.2 on page 188.) As you can see, there is no one way to change. It might be as simple as changing your instruction pace or as complex as designing a variety of activities to meet your students' diversity. You are the teacher. You choose the best strategy for change based on data you gather about the students you know and teach.

What Strategies Can You Use During Change?

In this chapter, we're addressing a more purposeful, deeper look at differentiation and sharing the most common types of strategies for changing instruction and practice in the classroom. You will notice that the strategies in this chapter have a slightly different format from the previous chapters. This is because they cover bigger differentiation concepts rather than just individual tools. Since all these changes are based on student data, they will likely involve purposeful student grouping. Therefore, the first strategy addresses grouping. We'll share grouping types and materials you might use to help manage groups. After that, we list these deeper differentiation strategies by the amount of teacher support each needs, beginning with near-total teacher support and ending with those strategies needing very little teacher support. These strategies will include a brief overview of the change strategy, how to do it, things you might need, and examples. It is not uncommon to blend strategies from the previous chapters into these change strategies.

Flexible Grouping

Flexible grouping is a change strategy for partners or small groups. During flexible grouping, students move in and out of groups for a specific purpose. The benefit is students having the opportunity participate in a variety of methods designed to meet their needs. Here, we'll provide a brief overview of the change strategy, how to do it, things you might need, and examples.

Teachers purposefully place students in groups for a variety of outcomes. The key is to ensure that the groups are flexible, not permanent, so they fit every type of change from right-now change to teacher-driven environmental change. Also remember to use readiness grouping, or ability grouping, sparingly (Marzano et al., 2001). See chapter 5 (page 81) for more. Table 7.1 provides an overview of the expected outcomes and the recommended grouping patterns for each outcome.

Directions

Follow these six steps.

1. Think through the logistics of your grouping. Consider questions like the following.

   - How many students will be in each group?

   - Will you assign roles: summarizer, leader, materials manager, questioner, and so on. Visit **go.SolutionTree.com/instruction** for role cards you can provide students.

   - Will you allow for student choice?

   - Do all the students know where to find and how to use all the materials?

   - Will all the students be able to do the tasks as they are, or will certain students need special help?

Table 7.1: *Purposeful Grouping Outcomes and Types*

Desired Outcome	Grouping Type	Notes and Strategies
Overall achievement and social skills improvement	Cooperative learning groups	Use all information at your disposal (academic, ethnicity, socioeconomic, gender, work behaviors, and so on) to design heterogeneous groups of four.
Increased attention and motivation	Interest groups	Allow students to make connections or analogies about their outside interests and the content.
	Work behavior groups	You may choose to group students homogenously or heterogeneously. Some work behaviors include leader, shy, quiet, talkative, sociable, and challenging.
Achievement gap closing and going beyond the standard for diverse learners	Readiness groups	Allow students to meet in homogeneous groups based on like needs.
Social skills growth and peer acceptance	Random groups	Use these when you want students to meet together briefly to complete a short task. Some examples of how to create random groups include numbering off, picking a card, mix and match, and seat location.
Efficient learning and content retention	Learning preferences group based on learning preferences or multiple intelligences	Learning preferences include visual, auditory, and kinesthetic methodologies, noise and lighting preferences, and so on.
		Multiple intelligences (Gardner, 1993) include verbal linguistic, logical-mathematical, musical rhythmic, visual spatial, bodily-kinesthetic, naturalist, intrapersonal, and interpersonal.

Visit ***go.SolutionTree.com/instruction*** *for a free reproducible version of this table.*

- How will you assess the learning?

- Do you need to change the room arrangement?

2. Determine the type of group you want for the expected outcome (table 7.1, page 163).

3. Design the groups' tasks. For example, you might have them design a group mind map about the causes of a civil war (be sure to state the criteria for success) or use manipulatives to represent a given equation. You could design different tasks to meet different groups' needs.

4. Model the roles and expectations for student behavior. We had two short and simple

rules: respect others and be responsible for performing your role and tasks.

5. Use the teacher checklist for grouping in figure 7.2 (or see the "Teacher Checklist for Grouping" reproducible on page 175).

6. Conclude by having the students complete the group evaluation sheet (figure 7.3 or see the "Group Evaluation Sheet" reproducible on page 176). This is important. It is critical for groups to work effectively together and must therefore be accountable for behaviors that enable productive work.

Directions: Use the following checklist for grouping.

Setting Up—Before Grouping
Check the following.
❑ Make sure materials are in the appropriate place.
❑ Think through role cards (what you want each role to look and sound like).
❑ Create and share the rubric (including behavior and academic expectations) or criteria for success.
❑ Create a student group list.
❑ Identify a method for grouping and how many students will be in the group.
❑ Write out group goals (work expectations).
❑ Have a checklist of activity procedures for students (group assignment details).
Reminding Students—Before and During Grouping
Check the following.
❑ Monitor noise level.
❑ Direct groups to where in the room they should remain during the activity.
❑ Identify what to do if there is a question.
❑ Show the group evaluation sheet that students will complete after group work and go over group etiquette.
❑ Explain role cards, which group they will be in, group goal, how much time they'll have, where materials are, and rubric expectations.
❑ Explain what groups should do when they complete assignments.
❑ Explain what to do with completed assignments.
Providing Closure—After Grouping
Check the following.
❑ Allow time for group reflection.
❑ Check that the group recorder completes the group evaluation sheet with input from other group members.
❑ Make sure the reporter explains what the group learns, questions it still has, or challenges it had.
❑ Create time for teams to set improvement goals for the next group activity.
❑ Assess student group work by using a rubric (individual effort and group effort).

Figure 7.2: Teacher checklist for grouping.

Directions: Student groups use the following sheet to evaluate themselves.

Group:				

Student names:				

Criteria	0 No Way	1 OK	2 Yes	3 Awesome
Our group stays on task.				
We help each other.				
We complement each other.				
We listen to each other.				
We keep our voices low.				
We accomplish the tasks well.				
We perform our management roles well.				

We find the following tasks too challenging:

We find the following tasks too easy:

We still have the following questions:

Our group can show improvement in this area:

Figure 7.3: Group evaluation sheet.

Examples

Consider the following examples.

- **Right-now change (regrouping):** About halfway through the lesson, the teacher realizes that all the class has the basics of the lesson, with some students appearing a bit more comfortable than others. The teacher regroups the students in partners, each consisting of one student who is doing well with the lesson and one student who is struggling, and has them take turns continuing to practice the skill while orally explaining their process.

- **Near-future change (regrouping):** After viewing the exit tickets, the teacher realizes that the students' knowledge levels are extremely diverse. Some students fully master the learning target, some still need a bit more practice, and a few others are confused and need more explicit instruction and practice. The teacher decides to regroup students by their readiness or ability levels and design tiered assignments focused on the learning target.

- **Last-chance change (regrouping):** After playing a game to review the unit's key concepts, the teacher becomes aware that while a small group of students appear ready for the unit exam, most of the class is still struggling with three specific areas. The teacher decides to provide an additional day of review before giving the test and sets up learning stations focused on the three areas where they are confused. Each station has an engaging, hands-on activity, and a brief formative assessment that students can self-check and use as a study guide. The students who demonstrate mastery that day have the following choices: participate in the station, be the station's expert leader, or continue learning with an anchor activity.

- **Student-driven change (regrouping):** After giving a quiz, the teacher allows the students to do an error analysis and self-reflection. The students agree that the biggest concern is key fact and information retention. They ask to meet with their multiple-intelligence groups to learn the material in their strongest modality.

- **Teacher-driven change (grouping plan):** At the beginning of the year, the teacher gives all the students a multiple-intelligence survey and an interest inventory. After analyzing the results, the teacher realizes that the morning class has a large percentage of visual spatial learners interested in drawing and video games, while the afternoon class has a large percentage of bodily-kinesthetic students interested in sports. Before considering their academic readiness, the teacher knows that the morning lessons will need to look different from the afternoon lessons. The teacher decides to plan a wide range of graphic organizers and interactive notebooks, as well as allow computer games for review for the morning class. For the afternoon class, the teacher decides to use a wide range of manipulatives to provide on-your-feet activities, and design sport-based review games.

 Preteaching

Preteaching

Preteaching is a change strategy for individuals, partners, small groups, or the whole group of students. During preteaching, students learn upcoming content. The benefit is that struggling students' brains are pre-exposed or primed for the upcoming content. Here, we'll provide a brief overview of the change strategy, how to do it, things you might need, and examples.

As discussed in chapter 3 (page 21), preteaching is an essential part of near-future change since research shows how valuable priming the brain is for memory and concept retention. Cognitive priming gives immediate and long-term transfer results and is worth the time (Wexler et al., 2016). Priming is essential since using prior knowledge is critical for learning. This proactive approach occurs when data tell you that some students need more background knowledge, directions or misconceptions clarification, and some stronger connections during the lesson. They'll need those new neural networks. The bottom line is: preteaching includes teaching skills or knowledge prior to an activity or lesson that requires them.

Directions

Follow these seven steps.

1. Break the standard into daily learning targets. Give a preassessment to determine student-readiness levels with each learning target within the standard.

2. Identify where each student is with each daily learning target.

3. Identify gaps in learning or misconceptions preventing the student from mastery.

4. Determine if you should preteach certain concepts or skills in order to prime the students' brains.

5. Develop preteaching minilessons for the gaps you see. Set up a comfortable area for the minilesson and make sure it has a whiteboard and marker (to show them the word), sticky notes, and pens or pencils (in case students show a picture of the word or write definitions in their own words).

6. Provide them an opportunity to demonstrate their learning and understanding. Consider students' learning modalities.

7. Design an assignment for other students (warm-up, independent work, or anchor activities as examples).

Examples

Consider the following examples.

- **Small-group warm-up:** During a science warm-up or drill, the teacher pulls eight students who are struggling with the prerequisite skills they need to successfully complete the lab. The teacher instructs on these skills by chunking the steps, and checks each student doing the skill to ensure he or she is ready for lab.

- **Modification:** The teacher creates a modified version of a graphic organizer (thinking map), directions for an experiment, directions for a research project, or reading-writing assignment

to better guide during groups. He or she pulls students into groups before the actual lesson to become more familiar with the modifications.

- **Prerequisite skill:** After preassessment reveals that some students lack a particular, very important skill required for a project (such as finding credible sources on the internet), the teacher pulls a small group during the lesson's warm-up. The teacher clarifies by explaining sequence, emphasizing vocabulary, and color coding the most important steps. He or she then lets those who want to become the expert leaders in their groups take over after the preteach.

- **Visualization:** The teacher asks students to visualize whatever content they are learning. For example, students might visualize a vocabulary word and then act out the word, or visualize each step in solving a word problem and then share the steps with their partner.

- **Review:** The teacher asks review questions and students show their answers on whiteboards. A quick show of the whiteboard enables the teacher to scan the audience to see who is getting it and who is not.

- **Vocabulary word preteaching:** Before doing the established activity, the teacher preteaches the most important vocabulary words in a novel way. Students identify words while reading, place them in context, and remember them better. Use some of the following strategies for preteaching vocabulary.

  - Role-playing or pantomiming

  - Categorizing words

  - Predicting how these words might be used in the reading

  - Connecting the vocabulary with other words and phrases they are familiar with

  - Doing a create-a-cloze activity

  - Matching words with pictures

  - Using gestures or playing charades

  - Showing real objects

  - Pointing to pictures or images

  - Doing quick drawings on the whiteboard

  - Elaborating on the word's meaning with examples and stories

- **Book tagging:** Students look through a book and put a sticky note on a page with a picture, graph, or diagram that is new or interesting to them. Or, you can require specific tags for marking (such as main idea, unknown vocabulary, and so on). The book tags let you know what the students find interesting, what they know, and what they don't know.

- **Flipped classroom:** Students read and learn about the content at home (Walvoord & Anderson, 1998). When they come to class, they are ready to apply the background knowledge. The teacher has students read articles, watch video clips, or watch a taped version of the teacher's instruction to fill in background knowledge that he or she identifies as missing in the preassessment.

- **Quick fact sheet:** Before reading historical fiction, students read a fact sheet about that time period so they understand the settings and mannerisms. The teacher emphasizes certain facts by explaining them with visuals, then asks questions to see if students have a better understanding of the concept after using the quick fact sheet.

- **Academic conversations:** The teacher preteaches mathematics words to make it easier for students to initiate academic conversations in groups. He or she offers students the sentence pattern, "Where does the *red* triangle go? It goes here" and "The triangle has three *vertices*. How many *vertices* does the rectangle have?" Through this process, students can learn about classification as well as colors and shapes. You can display a mathematical word wall that shows both the word and a graphic representation of the word, or make anchor charts to let students review and learn anytime they want

- **Play a game:** The game *Magic Letter, Magic Word* is a simple preteaching activity that teachers know won't take much time to develop for a small group that needs extra time with word meaning (Marzano & Simms, 2013). Teachers create a couple of key sentences that have vocabulary words missing except the first letter. The students must recall which word goes into the blank based on the cue and what they learned in previous days.

Reteaching

Reteaching

Reteaching is a change strategy for individuals, partners, small groups, or whole group. During reteaching, students relearn the content *in a different way*. The benefit is the opportunity for students to have their misunderstandings addressed immediately, rather than at the end of a unit of study. Here, we'll provide a brief overview of the change strategy, how to do it, things you might need, and examples.

Reteaching is an essential part of instruction that fits every type of change from right-now to teacher-driven environmental change. Reteaching is always preceded by some form of assessment that allows both student and teacher to determine errors or misconceptions. Reteaching allows the teacher to respond to a learning problem immediately. For reteaching to be effective, a teacher must use a different method or approach from the one he or she used initially—one that builds on the previous method but focuses specifically on the errors or misconceptions in student thinking. Teachers most commonly use this strategy when introducing new and challenging content or when reviewing previously taught content as a bridge for an upcoming lesson.

Directions

Follow these six steps.

1. Give an assessment.

2. Identify where each student is with the daily learning target.

3. Identify gaps in learning or misconceptions. Using the close the gap–reteaching template in figure 7.4, (page 169) record student names and mark with *X*s to indicate whether the errors were minor (quick and easy fix) or major (might take several lessons or a longer lesson).

What? (What did I teach? What data and errors did I see?)	So What? (What is needed?)	Now What? (How will I respond? List minilesson steps.)
Learning target taught: I can determine the meaning of unknown words by using context clues.	List skills, tools, strategies, questions, concepts they need:	Identify minilesson learning target:
Error 1: Not using the process of four steps to find clues.	Steps to thinking model/ think-aloud/chunk-chew—check each step until they get it	List steps I'll take to teach this skill. (Remember: I do, we do, two do, and you do.) ○ Show anchor chart of draw box. ○ Point to possible clues in text and explain why ○ Ask the three big questions ○ Four-step process with two paragraphs Write exit ticket:

Student Names	Minor Errors	Major Errors
Jamil		X
Raquel		X
Linda		X
Jerry		X
MaKenzie		X

What?	So What?	Now What?
Error 2: Breaking word into parts (affixes, roots)	List skills, tools, strategies, questions, concepts they need: Finding root words	Identify minilesson learning target: I can find the root words to help me guess at a meaning. List steps I'll take to teach this skill. (Remember: I do, two do, and you do.) ○ Show most common roots (handout) ○ Explain its definition ○ Create webs together ○ Practice ○ Whiteboards Write exit ticket: Guess word meanings based on finding its root, reading word in context, and possibly looking up meaning of root

Student Names	Minor Errors	Major Errors
Bartow		X
Lucy		X
Colin		X

Next steps after minilessons:

Figure 7.4: *Close the gap-reteaching template example.*

Visit go.SolutionTree.com/instruction for a free reproducible version of this figure.

4. Consider the skills, strategies, tools, questions, or concepts that the students will need for success and write them in the So What? column on the reteaching template.

5. Design a minilesson that addresses the errors the students made. Be sure to reteach the information differently than before. Consider reteaching in the student's strongest learning modality. Write how you will gradually release your responsibility in the Now What? column on the reteaching template. Notice the details in the reteaching example in figure 7.4 (page 169). Be very deliberate in reteaching so you can close the gap. Provide lots of chew points— opportunities for students to demonstrate their learning and understanding—during this minilesson.

6. Design assignments for the other students so you can have uninterrupted time with this group that needs you. Design a warm-up, independent work, or anchor activity.

Examples

Consider the following examples.

- **Error analysis:** The teacher provides a real (but anonymous) student writing and allows him to locate the common punctuation errors. Students work in groups to find them. He encourages the students to help each other find and explain the errors, saying they have to find four total.

- **Smaller chunks:** After an error analysis, the teacher decides how to take the misunderstood concept or skill so it's in its smallest chunk. For long division, that means doing only the first step with students and having them practice that one step with several different division problems. Then, she adds the next step. Students practice that step several times. After each practice and check, students give the teacher feedback on their level of confidence with each step.

- **Think-aloud:** Students didn't understand a process after the initial instruction, so the teacher models the process for them while doing a think-aloud. The teacher stops to discuss common misconceptions and describes which tools she is using and why. She also says aloud what she wonders about.

- **Sketch-it:** After presenting a chunk of material as a PowerPoint presentation, the teacher gives students the hard copy of the presentation and time to briefly sketch the key points they need to remember.

- **Kinesthetic teaching:** The third-grade teacher invites students to act out their position vocabulary words: *over, under, beside,* and *beneath.* Over time, students progress to acting out domain-specific vocabulary: *courage, justice, obstacle, promise.* Students continue progressing until they can act out key concepts in an entire unit about the three branches of government.

- **Organizational tools:** The students struggled with the amount of content they had to organize, so the teacher introduces thinking maps to help students organize and help the teacher and student to see misconceptions in action. (Interactive notebooks and Cornell Notes are also good strategies here.)

- **Mnemonic devices:** Students had trouble remembering the Great Lakes during their geography unit, so the teacher introduces the mnemonic *HOMES,* which helps them remember Huron, Ontario, Michigan, Eerie, and Superior.

- **Tactile teaching:** A kindergarten teacher reteaches blending using sandpaper letters. Students feel the two letters and blend the sound. During the science portion of class, the students use Wikki Stix to create and demonstrate the water cycle.

- **Color-coded key points:** Students who couldn't remember the steps in the scientific process should record their notes in their science journal using a different-color pencil for each step.

- **Targeting:** Teachers should use strategies that complement the students' learning preferences and strengths so they will acquire the concept or skill much faster. Teachers should match the most powerful strategies with student preferences for a quick reteach that they won't forget.

Tiered Assignments

Tiered assignments is a change strategy for individuals, partners, or small groups. Working at their readiness level helps struggling students close gaps; gives on-level students practice; and increases rigor for advanced students.

A preassessment or daily formative assessment helps you design the learning activities so they challenge students at the just-right level. Teachers won't use tiered assignments daily, but rather when the learning differences are diverse enough to require them, so they are often a near-future and last-chance change. Because tiering yields great results and allows you to more purposefully address the vast degrees of readiness in your classroom, every strategy in chapters 3–6 has suggestions for bumping it up and breaking it down to make tiering more doable.

Directions

The checklist in figure 7.5 will help you design learning activities so they are a good match with the group of students.

Short, easy-to-use ideas for any content are in the reproducibles "Ideas for Bumping It Up" and "Ideas for Breaking It Down" (pages 195 and 196). The Webb's Depth of Knowledge question stems (figure 5.6, page 94) has question stems for rigorous thinking. These cheat sheets are great to have on hand while planning.

Examples

Each task should have its own card with directions. Read the directions aloud for nonreaders. Consider the following examples.

- **Learning target:** *I can* sequence and summarize the plots, main events, and their influence on future events.

    - *Grade level*—The task card reads, With your group, draw the main events from the story. Put your drawings in order. Retell the story using transition words (*first, next, then, finally*). What do you think might happen next? Why?

    - *Bumping it up*—The task card reads, With your group, look at the photo. What do you think happened before this picture was taken? What will happen next? Retell the before, during, and after events using transition words (*first, next, then, finally*).

    - *Breaking it down*—The task card reads, With your group, put the pictures in order by following the sequence of the story. Retell the story by using transition words (*first, next, then, finally*). What do you think might happen next? Why?

An exemplar tiered lesson will:
❑ Focus on the standard or outcome with varying levels of complexity.
❑ Be created because students show a need, through preassessments or formative assessments, for these varying activities.
❑ Have activities for each group that are equally engaging and creative.
❑ Establish anchor activities so that when students complete the work, they will have something else to work on.
❑ Have students work cooperatively within groups with procedures, role cards, and group evaluation forms so each student stays on task, or have students work independently in their assigned tier.
❑ Have task cards or explanations for expectations at each tier.
❑ Analyze this work formatively. (Feel free to quiz students for grades a couple of days later, when they are ready for mastery level.)
❑ Support all students who have background knowledge that doesn't show mastery standard level. Use scaffolding to achieve the standard, which may not occur on the same day as others' mastery.

Figure 7.5: *Exemplar tiered lesson checklist.*

*Visit **go.SolutionTree.com/instruction** for a free reproducible version of this figure.*

- **Learning target:** I can identify and analyze characters in a story.

  - *Grade level*—The task card reads, With your group, use a Venn diagram to compare the main character at the beginning and end of today's story. Then, share what events cause the character to change using one of the following: a poster, interview, letter, or role-play.

  - *Bumping it up*—The task card reads, With your group, use a Venn diagram to compare the main character of today's story and the main character from last week's story from the beginning to the end of the story. Then, share what similar events or causes influenced each character's actions using one of the following: a poster, interview, letter, or role-play.

  - *Breaking it down*—The task card reads, Make a T-chart. On the left side, write three causes that affect the main character. On the right side, write the effects of each. Share your results using one of the following: a poster, interview, letter, or role-play.

- **Learning target:** I can identify a point of view and support my point of view in cohesive paragraphs using the main idea and supporting details.

  - *Grade level*—The task card reads, Read each statement. Choose *one* and decide whether you agree or disagree with it. Identify four reasons that support your thinking. Express your opinion in paragraph form and support your reasons with examples. The three statements are:

    a. Dogs make the best pets.

    b. Everyone should have a sibling.

    c. School helps you succeed in life.

  - *Bumping it up*—The task card reads, Read each statement. Choose one and decide whether you agree or disagree with it. Identify four reasons that support your thinking. Express your opinion in paragraph form and support your reasons with statistics, anecdotes, examples, or non-examples. The three statements are:

    a. Dogs make the best pets.

    b. Everyone should have a sibling.

    c. School helps you succeed in life.

  - *Breaking it down*—The task card reads, Read each statement. Choose one and decide whether you agree or disagree with it. On your graphic organizer, identify four reasons that support your thinking and support each reason with at least one example. Use your graphic organizer to share your opinion aloud. The three statements are:

    a. Dogs make the best pets.

    b. Everyone should have a sibling.

    c. School helps you succeed in life.

- **Learning target:** I can write letters whose language is tailored to the audience and purpose and that use appropriate conventions (parts of a letter, for example).

  - *Grade level*—The task card reads, With your group, write a letter convincing your parent or guardian to let you go to a school skating party. Be sure to offer more than one reason to support your request and to include all the parts of a letter.

  - *Bumping it up*—The task card reads, With your group, write a letter convincing your principal to host a school skating party. Be sure to provide at least three reasons to support your request and to include all the parts of a letter.

  - *Breaking it down*—The task card reads, With your group, write a letter convincing a friend to attend the school skating party. Be sure to offer more than one reason. Use the template on the computer to include all parts of the letter.

Learning Stations

Learning stations are a change strategy for individuals, partners, small groups, or the whole group. The benefit is that students will go only to the stations they specifically need to master and deepen their learning.

In chapter 4 (page 72), we presented rotation stations to explore chunks. In that strategy, small groups rotate through all the stations to acquire the day's chunked content. *Learning stations* are more purposefully designed. Not all students will participate in every learning station. They will go to the station they need based on data you have gathered. This might be a near-future change that you have created based on exit tickets, a last-chance change that you have created prior to giving a unit assessment, or a student-driven change based on student assessments.

Directions

Follow these seven steps.

1. Examine data such as preassessment, formative assessments, quizzes, and so on.

2. Determine specific areas where students may need more practice to achieve mastery.

3. Design a station to address these needs. We encourage teachers to write learning targets for the stations and post them at the station or on a chart in the front of the room. Use the "Learning Station–Planning Template" (page 177) reproducible to organize your plan.

4. Create activities that are hands-on, engaging, and allow students to practice. (Students not participating in these needs-based learning

stations may be working on learning contract, independent study, or anchor activities.)

5. Make task cards that explain exactly what the students need to do to be successful for each station and provide any materials they will need to work independently.

6. Design a formative assessment to check for understanding and degree of mastery.

7. Give each student a copy of the "Learning Station Self-Assessment" reproducible (page 178) so each is accountable for his or her work at each station. This is an important piece when you have multiple stations.

Example

Sean is struggling with reading comprehension. His fluency is low, which may be part of the problem. Together, Sean and the teacher have set a goal to add two or three words per minute to his fluency each week. In addition, his goal is to retell the key events in his story with 80 percent accuracy. Each station Sean goes to will include the activity, three comprehension questions for him to answer, and either paper or a recording device so Sean can retell the text and respond to the questions. One day each week, Sean will complete a one-minute timed reading with the teacher to check his fluency rate and monitor his improvement. Sean will participate in the following fluency stations.

- Poetry

- Reader's theater

- Independent reading

- Recorded stories where he reads along

Student-Driven Inquiry Learning

Student-driven inquiry learning is a change strategy for individual students. During it, students work independently on a chosen topic, the benefit of which is the student choosing what to learn, mastering his or her own learning, and deciding how to share that learning.

While it works for all students, student-driven inquiry learning is an especially good option for students who have aced a unit preassessment, show mastery on what you are about to teach, or finish assignments early. While you will still provide guidance and checkpoints for them, the students will be mostly independent learners. Students' passions should determine inquiry learning. You are the guide on the side, coaching this student with lots of questions. Remind the student that she oversees her own research. What a wonderful opportunity.

Directions

Follow these six steps.

1. Have data that show students mastered the current standard.

2. Allow students to brainstorm things they are passionate about and form inquiry questions that allow them to dive deeper into their passion. The reproducible "Jump-Start Inquiry or Passion Projects Brainstorming" (page 179) can guide them.

3. Help students organize their thinking about their inquiry project.

4. As students complete their research, have them examine the credibility of their sources using the reproducible "Credible and Accurate Resource Tracker" (page 180).

5. Provide or develop criteria for the students' final products. You can use the reproducible "Criteria for Success Cards" (page 181).

6. Allow students the opportunity to reflect on their process and self-assess with reproducibles ("Student Personal Accountability and Reflection Guide" on page 182 and "Student Effort Self-Assessment" on page 183).

Examples

Consider the following examples.

- **Inquiry projects:** Inquiry learning starts by students posing questions, problems, or scenarios and actively researching to find answers or solutions. Teachers facilitate, but do not drive, the student's learning.

- **Genius Hour:** Classrooms across the United States have embraced the Genius Hour (Grinberg, 2014), the Google practice (Genius Hour, n.d.) of allowing its staff to use 20 percent of its work week to be creative and work on projects that inspire them. Teachers are helping students think like a genius and research, create, invent, and discover new things to share not only with their class, but with the public.

Summary

A great dance instructor will always find a way to help each dancer master the moves. While some will need more time and practice, others might need a certain dance move modeled several times before they can imitate it. Great teachers know this about their learners, too. The more a teacher knows about his or her students, the better the changes will be regarding what to teach, how to teach, and how to close the gaps by using the best differentiated strategy for each student.

Teacher Checklist for Grouping

Directions: Use the following checklist for grouping.

Setting Up—Before Grouping
Check the following.
☐ Make sure materials are in the appropriate place.
☐ Think through role cards (what you want each role to look and sound like).
☐ Create and share the rubric (including behavior and academic expectations) or criteria for success.
☐ Create a student group list.
☐ Identify a method for grouping and how many students will be in the group.
☐ Write out group goals (work expectations).
☐ Have a checklist of activity procedures for students (group assignment details).

Reminding Students—Before and During Grouping
Check the following.
☐ Monitor noise level.
☐ Direct groups to where in the room they should remain during the activity.
☐ Identify what to do if there is a question.
☐ Show the group evaluation sheet that students will complete after group work and go over group etiquette.
☐ Explain role cards, which group they will be in, group goal, how much time they'll have, where materials are, and rubric expectations.
☐ Explain what groups should do when they complete assignments.
☐ Explain what to do with completed assignments.

Providing Closure—After Grouping
Check the following.
☐ Allow time for group reflection.
☐ Check that the group recorder completes the group evaluation sheet with input from other group members.
☐ Make sure the reporter explains what the group learns, questions it still has, or challenges it had.
☐ Create time for teams to set improvement goals for the next group activity.
☐ Assess student group work by using a rubric (individual effort and group effort).

Group Evaluation Sheet

Directions: Student groups use the following sheet to evaluate themselves.

Group name:				
Student names:				

Criteria	0 No Way	1 OK	2 Yes	3 Awesome
Our group stays on task.				
We help each other.				
We complement each other.				
We listen to each other.				
We keep our voices low.				
We accomplish the tasks well.				
We perform our management roles well.				

We find the following tasks too challenging:

We find the following tasks too easy:

We still have the following questions:

Our group can show improvement in this area:

Learning Station–Planning Template

Station:	Station:
Standards we will address:	Standards we will address:
Format I will use: • File folder • Dice • Board game • Paper and pencil • Spinner • Sentence strips • Other: _____	Format I will use: • File folder • Dice • Board game • Paper and pencil • Spinner • Sentence strips • Other: _____
Assessment method: • Rubric • Self-evaluation • Paper and pencil • Observation • Learning log • Conference • Menu • Contract • Presentation • Other: _____	Assessment method: • Rubric • Self-evaluation • Paper and pencil • Observation • Learning log • Conference • Menu • Contract • Presentation • Other: _____
Materials I need:	Materials I need:

Learning Station Self-Assessment

Name:

Rating symbols to use:

Scale: 0 = Not yet; 1 = Very few times; 2 = Often; 3 = Almost always

	Station 1	Station 2	Station 3	Station 4	Station 5
Monday					
Tuesday					
Wednesday					
Thursday					
Friday					

• I used my time well and focused on the task. • I met the literacy station goal. • I helped others achieve their goals. ⭐	• I used my time and focused fairly well. • I halfway met the literacy station goal. • I helped some students achieve their goal. ✓	• I didn't use my time well yet. • I didn't meet the goal yet. • I distracted other students. (Explain verbally why you made these choices to teacher.) NY Not Yet

Jump-Start Inquiry or Passion Projects Brainstorming

Directions: Answer the following questions to jump-start your brainstorming session.

What's your passion?

What are you good at doing?

What do you love to do?

What do you love to learn?

What things do you wonder about?

If you could invent new classes at school, what would they be?

If you could invent anything new, what would it be?

Credible and Accurate Resource Tracker

Name of researcher: _____

Research topic: _____ Date: _____

Resource Information *(MLA style)*	Credibility Ranking and Explanation *1 = Not very credible* *2 = Credible* *3 = Very credible*	Information Used From This Resource *(quotes and page numbers)*	Integration of Information *(paraphrasing, direct quote, block quote)*	New Questions

Source: Jensen, E., & Nickelsen, L. (2014). Bringing the Common Core to life in K–8 classrooms: Thirty strategies to build literacy skills. Bloomington, IN: Solution Tree Press.

Criteria for Success Cards

Use these cards while you check your near-final versions of your student-driven inquiry learning.

PowerPoint Presentation
Criteria for Success

Check each box after completion:

- ❑ My visuals focus on the content.
- ❑ My content is accurate.
- ❑ I included citations from resources where needed.
- ❑ My visuals and words are coordinated.
- ❑ My content is represented sequentially.
- ❑ My creativity is evident.
- ❑ When presented, the technology works fluently.
- ❑ Other: _____

Mind Map
Criteria for Success

Check each box after completion:

- ❑ I used paper, Coogle, or MindMeister.
- ❑ My visuals and symbols match the content they are next to.
- ❑ My chunks have relevant information in them.
- ❑ My citations are near the content.
- ❑ My details are attached to the main ideas.
- ❑ Other: _____

Anchor Chart
Criteria for Success

Check each box after completion:

- ❑ My chart paper has the main idea of what I learned.
- ❑ My chart paper has a few details that are the most important.
- ❑ I used strong visuals to bring my content together.
- ❑ I can explain what I learned by sharing this anchor chart.
- ❑ I used key terms correctly.
- ❑ My spelling is accurate.
- ❑ Other: _____

Poem
Criteria for Success

Check each box after completion:

- ❑ I showed what I learned about my research through the content of this poem.
- ❑ I have a picture that represents the content in the poem.
- ❑ I included the type of poem and followed the special rules for that poem.
- ❑ My words rhyme when they are supposed to.
- ❑ Other: _____

Student Personal Accountability and Reflection Guide

Check one of the following.	Scale:
❑ Project ❑ Assignment ❑ End-of-week work ❑ Other: _____	N/A = Not applicable 0 = Below average 1 = Average 2 = Above average 3 = Exceptional

Evaluation Statements	My Rating	Comments and Explanation of Rating (How to grow)
I worked as hard as I could possibly work.		
I set high standards for myself and checked to ensure I met them.		
I spend enough time to do the quality work that I need to do.		
I regulate my procrastination, distractions, and temptations (including social networking) in order to complete my work.		
I use a variety of resources and ensure they are credible.		
I ask questions when directions or content are unclear.		
I review my work often to ensure the least amount of errors.		
I ask for examples of what is necessary in order to do my best.		
I am proud of the work I did and would share it with others.		

Write comments here. (If you rated yourself a 0 or a 1 on the preceding criteria, please explain why. See the following ideas.)

- Was it a lack of something specific?
  - Healthy lifestyle—Did you have enough sleep, water, nutritious food, or exercise?
  - Vision—Did you not understand the expectations or get insufficient quality examples?
  - Time—Did you create a schedule and prioritize the things that you needed to accomplish? Did you take brain breaks? Did you limit social media time? Did you just run out of time to review it again?
  - Resources—Did you know what was available? (Possible resources include internet, apps, people, equipment, and books.) Did you ask questions to find resources? Were the resources confusing?
  - Knowledge—Did you ask questions? Why or why not? Were you afraid to ask questions or feel that it took too much time?
- Were you stuck? Did you use your metacognitive fix-it activities?
- How was your attitude about the assignment? Did you get tired of working on the assignment? Were you able to find someone who could offer support and feedback?

Student Effort Self-Assessment

Directions: Think about the following statements and select the option that best reflects your efforts to meet the statement.

Statement	Options	Comments
I put in a sufficient amount of time to do my best work on this assignment.	Yes or No	
I got rid of distractions so I could focus on this assignment.	Yes or No	
I corrected and improved my work after getting feedback from at least two other people.	Yes or No	
I reached out for help if I needed it.	Yes or No	
I used many reliable resources to complete this assignment.	Yes or No	
I stuck with this assignment even when I was struggling.	Yes or No	
Other:	Yes or No	

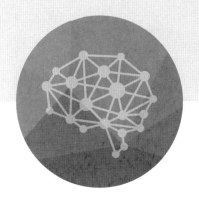

Finesse the Chunk, Chew, Check, and Change Cycle: A Beautiful Classroom Dance

You have studied the moves. You have learned how to chunk the content, discovered ways for students to chew the content, seen ways to formally and informally check for understanding, and explored how to change instruction based on what you learned from data checkpoints. You've read about dozens of strategies that you can easily implement in your daily lesson plans. Now it's time to start the music and set things into motion.

This chapter is about coordinating the entire cycle by bringing everything together. This chapter will make it easier for you to implement the whole process. We start by showing you what this might look like in a couple of classroom scenarios. In addition, we will provide a cheat sheet for planning with the instructional cha-chas cycle. These forms will guide your thinking and act as a checklist to help you implement the whole process faster. A completed lesson plan helps you see how all of this comes together.

We end this chapter by providing a template with which you can self-assess to determine how well you are implementing the instructional cha-chas. Which step is your strength? Which step provides a growth opportunity: chunk, chew, check, or change?

Classroom Scenarios

What might the instructional cha-chas cycle look like in your classroom? Let's look at a couple of classroom scenarios.

Scenario One

Mr. Parker, a fifth-grade teacher, is teaching his students about past-tense verbs. He models two different verbs (chunk using an *I do*) and then partners his students and provides them with six more verbs (chew using a *two do*). As he walks around the room recording the results of his formative assessment (check), he realizes that 100 percent of the students correctly formed the past-tense form of the verbs (examine the results of the check). Rather than continue with the remaining eight verbs, he pulls the class together and introduces irregular verbs (which is tomorrow's lesson). He made a right-now change and accelerated the lesson rather than having the students continue with something they had clearly mastered.

Scenario Two

Ms. Jones's second-grade students are learning to recognize main ideas in informational text. Ms. Jones begins by reading aloud the first paragraph from the text and uses the think-aloud process to show students how she determines the main idea of the paragraph (chunk using an *I do*). Next, she reads aloud the second paragraph and has students discuss in groups what they believe the main idea is (chunk using a *we do* and students chew). She selects a student from each team to share their thinking (check).

She notices that one table has had trouble identifying the main idea (examine the results of the check), so after reading aloud the third paragraph (chunk), she joins this group during the discussion, helping them to identify the main idea before asking teams to share their thinking (check). She made a right-now change to join the struggling group and provide more support.

She realizes that three of the students in the group are still having difficulty (examine the results of the check), so she partners the rest of the students to complete the remaining paragraphs of the text, while she works with the three students who are struggling using a less complex text. She made another right-now change by regrouping students and changing the text for the three students who are struggling. She asks the partners to record their main ideas on their paper and turn them as their exit ticket (check). Based on the results of the exit tickets, Ms. Jones plans the next day's lesson (examine the results of the check) where she will regroup the students based on that checkpoint data. Two groups will create their own mini informational paragraph and then challenge the other team to find their main idea. Two other groups will be reading texts of different complexities and identifying main ideas. She made a near-future change by designing a tiered activity for the following day.

Cheat Sheet for Planning With the Instructional Cha-Chas Cycle

Figure 8.1 lists each step's key elements. You can use this cheat sheet to stay on track as you implement each step. We recommend keeping copies on hand of the reproducibles "Planning With the Instructional Cha-Chas Cycle" (page 193) and the "Ideas for Bumping It Up" (page 195) and "Ideas for Breaking It Down" (page 196) for daily use.

The checklist will help you plan more efficiently so the process becomes a quick routine in your classroom, making planning part of your daily routine. When you plan this way, you teach powerfully and students love learning. They get to say "I got it" on a daily basis. When you teach this way, you will see more engaged

Directions: Use the following checklist to gauge your planning of the instructional cha-chas cycle.

Plan
❑ Start with the standard that students need to master.
❑ Break down the standard into learning targets. There should be a sequence of several learning targets that helps students achieve the big, broad standard.
❑ Make sure the learning targets are such that most students can achieve the learning targets during that lesson that day. Remember that the entire lesson will be structured around this learning target.
❑ Design the main formative assessment for this lesson. What do you want your students to learn, understand, and be able to do by the end of this lesson? The main formative assessment should be evidence that the students mastered the learning target.
❑ Create the criteria for success for this main formative assessment. What are the details and characteristics of this formative assessment? How does it guide students toward mastery? Students should know exactly what you want to see and hear as evidence of learning target mastery.
❑ Share the criteria for success with students in some of the following ways: rubric, student checklist, exemplar and nonexemplar, peer assessment, template, or self-assessment.
❑ Decide whether to give a preassessment. What type of preassessment will provide the data you need to effectively plan?
❑ Examine students' preassessment data or any other academic data. Do any students already know the content? What will you have them do? What will you do if half the class already understands? Is there any background knowledge missing?

❑ Examine student data, including interests, learning preferences, and multiple intelligences. What materials can you use? What methods of instruction and practice can you use to address these learners? Do any students need additional or different resources or support?

Chunk

❑ Separate your lesson into manageable chunks using the appropriate time limit for your students.

❑ Introduce the most important information first in a novel and interesting way. How will you engage students in the learning?

❑ Activate students' prior knowledge with questions.

❑ Introduce any key terms in a manner that increases retention: visuals, kinesthetic signs (like pointing to four things when you define a noun as a person (point), place (point), thing (point) and idea (one had in the air by your head to represent an idea), and so on.

❑ Provide several opportunities for student processing during the middle chunks of the lesson so as not to overload their working memory.

❑ Move questioning from simple to more complex.

❑ Use CARER (coherent content, active students, relevant content, emotion-evoking strategies or tools, and retrieving the information often; Jensen, 2018) to ensure high engagement and content memory.

❑ Close the lesson and check for student mastery level with questions, exit tickets, and so on that formally provide data about each student.

Chew

❑ For every chunk, include a chew. Are students talking about the content?

❑ Include chews for different learning modalities. Do the chews support the visual, auditory, and kinesthetic learners?

❑ Include chews that address different intelligence types. Is there an opportunity for both the interpersonal and intrapersonal leaner? Have you included support for other intelligences?

❑ Provide opportunities for processing in groups. Do you have students grouped heterogeneously to strengthen both academics and social skills? Do you have them grouped homogeneously to close gaps (by readiness), strengthen retention (by learning preference), or increase motivation (by interest)?

Check

❑ For every chew, include a check. Do you design all your checks to measure student progress toward the learning target? How do you know if the students are mastering the content?

❑ Provide a variety of checks, including formal and informal and oral, written, and demonstration. How did you document the assessment data?

❑ Provide both short-and-sweet and long-and-deep checks.

❑ Accompany every check with actionable feedback. Which type of feedback will you give: verbal, written, visual demonstration, or a grade?

Change

❑ Reflect on the results of every check. Are the students mastering the content?

❑ Make changes to support your students. Will the change be right-now, near-future, last-chance, student-driven, or teacher-driven environmental change?

❑ Decide when you will provide the change. Will this occur during class time or beyond the class time?

❑ Choose the correct change for the situation. Will you adjust your pacing; change student grouping; preteach or reteach; tier the assignment; pull a small group; provide learning stations; allow for student self-assessment and goal setting; offer student-driven inquiry learning; or have students work on other student-driven continued learning activities?

Figure 8.1: Planning with the instructional cha-chas.

students. This process has the potential to double the speed of your students' learning (Hattie, 2009).

The completed, detailed version of the lesson plan you have been following throughout the book is in figure 8.2. Here, you can see how everything comes together including the plan for change, highlighted in gray. Visit **go.SolutionTree.com/instruction** for a blank lesson-plan template to use as you implement the instructional cha-chas cycle or use the reproducible "Daily Lesson Plan" (page 197). You do not need to include the level of detail for each step that you see here. The purpose for that detail here is to help you clearly understand each piece of the lesson plan. When you use the lesson-plan template on your own, you can record as much or as little detail as you need. Eventually, you will write your lesson plans with shorter phrases as you get used to the format. Figure 8.3 (page 190) is an example of a shortened version of the completed template.

Daily Lesson Plan

Subject or unit: Reading: Main Idea—Details **Grade:** 5

Standard: Determine two or more main ideas of a text and explain how they are supported by key details; summarize the text (RI.5.2).

Learning target (do and know): I can describe or graphically represent the relationship between main idea and details.

Main formative assessment (show): Students complete "The Main Idea and Detail Tabletop Graphic Organizer" (page 104) to show how the details (table legs) support the main idea (tabletop) based on a given paragraph.

Criteria for success (check type):	Criteria for success (explain details): Students self-assess their work and complete a checklist with the following criteria for success.
☐ Rubric	
☑ Self-assessment	☐ I can write accurate details on the legs.
☑ Checklist	☐ I can write the accurate main idea on the tabletop.
☐ Peer assessment	
☐ Exemplars	☐ I can write an explanation, in complete sentences, of how the details and main idea are connected.
☐ Nonexemplars	
☐ Verbal	
☐ Other: _____	

The Chunk Explained: What Teacher Will Do	The Chew Explained: What Students Will Do *(Place the main formative assessment from preceding section in the appropriate chunk.)*	Check for Understanding *(Check those that apply.)*
Beginning chunks (I do): Review the definition of *main idea*. Move your arms as large as possible, creating an invisible square, or frame, in the air: the big picture. Define details and make little circles with your hands going into the invisible square that you just motioned. Explain that the little details create the big picture; they help you visualize what the picture looks like.	Students show the body movement that represents the definition of the main idea (arms folded on top of each other to represent a strong tabletop). Students practice showing the details (table legs). Students create the tabletop and then take one arm to represent the table legs. ☑ Individual ☐ Partners ☐ Small-group total: _____	☐ Exit ticket or final stretch check ☐ Electronic tools ☐ Whiteboards for quick checks ☐ Turn-and-talk ☐ Documented teacher observation ☐ Writing ☐ Self-assessment or peer assessment ☐ Main formative assessment evidence ☑ Other: _Quick view_

Middle chunk (we do, two do): Say, "There are many visuals that we can create to help us understand the relationship between main idea and details. I use the visual of an imaginary frame to represent main idea. The circles inside it represent details. Today, we are going to show another visual: a tabletop with legs supporting it." Show an anchor chart (a large visual, usually on chart paper) of a tabletop that shows the top of the table labeled Main Idea and the table legs labeled Details. Then, show a paragraph from any of your texts and how the main idea of the paragraph gets written on the tabletop and the details of the paragraph are written on the individual legs supporting the tabletop. Make sure all students can explain that details are the legs of the table that support the tabletop, which represents the main idea. Share many anchor chart examples: paragraph being separated on the tabletop graphic organizer with main idea on top and details written on the legs.	Students create a kinesthetic table on the floor after receiving sentence strips with details and one main idea. Students determine who is the main idea. The rest of the students are details that support it. Their bodies create a table on the floor with the sentence strip on their bellies. Teacher checks and gives feedback before they rotate sentence strips. ❏ Individual ❏ Partners ☑ Small-group total: _5 or 6_ **Bump it up:** Two groups of students need to be challenged. I will add two irrelevant details to their sentence strip pile and they will need to decipher which two detail sentences don't belong in that main idea tabletop grouping.	❏ Exit ticket or final stretch check ❏ Electronic tools ❏ Whiteboards for quick checks ❏ Turn-and-talk ☑ Documented teacher observation ❏ Writing ❏ Self-assessment or peer assessment ❏ Main formative assessment evidence ❏ Other: _____
Ending chunk (you do): Summarize the day's learning by pointing out what each group does during the lesson and giving positive feedback to each group. Explain the exit ticket by modeling how to bring the pieces together with a different paragraph (not the one you use to assess students).	Students read a paragraph that is under the document camera. You can read it to them. Main formative assessment: Students complete the drawing by writing the main idea on the top of the table and writing three or four details on the legs. Then, they describe the relationship between the main idea and details on the lines at the bottom of the paper. Each student turns one in. ☑ Individual ❏ Partners ❏ Small-group total: _____	*(Analyze the main formative assessment by determining if the criteria for success are in place.)* Hand out exit tickets.

Change

(Explain how you might regroup, preteach, reteach, tier, design stations, facilitate individual goal setting, urge independent inquiry, employ continuous learning, or have students self-assess.)

Based on the student data from this lesson, I will do the following to respond to student needs.

The exit ticket revealed that five students still struggle with details supporting the main idea and what the main idea is truly all about. They placed a detail on the tabletop and the main idea on a leg. So, I will reteach this concept tomorrow using the same visual, but using shorter, easier-to-read paragraphs. I will do the following things with this small group: read the paragraph together, ask group members for the big picture about details and main idea, and ask for the details that explain this big picture. I will break students into smaller groups while they work. To bump it up, other students will design their own paragraphs, swap with a friend, and then graphically represent their friend's paragraph on the tabletop.

Source for standard: NGA & CCSSO, 2010a.

Figure 8.2: *Example of a completed daily lesson plan with differentiation points.*

Daily Lesson Plan

Subject or unit: Writing **Grade:** 2

Standard: Write informative/explanatory texts in which they introduce a topic, use facts and definitions to develop points, and provide a concluding statement or section (W.2.2.).

Learning target (do and know): I can sum up information about my animal's habitat.

Main formative assessment: Sticky notes, fact strips, and books flagged.

Criteria for success (check type):	Criteria for success (explain details):
❑ Rubric	❑ I will use relevant information (text or pictures)—about my animal's habitat.
❑ Self-assessment	
☑ Checklist	❑ I will use two to three details from the text describing my animal's habitat in my own words.
❑ Peer assessment	
☑ Exemplars	❑ I will include a pro and a con about my animal's habitat.
❑ Nonexemplars	
❑ Verbal	❑ I will use neat handwriting so I can reread what I wrote.
❑ Other: _____	
	❑ I will use correct punctuation.
	❑ I will spell words correctly.

The Chunk Explained: What Teacher Will Do	The Chew Explained: What Students Will Do *(Place the main formative assessment from the preceding section in the appropriate chunk.)*	Checking for Understanding *(Check those that apply.)*
Beginning chunk (I do): Model paraphrasing with teacher text and fact strips. Read aloud the animal text to the class. Do a teacher think-aloud while modeling. Teacher shares what he or she would write and shows students how to do it.	After hearing the animal text, students turn and talk about what they would write on fact strips. ❑ Individual ❑ Partners ❑ Small-group total: _____	❑ Exit ticket or final stretch check ❑ Electronic tools ❑ Whiteboards for quick checks ☑ Turn-and-talk ❑ Documented teacher observation ❑ Writing ❑ Self-assessment or peer assessment ❑ Main formative assessment evidence ❑ Other: _____
Middle chunk (we do): Guided small-group writing focuses on habitat sections of text.	In small groups, students share their paraphrased facts. Peers give feedback: Does it sound paraphrased? Does this fit in the habitat section?	❑ Exit ticket or final stretch check ❑ Electronic tools ❑ Whiteboards for quick checks ☑ Turn-and-talk ❑ Documented teacher observation ❑ Writing ☑ Self-assessment or (peer assessment) ❑ Main formative assessment evidence ❑ Other: _____

| Middle chunk (two do): Partners on same animal gathered more notes on habitat.

Differentiated instruction moment: The teacher provides graphic organizers for some partnerships. | Students collaborate to find stronger facts on habitat for their animal. They check one another's notes about their animal's habitat. | ❏ Exit ticket or final stretch check
❏ Electronic tools
❏ Whiteboards for quick checks
☑ Turn-and-talk
❏ Documented teacher observation
❏ Writing
❏ Self-assessment or peer assessment
❏ Main formative assessment evidence
❏ Other: _____ |
| Ending chunk (you do): Students independently finish their notes on habitat and then begin the same cycle on their animal's physical features and what it eats (added to the next lesson). | Students continue paraphrasing notes independently and use the criteria for success checklist before meeting with the teacher to move on.*
❏ Individual
❏ Partners
❏ Small-group total:_____ | ❏ Exit ticket or final stretch check
❏ Electronic tools
❏ Whiteboards for quick checks
☑ Turn-and-talk
☑ Documented teacher observation
❏ Writing
❏ Self-assessment or peer assessment
❏ Main formative assessment evidence
❏ Other: _____ |

*Note: After this checkpoint, students compile notes to complete their writing and use criteria for success.

Source for lesson: D. Hafner, E. Kirby, & J McKinlay, Maryvale Primary School, Buffalo, New York, 2018.

Source for standard: NGO & CCSSO, 2010a.

Figure 8.3: *Example of completed daily lesson plan with differentiation points—shortened version.*

Self-Assessment for Strengths and Growth Opportunities

The "Teacher Self-Assessment for the Instructional Cha-Chas Cycle" reproducible (page 199) will guide your journey of implementing the four steps. Chew and check are in the same box because their processes merge. While the students are chewing, you're checking for understanding.

Be honest with yourself when you take the assessment. Then determine *one* area that you want to focus on to improve. Set a goal and study the chapter that explains that step. Ask another teacher or coach to help you implement that step routinely and effectively. Take the self-assessment to continuously improve. We recommend creating a goal based on one area (chunk) that you want to improve and create the specific strategies for doing so. That might mean designing smaller chunks for better digestion, using visuals, songs, or movement, creating relevant examples, or other approaches. Once you achieve this goal, retake the assessment to determine your next goal within the instructional cha-chas. Routines are powerful. Make chunk, chew, check, and change a daily routine in your subject areas and you will see gaps close.

Summary

For a dance recital to come together, the choreography must be well planned so that one dance connects to the next. This is how lessons should look while teaching from day to day. The materials in this chapter help your lesson flow, which helps students reach the standards. You may need to adjust the plan along the way to help students get it—and they may get there on different days and in different ways—but this is what the instructional cha-chas is all about: success for all students.

Planning With the Instructional Cha-Chas Cycle

Directions: Use the following checklist to gauge your planning of the instructional cha-chas.

Plan
❑ Start with the standard that students need to master.
❑ Break down the standard into learning targets. There should be a sequence of several learning targets that helps students achieve the big, broad standard.
❑ Make sure the learning targets are such that most students can achieve the learning targets during that lesson that day. Remember that the entire lesson will be structured around this learning target.
❑ Design the main formative assessment for this lesson. What do you want your students to learn, understand, and be able to do by the end of this lesson? The main formative assessment should be evidence that the students mastered the learning target.
❑ Create the criteria for success for this main formative assessment. What are the details and characteristics of this formative assessment? How does it guide students toward mastery? Students should know exactly what you want to see and hear as evidence of learning target mastery.
❑ Share the criteria for success with students in some of the following ways: rubric, student checklist, exemplar and nonexemplar, peer assessment, template, or self-assessment.
❑ Decide whether to give a preassessment. What type of preassessment will provide the data you need to effectively plan?
❑ Examine students' preassessment data or any other academic data. Do any students already know the content? What will you have them do? What will you do if half the class already understands? Is there any background knowledge missing?
❑ Examine student data, including interests, learning preferences, and multiple intelligences. What materials can you use? What methods of instruction and practice can you use to address these learners? Do any students need additional or different resources or support?

Chunk
❑ Separate your lesson into manageable chunks using the appropriate time limit for your students.
❑ Introduce the most important information first in a novel and interesting way. How will you engage students in the learning?
❑ Activate students' prior knowledge with questions.
❑ Introduce any key terms in a way that increases retention: visuals (such as images and maps), kinesthetic signs (for example, using your finger to point to four things when you define a noun as a person [point to self], place [point to floor], thing [point to desk], and idea [point to head]), and so on.
❑ Provide several opportunities for student processing during the middle chunks of the lesson so as not to overload their working memory.
❑ Move questioning from simple to more complex.
❑ Use CARER (coherent content, active students, relevant content, emotion-evoking strategies or tools, and retrieving the information often; Eric Jensen, personal communication, 2018) to ensure high engagement and content memory.
❑ Close the lesson and check for student mastery level with questions, exit tickets, and other formal assessments that provide data about each student.

Chew
❑ For every chunk, include a chew. Are students are talking about the content?
❑ Include chews for different learning modalities. Do the chews support the visual, auditory, and kinesthetic learners?

❑ Include chews that address different intelligence types. Is there an opportunity for both the interpersonal and intrapersonal learner? Have you included support for other intelligences?

❑ Provide opportunities for processing in groups. Do you have students grouped heterogeneously to strengthen both academics and social skills? Do you have them grouped homogeneously to close gaps (by readiness), strengthen retention (by learning preferences), or increase motivation (by interest)?

Check

❑ For every chew, include a check. Do you design all your checks to measure student progress toward the learning target? How do you know if the students are mastering the content?

❑ Provide a variety of checks, including formal and informal and oral, written, and demonstration. How did you document the assessment data?

❑ Provide both short-and-sweet and long-and-deep checks.

❑ Accompany every check with actionable feedback. Which type of feedback will you give: verbal, written, visual demonstration, or a grade?

Change

❑ Reflect on the results of every check. Are the students mastering the content?

❑ Make changes to support your students. Will the change be right-now, near-future, last-chance, student-driven, or teacher-driven environmental change?

❑ Decide when you will provide the change. Will this occur during class time or beyond the class time?

❑ Choose the correct change for the situation. Will you adjust your pacing; change student grouping; preteach or reteach; tier the assignment; pull a small group; provide learning stations; allow for student self-assessment and goal setting; offer student-driven inquiry learning; or have students work on other student-driven continued learning activities?

Ideas for Bumping It Up

These short, easy-to-use ideas for bumping it up, or introducing more challenge, work for any content.

Use more challenging verbs with the content they are to learn.
Make the objective or activity more abstract. Allow them to fill in the missing or inferred pieces.
Allow them to generate open-ended questions about the learning.
Ask them to evaluate real community problems and brainstorm potential solutions (while still focusing on the standards at hand).
Ask them to help you create the evaluation rubric for the project. Challenge them to think creatively.
For writing assignments, encourage them to use more sophisticated vocabulary, more elaborate figurative language, and more complex sentences.
Ask them to make more sophisticated connections with content: connections to nation, world, current events, scientific elements in these locations, and the like.
Allow them to create their own mind maps, note organization, and so on rather than creating them yourself.
Ask them to write the next day's warm-up on their daily exit tickets.
Ask them to create tips and memory strategies for concepts they just learned so they can teach them to all students.
Make mistakes on purpose and ask them to evaluate what went wrong.
Ask them to synthesize information by creating a completely different way to show the new learning: a website, graphic, mind map, newspaper article, or program, for example.

Ideas for Breaking It Down

These short, easy-to-use ideas for breaking it down, or scaffolding, work for any content.

Create templates or partial notes to help them organize their thinking or learning.
Reteach with a different strategy, preferably with their dominant learning preference.
Choose a study buddy for them who can offer peer support when you are helping others.
Create a so-called *supplies-for-support table* that has all kinds of tools they might need immediately but not have within their reach: protractor, manipulatives, sticky notes, ruler, calculator, times tables, dictionary, thesaurus, booted internet, sentence strips, Unifix cubes, Judy Clocks, Wikki Stix, play money, fraction rulers, number lines, and so on.
Show a poor example of what you are expecting (a nonexemplar) and an exemplar of what you expect.
Create a specific, short rubric with clear vocabulary so they know what you expect.
Color-code information. Different-color highlighters or sticky notes can distinguish between parts of speech, types of sentences, sentence value, most important details versus added details, and so on. Give them the pieces so they can rearrange them into new ideas.
Have them complete a create-a-cloze paragraph to show their background knowledge or learning.
Provide plenty of question stems when they are designing their own questions.
Provide plenty of sentence starters to help them formulate their thoughts on paper.
Allow them to verbalize to you what they learned rather than write their thoughts.
Allow them to find visuals to understand concepts.
Use visuals whenever possible: time lines, diagrams, photos, pictures, images, and so on.

Daily Lesson Plan

Subject or unit: **Grade:**

Standard:

Learning target (do and know):

Main formative assessment (show):

Criteria for success (check type):

- ❑ Rubric
- ❑ Self-assessment
- ❑ Checklist
- ❑ Peer assessment
- ❑ Exemplars
- ❑ Nonexemplars
- ❑ Verbal
- ❑ Other: _____

Criteria for success (explain details): Students self-assess their work and complete a checklist with the following criteria for success.

- ❑
- ❑
- ❑

The Chunk Explained: What Teacher Will Do	The Chew Explained: What Students Will Do *(Place the main formative assessment from preceding section in the appropriate chunk.)*	Check for Understanding *(Check those that apply.)*
Beginning chunks (I do):		❑ Exit ticket or final stretch check
		❑ Electronic tools
		❑ Whiteboards for quick checks
		❑ Turn-and-talk
		❑ Documented teacher observation
		❑ Writing
		❑ Self-assessment or peer assessment
		❑ Main formative assessment evidence
	❑ Individual ❑ Partners ❑ Small-group total: _____	❑ Other: _____

Middle chunks (we do, two do):		❑ Exit ticket or final stretch check
		❑ Electronic tools
		❑ Whiteboards for quick checks
		❑ Turn-and-talk
		❑ Documented teacher observation
		❑ Writing
		❑ Self-assessment or peer assessment
	❑ Individual	❑ Main formative assessment evidence
	❑ Partners	❑ Other: _____
	❑ Small-group total: _____	
Ending chunk (you do):		*(Analyze the main formative assessment by determining if the criteria for success are in place.)*
	❑ Individual	
	❑ Partners	
	❑ Small-group total: _____	

Change
(Explain how you might regroup, preteach, reteach, tier, design stations, facilitate individual goal setting, urge independent inquiry, employ continuous learning, or have students self-assess.)

Teacher Self-Assessment for the Instructional Cha-Chas Cycle

Directions: Teachers use the following tool to self-assess their journey implementing the instructional cha-chas.

	Scale: 0 = Not yet, 1 = Very few times, 2 = Often, 3 = Almost always	Explanation (if needed)
Plan It		
I write my learning targets in student-friendly language beginning with I can, so every student can see and refer to it.		
My learning targets are specific steps to the standard. They are not the standard but a step toward the standard.		
I plan the main formative asessment and its criteria for success before I start teaching. I ensure all criteria align and are rigorous and manageable.		
Most students can accomplish my learning targets by the end of the lesson.		
I establish and model the criteria for success.		
I would like my planning to grow in the following way:		
Chunk It		
I share my learning target with my students verbally and in writing.		
I explain or define certain words within the learning target.		
I activate students' prior knowledge, provide relevant examples, explain why the day's lesson is important, help students make important connections, and tie content to their interests.		
I model, explain, and think aloud to demonstrate the thinking they might engage in.		
I explicitly define vocabulary words and ask students to connect with the words, create a visual in their head with the words (or show them a visual), and ask them to act out the words.		
I use anchor charts to show them how many pieces come together to form a bigger picture.		

Chunk It		
I use music, video clips, compelling pictures, and kinesthetic tools to reinforce the content.		
I teach for an appropriate amount of time for my students' age and attention span. Then, I ask them to chew it by processing, reviewing, and retrieving.		
I differentiate the content based on preassessment or formative assessment data to provide a just-right challenge and move students forward.		
I would like my chunks to grow in the following way:		

Chew It and Check It		
The main formative assessment is engaging, rigorous, and fully aligned to the learning target.		
My lessons have many formative assessments to engage and give students an opportunity to reinforce the learning. I use that to check their progress toward the learning target.		
My students self-assess their progress toward learning target mastery. Along with formative assessment data, I use these data to move instruction forward.		
My students process the chunks in a variety of ways: independently, with a partner, and in small groups.		
I have a variety of quick formative assessments after each chunk: turn-and-talk, whiteboard moments, quick writes, quick draws, question-and-answer, self-assessment indicators (thumbs up, thumbs down), and others.		
I have at least two checkpoints (small formative assessments) planned mid-lesson to determine where each student is with the learning target.		
Feedback: I view mistakes as opportunities for learning. I encourage students to challenge one another's answers respectfully.		
Feedback: My students are not afraid to ask for help. They know what resources to use in order to figure things out on their own. I promote independence with my cues, prompts, reminders, examples, and criteria for success.		
Feedback: I provide support when my students ask for or need it. I preteach or reteach when data tell me I should. My feedback reflects the daily data collection.		

Feedback: I encourage students to peer-assess and self-assess often. I give them the tools to do this.		
Feedback: My feedback to students is related to the learning target; explains what they are doing correctly and well; and then ends with a suggestion, strategy, or question for getting to the learning target.		
My closure or exit ticket directly assesses where the students are with the learning target.		
I collect and use data from my formative assessments daily to determine my next instruction.		

I would like my chews and checks to grow in the following way:

Change It

I encourage students to revise and resubmit assignments. I have a redo and retake policy that doesn't allow students to take advantage of these second chances.		
I change my instruction the next day either with a full reteach lesson with different strategies from original teaching, or with a different lesson for whole group (if data indicate that need).		
I change my instruction right now by reteaching. I respond to what I saw or heard by grouping students and giving them what they need in that moment.		
I change my instruction before I start the unit and prepare lessons based on the preassessment data and observations.		
I look at data and determine how to enrich the students who understand.		
I study student errors and ensure I address them during the reteach lesson.		
When I need to reteach or spend more time with a group, all other students know what anchor activities to do. Those activities are curriculum based and engaging and have criteria for success.		

I would like my changes to grow in the following way:

Teaching With the Instructional Cha-Chas © 2019 Solution Tree Press • SolutionTree.com
Visit **go.SolutionTree.com/instruction** to download this page.

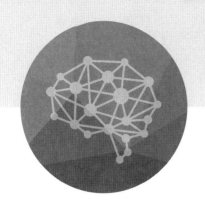

Swing Into Action With the Four Steps: Time for Your Solo

Dancers are unique. Some are meticulous; others dance freely. Some prefer ballroom; others prefer tap. Students, just like dancers, are unique. Our classes are filled with students who come from different backgrounds, who learn in different ways, and who care about different things. The truly effective teacher has learned to differentiate, meeting students where they are and helping them get to where they need to go, and beyond.

Not everyone is attentive to details or mechanically inclined, and we are therefore grateful to the teachers who educated the surgeons who operate on our bodies and the mechanics who work on our cars. We hope those surgeons and mechanics stay up-to-date on research so they can implement necessary changes. Just as we expect them to continue growing in their field, we teachers need to continue growing in ours.

Teachers show their students every day what it means to be a lifelong learner. You teach them to strive and persevere; give them the opportunity to practice the skills they will use for a lifetime; celebrate their achievements; and, when they fail, help them pick up the fragmented pieces of their learning and turn them over for examination until they can see a pattern. A teacher's willingness to participate, provide feedback, adapt, and make modifications guarantees student success.

And we realize that just as there is no one-size-fits-all student, teacher, or classroom, there is no one-size-fits-all way to differentiate. Everything will depend on the prior knowledge, interests, and abilities that you and your students bring to the situation.

We hope that *Teaching With the Instructional Cha-Chas* has provided you the means to *chunk* information to make it relative and meaningful to your students. We hope we have provided you with new ideas for your students to *chew* on during their learning for greater retention when you *check* for understanding. And we hope we have shown you that it isn't hard to *change* your instruction, grouping, practice, or assessments to meet all your students where they are and move them forward in their learning. We hope that we help you enjoy your classroom dance.

References and Resources

21st Century Learning Academy. (2011). *The 40 reflection questions*. Accessed at https://backend.edutopia.org/sites /default/files/pdfs/stw/edutopia-stw-replicatingPBL-21stCAcad-reflection-questions.pdf on October 31, 2018.

Adesope, O. O., Trevisan, D. A., Sundararajan, N. (2017). Rethinking the use of tests: A meta-analysis of practice testing. *Review of Educational Research*, *87*(3), 659–701.

Agarwal, P. K., Roediger, H. L., McDaniel, M. A., & McDermott, K. B. (2013). *How to use retrieval practice to improve learning*. St. Louis, MO: Washington University, Institute of Educational Sciences.

Anderson, L. W., & Krathwohl, D. R. (Eds.). (2001). *A taxonomy for learning, teaching, and assessing: A revision of Bloom's taxonomy of educational objectives*. Boston: Allyn & Bacon.

Andrade, H., & Valtcheva, A. (2009). Promoting learning and achievement through self-assessment. *Theory Into Practice*, *48*(1), 12–19.

Apple. (2017). *Use the voice memos app*. Accessed at https://support.apple.com/en-us/ HT206775 on June 21, 2018.

Arnold, K. M., & McDermott, K. B. (2013). Free recall enhances subsequent learning. *Psychonomic Bulletin & Review*, *20*(3), 507–513.

Atkin, J. M., Black, P., & Coffey, J. (Eds.). (2001). Classroom assessment and the National Science Education Standards. Washington, DC: National Academy Press.

Bäckman, L., & Nyberg, L. (2013). Dopamine and training-related working-memory improvement. *Neuroscience and Biobehavioral Reviews*, *37*(9), 2209–2219.

Barrett, S. L. (1992). *It's all in your mind: A guide to understanding your brain and boosting your brain power*. Minneapolis, MN: Free Spirit Publishing.

Beck, I. L., McKeown, M. G., & Kucan, L. (2002). *Bringing words to life: Robust vocabulary instruction*. New York: Guilford Press.

Bender, W. N. (2008). *Differentiating instruction for students with learning disabilities: Best teaching practices for general and special educators* (2nd ed.). Thousand Oaks, CA: Corwin Press.

Black, P., & Wiliam, D. (1998). Assessment and classroom learning. *Assessment in Education Principles, Policy and Practice*, *5*(1), 7–74.

Black, P., & Wiliam, D. (2010). Inside the black box: Raising standards through classroom assessment. *Phi Delta Kappan*, *92*(1), 81–90.

Bloom, B. S. (Ed.). (1956). *Taxonomy of educational objectives: The classification of educational goals; Handbook I: Cognitive domain*. New York: McKay.

Botto, M., Basso, D., Ferrari, M., & Palladino, P. (2014). When working memory updating requires updating: analysis of serial position in a running memory task. *Acta Psychologica*, *148*, 123–129.

Bousfield, W. A. (1953). The occurrence of clustering in the recall of randomly arranged associates. *Journal of General Psychology*, *49*(2), 229–240.

Brookhart, S. M. (2010). *Formative assessment strategies for every classroom* (2nd ed.). Alexandria, VA: Association for Supervision and Curriculum Development.

Brookhart, S. M., & Moss, C. M. (2012). *Learning targets: Helping students aim for understanding in today's lesson.* Alexandria, VA: Association for Supervision and Curriculum Development.

Burke, K. (2010). *Balanced assessment: From formative to summative.* Bloomington, IN: Solution Tree Press.

Burns, M. (2018, June 15). *Tech tools and tips for think alouds* [Blog post]. Accessed at https://classtechtips.com/2018/06/15/tips-for-think-alouds on August 28. 2018.

Caine, G., Caine, R. N., & Crowell, S. (1994). *Mindshifts: A brain-based process for restructuring schools and renewing education.* Tucson, AZ: Zephyr Press.

Cash, R. M. (2011). *Advancing differentiation: Thinking and learning for the 21st century.* Minneapolis, MN: Free Spirit.

Chapman, C., & King, R. (2005). *Differentiated assessment strategies: One tool doesn't fit all.* Thousand Oaks: CA: Corwin Press.

Chappuis, J. (2009). *Seven strategies of assessment for learning.* Upper Saddle River, NJ: Pearson Education.

Ciani, K. D., & Sheldon, K. M. (2010). A versus F: The effects of implicit letter priming on cognitive performance. *British Journal of Educational Psychology, 80*(1), 99–119.

Coil, C. (2004). *Standard-based activities and assessments for the differentiated classroom.* Marion, IL: Pieces of Learning.

Coil, C., & Merritt, D. (2001). *Solving the assessment puzzle piece by piece.* Marion, IL: Pieces of Learning.

Costa, A. L. (2001). *Developing minds: A resource book for teaching thinking* (3rd ed.). Alexandria, VA: Association for Supervision and Curriculum Development.

Cowan, N. (2015, July). George Miller's magical number of immediate memory in retrospect: Observations on the faltering progression of science. *Psychological Review, 122*(3), 536–541.

Cranney, J., Ahn, M., McKinnon, R., Morris, S., & Watts, K. (2009). The testing effect, collaborative learning, and retrieval-induced facilitation in a classroom setting. *European Journal of Cognitive Psychology, 21*(6), 919–940.

Davis, M., & Whalen, P. J. (2001). The amygdala: Vigilance and emotion. *Molecular Psychiatry, 6*(1), 13–34.

Delaware Department of Education. (n.d.). *Curriculum development for English and language arts (ELA).* Accessed at www.doe.k12.de.us/Page/2425 on June 11, 2018.

Depka, E. (2017). *Raising the rigor: Effective questioning strategies and techniques for the classroom.* Bloomington, IN: Solution Tree Press.

Diamond, M. C. (2001). Response of the brain to enrichment. *Annals of the Brazilian Academy of Sciences, 73*(2), 211–220.

Dweck, C. S. (2000). *Self-theories: Their role in motivation, personality, and development.* Abingdon, United Kingdom: Psychology Press.

Ebbinghaus, H. (1913). *On memory: A contribution to experimental psychology.* New York: Teachers College.

Ericcson, K. A., Chase, W. G., & Faloon, S. (1980). Acquisition of a memory skill. *Science, 208*(4448), 1181–1182.

Erickson, K. I., Voss, M. W., Prakash, R. S., Basak, C., Szabo, A., Chaddock, L., et al. (2011). Exercise training increases size of hippocampus and improves memory. *Proceedings of the National Academy of Sciences of the United States of America, 108*(7), 3017–3022.

Esteban-Cornejo, I., Tejero-Gonzalez, C. M., Sallis, J. F., & Veiga, O. L. (2015). Physical activity and cognition in adolescents: A systematic review. *Journal of Science and Medicine in Sport, 18*(5), 534-539.

evaluation. (2018). In *Dictionary.com.* Accessed at www.dictionary.com/browse/evaluate?s=t on June 21, 2018.

Fisher, D., & Frey, N. (2008). *Better learning through structured teaching: A framework for the gradual release of responsibility*. Alexandria, VA: Association for Supervision and Curriculum Development.

Fisher, D., & Frey, N. (2015). *Unstoppable learning: Seven essential elements to unleash student potential*. Bloomington, IN: Solution Tree Press.

Fisher, D., Frey, N., & Pumpian, I. (2012). *How to create a culture of achievement in your school and classroom*. Alexandria, VA: Association for Supervision and Curriculum Development.

Fonollosa, J., Neftci, E., & Rabinovich, M. (2015). Learning of chunking sequences in cognition and behavior. *Public Library of Science Computational Biology, 11*(11): e1004592. Accessed at http://journals.plos.org /ploscompbiol/article?id=10.1371/journal.pcbi.1004592 on August 28, 2018.

Fountas, I., & Pinnell, G. S. (1996). *Guided reading, good first teaching for all children*. Portsmouth, NH: Heinemann.

Fountas, I., & Pinnell, G. S. (2000). *Guiding readers and writers (grades 3–6): Teaching, comprehension, genre, and content literacy*. Portsmouth, NH: Heinemann.

Fuchs, L. S. & Fuchs, D. (1986, November 1). Effects of systematic formative evaluation: A meta-analysis. *Exceptional Children, 53*(3), 199–208.

Gardner, H. (1993). *Frames of mind: The theory of multiple intelligences*. New York: Basic Books.

Genius hour. (n.d.). *What is genius hour?* Accessed at www.geniushour.com/what-is-genius-hour on June 22, 2018.

Graves, M. (2006). *The vocabulary book: Learning and instruction*. New York: Teachers College Press.

Grinberg, E. (2014). *'Genius hour': What kids can learn from failure*. Accessed at www.cnn.com/2014/03/09/living /genius-hour-education-schools/index.html on July 9, 2018.

Haapala, E. A., Väistö, J., Lintu, N., Westgate, K., Ekelund, U., Poikkeus, A.-M., et al. (2017). Physical activity and sedentary time in relation to academic achievement in children. *Journal of Science and Medicine in Sport, 20*(6), 583–589.

Haskins, J. (1992). *The day Martin Luther King, Jr. was shot*. New York: Scholastic.

Hattie, J. (2009). *Visible learning: A synthesis of over 800 meta-analyses relating to achievement*. New York: Routledge.

Heacox, D. (2009). *Making differentiation a habit: How to ensure success in academically diverse classrooms*. Minneapolis, MN: Free Spirit.

Heacox, D., & Cash, R. M. (2014). *Differentiation for gifted learners: Going beyond the basics*. Minneapolis, MN: Free Spirit.

Henkes, K. (1996). *Lilly's purple plastic purse*. New York: Greenwillow Books.

Herrell, A. L., & Jordan, M. (2012). *50 strategies for teaching English language learners*. Boston: Pearson.

Jeffrey, G. (2007). *Martin Luther King Jr.: The life of a civil rights leader*. New York: Rosen.

Jensen, E. (2005). *Teaching with the brain in mind* (2nd ed.). Alexandria, VA: Association for Supervision and Curriculum Development.

Jensen, E., & Nickelsen, L. (2008). *Deeper learning: 7 powerful strategies for in-depth and longer-lasting learning*. Thousand Oaks, CA: Corwin Press.

Jensen, E., & Nickelson, L. (2014). *Bringing the Common Core to life in K–8 classrooms: Thirty strategies to build literacy skills*. Bloomington, IN: Solution Tree Press.

Johnson, D. W., Johnson, R. T., & Holubec, E. J. (1994). *The new circles of learning: Cooperation in the classroom and school*. Alexandria, VA: Association for Supervision and Curriculum Development.

Kohl, H. W., & Cook, H. D. (Eds.). (2013). *Educating the student body: Taking physical activity and physical education to school*. Washington, DC: National Academies Press.

Larsen, D. P., Butler, A. C., & Roediger, H. L. (2009). Repeated testing improves long-term retention relative to repeated study: A randomised controlled trial. *Medical Education, 43*(12), 1174–1181.

Leahy, S., & Wiliam, D. (2012). From teachers to schools: Scaling up professional development for formative assessment. In J. Gardner (Ed.) *Assessment and learning* (2nd ed.). London: SAGE.

Lipnevich, A. A., & Smith, J. K. (2008, June). *Response to assessment feedback: The effects of grades, praise, and source of information* [Research report]. Educational Testing Service. Accessed at www.ets.org/Media/Research/pdf / RR-08-30.pdf on September 3, 2018.

Liu, T., & Hou Y. (2013). A hierarchy of attentional priority signals in human frontoparietal cortex. *Journal of Neuroscience, 33*(42), 16606–166616.

Luchicchi, A., Bloem, B., Viaña, J. N. M., Mansvelder, H. D., & Role, L. W. (2014). Illuminating the role of cholinergic signaling in circuits of attention and emotionally salient behaviors. *Frontiers in Synaptic Neuroscience, 6,* 24.

Martin, A., & van Turennout, M. (2002). Searching for the neural correlates of object priming. In L. R. Squire & D. L. Schacter (Eds.), *Neuropsychology of memory* (3rd ed., pp. 239–247). New York: Guildford Press.

Marzano, R. J. (2000). *Transforming classroom grading.* Alexandria, VA: Association for Supervision and Curriculum Development.

Marzano, R. J. (2010). Art and science of teaching/reviving reteaching. *Educational Leadership, 66*(2), 82–83.

Marzano, R. J., Pickering, D. J., & Pollock, J. E. (2001). *Classroom instruction that works: Research-based strategies for increasing student achievement.* Alexandria, VA: Association for Supervision and Curriculum Development.

Marzano, R. J., & Simms, J. A. (2013). *Vocabulary for the Common Core.* Bloomington, IN: Marzano Resources.

McDermott, K. B., Agarwal, P. K., D'Antonio, L., Roediger, H. L., III, & McDaniel, M. A. (2014). Both multiple-choice and short-answer quizzes enhance later exam performance in middle and high school classes. *Journal of Experimental Psychology: Applied, 20*(1), 3–21.

McKnight, K. S. (2017). *Literacy and learning centers for the big kids: Building literacy skills and content knowledge, grades 4–12.* Antioch, IL: Engaging Learners.

Medina, J. (2014). *Brain rules: 12 principles for surviving and thriving at work, home, and school.* (2nd ed.). Seattle, WA: Pear Press.

Meyer, A., Rose, D. H., & Gordon, D. (2014). *Universal design for learning: Theory and practice.* Wakefield, MA: CAST.

Michigan State University's Center for Language and Research. (n.d.). *FAQs.* Accessed at https://clear.msu.edu /resources/rich-internet-applications/smile/faqs on June 25, 2018.

Miller, G. A. (1956). The magical number seven, plus or minus two: Some limits on our capacity for processing information. *Psychological Review, 63*(2), 81–97.

Moss, C. M., & Brookhart, S. M. (2009). *Advancing formative assessment in every classroom: A guide for instructional leaders.* Alexandria, VA: Association for Supervision and Curriculum Development.

Myers, N. E., Stokes, M. G., Walther, L., & Nobre, A. C. (2014). Oscillatory brain state predicts variability in working memory. *Journal of Neuroscience, 34*(23), 7735–7743.

National Governors Association Center for Best Practices & Council of Chief State School Officers. (2010a). *Common Core State Standards for English language arts and literacy in history/social studies, science, and technical subjects.* Washington, DC: Authors. Accessed at www.corestandards.org/assets/CCSSI_ELA%20Standards.pdf on October 16, 2018.

National Governors Association Center for Best Practices & Council of Chief State School Officers. (2010b). *Common Core State Standards for mathematics.* Washington, DC: Authors. Accessed at www.corestandards.org/ assets/CCSSI_Math%20Standards.pdf on June 11, 2018.

National Reading Panel. (2000). *Teaching children to read: An evidence-based assessment of the scientific research literature on reading and its implications for reading instruction.* Accessed at www.nichd.nih.gov/sites/default/files/publications/pubs/nrp/Documents/report.pdf on August 28, 2018.

Nishida, H. (2013). The influence of chunking on reading comprehension: Investigating the acquisition of chunking skill. *The Journal of Asian TEFL, 10*(4), 163–183.

Nickelson, L. (2003). *Comprehension activities for reading in social studies and science.* New York: Scholastic.

Ogle, D. M. (1986). K-W-L: A teaching model that develops active reading of expository text. *Reading Teacher, 39*(6), 564–570. Accessed at www.jstor.org/stable/20199156 on June 14, 2018.

Palincsar, A. S. (1986). Metacognitive strategy instruction. *Exceptional Children, 53*(2), 118–124.

Palincsar, A. S., & Brown, A. L. (1984). Reciprocal teaching of comprehension-fostering and comprehension-monitoring activities. *Cognition and Instruction, I*(2), 117–175.

Pauk, W., & Owens, R. (2011). *How to study in college.* Boston, MA: Wadsworth.

Pearson, P. D., & Gallagher, M. C. (1983). The instruction of reading comprehension. *Contemporary Educational Psychology, 8*(3), 317–344.

Pinnell, G. S., & Scharer, P. L. (2003). *Teaching for comprehension in reading, grades K–2.* New York: Scholastic Professional Books.

Polacco, P. (1994). *Pink and say.* New York: Philomel Books.

Popham, W. J. (2013). *Transformative assessment.* Boston: Houghton Mifflin Harcourt.

Poulose, S. M., Miller, M. G., Scott, T., & Shukitt-Hale, B. (2017). Nutritional factors affecting adult neurogenesis and cognitive function. *Advances in Nutrition, 8*(6), 804–811.

Pressley, M., & Afflerbach, P. (1995). *Verbal protocols of reading: The nature of constructively responsive reading.* Hillsdale, NJ: Lawrence Erlbaum.

Ratey, J. J., & Hagerman, E. (2008). *Spark: The revolutionary new science of exercise and the brain.* New York: Little, Brown.

Roffman, J. L., Tanner, A. S., Eryilmaz, H., Rodriguez-Thompson, A., Silverstein, N. J., Ho, N. F., et al. (2016). Dopamine D_1 signaling organizes network dynamics underlying working memory. *Science Advances, 2*(6), e1501672.

Rosenshine, B. (2012). Principles of instruction: Research-based strategies that all teachers should know. *American Educator.* Accessed at https://files.eric.ed.gov/fulltext/EJ971753.pdf on September 4, 2018.

Sadler, D. R. (1989). Formative assessment and the design of instructional systems. *Instructional Science, 18*(2), 119–144.

Schimmer, T. (2016). *Grading from the inside out: Bringing accuracy to student assessment through standards-based mindset.* Bloomington, IN: Solution Tree Press.

Serravallo, J. (2015). *The reading strategies book: Your everything guide to developing skilled readers.* Portsmouth, NH: Heinemann.

Shavelson, R. J. (2006). *On the integration of formative assessment in teaching and learning with implications for teacher education* [Paper]. Accessed at www.stanford.edu/dept/SUSE/SEAL on August 2, 2018.

Shing, Y. L., & Brod, G. (2016). Effects of prior knowledge on memory: Implications for education. *Mind, Brain, and Education, 10*(3), 153–161.

Sleiman, S. F., Henry, J., Al-Haddad, R., El Hayek, L., Haidar, E. A., Stringer, T., et al. (2016, June 2). *Exercise promotes the expression of brain derived neurotrophic factor (BDNF) through the action of the ketone body β-hydroxybutyrate.* Accessed at https://elifesciences.org/articles/15092 on August 20, 2018.

Smith Micro Software. (2016). *Sock puppets* (Version 2.0.4) [Mobile application software]. Accessed at https://itunes.apple.com/us/app/sock-puppets/id394504903?mt=8 on June 20, 2018.

Sousa, D. A. (2005). *How the brain learns to read.* Thousand Oaks, CA: Corwin Press.

Sousa, D. A. (2017). *How the brain learns* (5th ed.). Thousand Oaks, CA: Corwin Press.

Stead, T. (2006). *Reality checks: Teaching reading comprehension with nonfiction, K–5.* Portland, ME: Stenhouse.

Stiggins, R. J. (2000). *Student-involved classroom assessment* (3rd ed.). Upper Saddle River, NJ: Prentice Hall.

Tate, M. L. (2003). *Worksheets don't grow dendrites: 20 instructional strategies that engage the brain.* Thousand Oaks, CA: Corwin Press.

Tomlinson, C. A. (2001). *How to differentiate instruction in mixed-ability classrooms* (2nd ed.). Alexandria, VA: Association for Supervision and Curriculum Development.

Tomlinson, C. A. (2014). *The differentiated classroom: Responding to the needs of all learners* (2nd ed.). Alexandria, VA: Association for Supervision and Curriculum Development.

Tomlinson, C. A., & Allan, S. D. (2000). *Leadership for differentiating schools & classrooms.* Alexandria, VA: Association for Supervision and Curriculum Development.

Tovani, C. (2000). *I read it, but I don't get it: Comprehension strategies for adolescent readers.* Portland, ME: Stenhouse.

Turville, J., Allen, L., & Nickelsen, L. (2010). *Differentiating by readiness: Strategies and lesson plans for tiered instruction grades K–8.* Larchmont, NY: Eye on Education.

Vagle, N. D. (2015). *Design in five: Essential phases to create engaging assessment practice.* Bloomington, IN: Solution Tree Press.

van Praag, H., Kempermann, G., & Gage, F. H. (1999). Running increases cell proliferation and neurogenesis in the adult mouse dentate gyrus. *Nature Neuroscience, 2*(3), 266–270.

Vosniadou, S., Ioannides, C., Dimitrakopoulou, A., & Papademetriou, E. (2001). Designing learning environments to promote conceptual change in science. *Learning and Instruction, 11*(4–5), 381–419.

Walvoord, B. E., & Anderson, V. J. (1998). *Effective grading: A tool for learning and assessment in college.* Hoboken, New Jersey: Jossey-Bass.

Webb, N. L. (1997). *Criteria for alignment of expectations and assessments in mathematics and science education* (Research Monograph No. 6). Madison: University of Wisconsin-Madison, National Institute for Science Education.

Webb, N. L. (1999). *Alignment of science and mathematics standards and assessments in four states* (Research Monograph No. 18). Madison: University of Wisconsin-Madison, National Institute for Science Education.

Wexler, B. E., Iseli, M., Leon, S., Zaggle, W., Rush, C., Goodman, A., et al. (2016, September 12). Cognitive priming and cognitive training: Immediate and far transfer to academic skills in children. *Scientific Reports, 6.* Accessed at www.nature.com/articles/srep32859 on August 2, 2018.

Wiliam, D. (2011). *Embedded formative assessment.* Bloomington, IN: Solution Tree Press.

Wiliam, D. (2016). The secret of effective feedback. *Educational Leadership, 73*(7), 10–15.

Wiliam, D., & Leahy, S. (2015). *Embedding formative assessment: Practical techniques for K–12 classrooms.* West Palm Beach, FL: Learning Sciences International.

Winebrenner, S. (2006). *Teaching kids with learning difficulties in the regular classroom: Ways to challenge & motivate struggling students to achieve proficiency with required standards* (Rev. ed). Minneapolis, MN: Free Spirit.

Wormeli, R. (2018). *Fair isn't always equal: Assessment and grading in the differentiated classroom* (2nd ed.). Portland, ME: Stenhouse.

Zweirs, J., & Crawford, M. (2011). *Academic conversations: Classroom talk that fosters critical thinking and content understandings.* Portland, Maine: Stenhouse.

Index

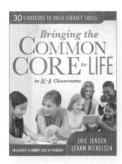

Bringing the Common Core to Life in K–8 Classrooms
Eric Jensen and LeAnn Nickelsen

Actively engage students in their own learning. Discover strategies to promote student mastery of the Common Core State Standards for English language arts across the curriculum. Explore techniques to lead students in close reading, activate their background knowledge to prepare them for learning, and gain insight into habit formation. You'll develop the know-how to effectively structure teaching to empower all students.
BKF442

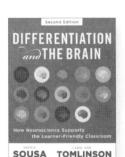

Differentiation and the Brain, Second Edition
David A. Sousa and Carol Ann Tomlinson

Students are becoming more academically and culturally diverse, making it more important than ever to shift away from a one-size-fits-all approach to teaching and learning. The second edition of this best-selling resource will help you create truly effective, brain-friendly classrooms for all learners. The authors share an array of updated examples, scenarios, and exercises, as well as the latest research from cognitive psychology, neuroscience, and pedagogy.
BKF804

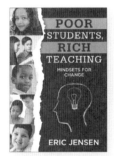

Poor Students, Rich Teaching
Eric Jensen

Discover practical and research-based strategies to ensure all students, regardless of circumstance, are college and career ready. This thorough resource details the necessary but difficult work that teachers must do to establish the foundational changes essential to positively impact students from poverty. Organized tools and resources are provided to help teachers effectively implement these essential changes.
BKF603

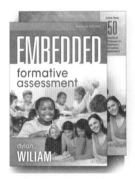

Embedded Formative Assessment, Second Edition and
The Handbook for Embedded Formative Assessment
Dylan Wiliam

The second edition of the best-selling *Embedded Formative Assessment* presents new research, insights, and formative assessment strategies and techniques teachers can immediately apply in their classrooms. As a companion, *The Handbook for Embedded Formative Assessment* has one main purpose: to help teachers develop the practice of formative assessment by providing tried-and-tested classroom formative assessment techniques and giving evidence that shows how these techniques positively impact student achievement.
BKF790, BKF803

The New Art and Science of Teaching and
The Handbook for the New Art and Science of Teaching
Robert J. Marzano

Built on the foundation of 50 years of research, *The New Art and Science of Teaching* framework has helped educators around the globe transform instruction. In *The New Art and Science of Teaching* series, subject-matter experts break down how to make the most of this groundbreaking model and its strategies in the areas of reading, writing, assessment, science, mathematics, and more.
BKF776, BKF844

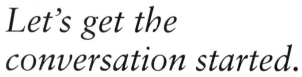